THE "DISCOVERY" OF SUDDEN INFANT DEATH SYNDROME

Lessons in
the Practice of
Political Medicine

Abraham B. Bergman, M.D.

UNIVERSITY OF WASHINGTON PRESS

Seattle and London

Copyright © 1986 by Praeger Publishers, a division of CBS Inc., 521 Fifth Avenue,
New York NY 10175 USA.

First paperback edition published 1988 by the University of Washington Press.

Printed in the United States of America

Library of Congress Cataloging-in-Publication Data

Bergman, Abraham B., 1932–
    The "discovery" of sudden infant death syndrome: lessons in the
practice of political medicine.
    Reprint. Originally published: New York: Praeger, 1986.
    Bibliography: p.
    Includes index.
    1. Sudden infant death syndrome—Political aspects—United States. 2. Sudden
infant death syndrome—Government policy—United States.
I. Title.
RJ320.S93B47   1988   362.1'9892   87-34542
ISBN 0-295-96601-7 (pbk.)

FOREWORD

This is an important book. It documents the discovery of one of the most neglected diseases in child health. Sudden Infant Death Syndrome is the most important single cause of death in the first year of life after the newborn, and until the 1970s it was the most ignored disease in the United States. All this changed as a result of the dedicated and remarkable group of people, mostly parents, who had suffered through the loss of a child from this syndrome, and their dedicated medical advisor, Dr. Bergman. A major accomplishment of the 1960s and 1970s was the definition of this clinical syndrome and its separation from other causes of death in children. But the remarkable parts of this book are the graphic details of the terrible burden placed upon parents who suffered the loss of their children. Doctors did not talk to them about it. In many instances they were accused of child abuse, and were even imprisoned. A good deal of the book details the successful way in which this hardy band got through the political system to win an appropriation for the development of parent support groups. It documents, for naive enthusiasts, the many pitfalls between a good idea and its implementation. It will warn those who think they can get a bill passed and implemented, no matter how logical and good the bill may seem, that to be successful one must expend an enormous amount of time and energy, be skillful in the political process, know the right people, and deal with media. One quote from the book, in this regard, stands out: "Media attention is an absolute necessity for successful public-interest lobbying."

Equally important to the successful lobbying effort was the campaign to sensitize health professionals to care more humanely for these bereaved families. While that battle will never be completely won, there is no doubt that physicians know about Sudden Infant Death Syndrome, and they are more likely than in the past to deal effectively with the grief of these parents. Perhaps, the most important thing to me from this book is the tribute it pays to the remarkable talents of "ordinary" people who do extraordinary things when motivated for the public good.

Finally, in the last section of the book, Bergman tells of his own shortcomings, especially when faced with new personnel in public positions who know none of the history of his successful struggles. The difficulties of having persistence, dealing with burnout, and not becoming arrogant about those who now occupy public positions is a lesson for all who wish to do public-interest lobbying. Bergman does not pull punches. He tells who his good guys and bad guys are in straight fashion throughout the book. It reads somewhat like Mayor Koch's autobiography, in that regard.

The final chapter, showing the decline in support for the SIDS program, mirrors the decline and support of the human services portion of the federal budget during the 1980s. It is a warning to all that there are no permanent victories in the battle for allocation of federal funds for public good. There are always competing pressures, and the battle goes to those who are persistent as well as skillful. For those of us who think we are on the side of angels when we advocate for better child health, reading this book is a must. It will discourage some from beginning the battle, but it will make more successful those who have the guts to rise again and fight another day.

Robert J. Haggerty, M.D.
President
William T. Grant Foundation

PREFACE

"What did I do? Healthy babies don't just die. Please help me understand how I killed my little girl."

"I read an article on infant deaths and would like more information. I had a 3 month old baby boy die about 39 years ago and at that time we had two doctors examine him and both only said, 'it is just one of those things.' They did say that they probably couldn't have saved him. I have always wanted more information."

"He was a twin and my other son has always been very healthy. The one who died had been healthy also but he had the flu a week prior to his death. Do you think he could have had pneumonia and I did not know it, I was so young and inexperienced? When the other baby got sick afterwards I went to a different doctor. I had lost faith in the doctor who could not give me any comfort at all about my baby who died so suddenly. I have never forgotten this and although I am a great-grandmother now I still would like to know why my baby died. Thank you."

"We lost our little boy and I have just read a column about what maybe killed him. He didn't have an autopsy but everything I have read or heard about crib death points to that as the cause of his going away. He was 7 months old and had a little cold but his last night on earth he seemed perfectly healthy and happy. I found him the next morning dead.

"It is so hard to write about it now as I feel absolutely horrified. I have another little boy and a loving husband and I know that somehow I must go on. I feel that reading this column must be God's answer to me. I feel so guilty and heartbroken and responsible for all this. He was so perfect. Can you please help our family to go on and maybe you can show me the way to do this. I am sending you a picture of the baby so you can see how sweet he was. This terrible thing of crib death must be stopped. How does a mother go on? I want more children but then I ask myself if my mistakes harmed the baby and how will I ever really know what mistakes I made so I won't do it again. Please help me."

"I had a baby die of crib death three years ago. We didn't have an autopsy and we were told that she died of a virus in the lungs. We never did get a certificate or anything. The doctor who was taking care of the baby didn't tell us anything either. He just said we should have other children and forget about the baby who died.

"I can't forget about the baby. She was my only daughter and I loved her so much. My mother thinks that I maybe shouldn't have put new blankets on the crib but I wanted her to have everything new and pink, so I did. Do you think that the blankets killed her? I know that I did something wrong because babies don't just die like that. She was blond and blue-eyed and so pretty and was never sick at all and she was only 2 months old. My husband won't talk about it—he thinks it is something in our genes that killed her. Why did she die and our sons live, then? What did I do wrong? Please help me."

"Our daughter lost her only baby at the age of 7 months from crib death and was subjected to such an investigation by the D.A. and the sheriff, also at the hospital. She was in such a state of shock herself that she had to be tranquilized and hospitalized. She has never nor will she ever forget the torture while standing over her dead baby boy that both she and her husband adored. I wish we could help more in devising a better system of dealing with these families. No one should have to go through what my daughter experienced."

Letters to the author

CONTENTS

LIST OF APPENDIXES

INTRODUCTION

Sudden infant death syndrome (SIDS), commonly known as crib death, claims between 6,000 and 7,000 babies a year in the United States. It is responsible for between 2 and 3 deaths out of every 1,000 live births. After the first week of life, where deaths associated with prematurity predominate, SIDS is the most important single cause of death of infants under 1 year of age. It ranks second only to injuries as the greatest cause of death in children less than 15 years of age, taking more lives in that age period than better known entities such as leukemia, heart disease, cystic fibrosis, or muscular dystrophy. Despite the magnitude of the problem, until the mid 1970s SIDS must have been the most ignored disease in history. Virtually no research was being conducted, and the families of victims were told nothing about why their babies died. As illustrated by the four cases cited in the preface, the grief and guilt were omnipresent.

Significant changes came about in the 1970s. Though the toll of deaths continued unabated, a substantial scientific research effort was launched, aimed at finding the cause or causes of SIDS. Surviving family members, though still devastated by the sudden and unexpected loss of treasured infants, began to receive accurate information and support through their travail. SIDS, previously ignored by health professional educators, is now routinely mentioned in curricula and textbooks.

How did these changes come about? Assuredly not through any actions of the high priests of science and medicine, nor through the initiatives of government policy makers. Change was wrought by a small band of parents who had lost babies to SIDS, aided by a few good-hearted physicians by means of an *organized political campaign*. The campaign was launched in 1972 by an organization called the National SIDS Foundation (NSIDSF) and was conducted simultaneously at the local, state, and national levels.

The purpose of this book is to describe the political campaign with emphasis on the grass-roots techniques that were employed. I view it as a cookbook for other neglected health problems or social causes. Because I was an active participant in the battle, I write in the first person and lay no claim to scientific objectivity. I don't know all that went on with the "other side." Portions of this book were originally prepared as a case study for a course in health policy and management at the Harvard University School of Public Health.

In my work with NSIDSF I never cease to be amazed and inspired by the "little people" who not only lost infants but were treated so shabbily by our health care establishment, and yet fought back and won. Suzy Behr ran an employment agency in Omaha. Judy Smith had an early morning paper route in Houston. Donna Gimeno worked in a plastics factory in Denver. Sherryl Collins owned a tiny farm outside of Milwaukee. Pat Mounteer worked as a waitress in an all-night restaurant in Salt Lake City. These unsung heroines and scores like them helped lead chapters of the National Sudden Infant Death Syndrome Foundation while the health professionals, the academics, and the government officials all stood by and turned up their noses.

It is to these gutsy volunteers of the NSIDSF that this book is dedicated.

Abraham B. Bergman, M.D.

THE "DISCOVERY" OF
SUDDEN INFANT DEATH SYNDROME

1

SIDS—
HISTORICAL ASPECTS

And this woman's child died in the night because she overlaid it—and she rose at midnight and took my son from beside me, while thine hand maid slept and laid it on her bosom and laid her dead child on my bosom.

1 Kings 3:19, 22

Up to the time I started working in the field, my knowledge about SIDS was similar to that of most physicians—zero. I had heard of the entity—once—several days before I started medical school in 1954. Catering to self-styled intellectuals, a medical school fraternity at Western Reserve University in Cleveland had a series of scientific lectures during rush week. One such talk was given by the brilliant and colorful forensic pathologist, Lester Adelson, who described a mysterious malady of infants called "crib death." Adelson, while working in the Cleveland coroner's office, had studied several hundred of these cases (1956). That was the first and last time I ever heard about crib death during my *entire* medical education.

I am now dimly aware of having been involved with crib death cases during my internship and residency at the Boston Children's Hospital. I sometimes was called to the emergency room to pronounce babies dead who arrived "too late." The sum and substance of my medical intervention was to place a stethoscope on a quiet chest and mumble, "I'm sorry, he's dead." The reason that the specifics escape my consciousness is because these unfortunate babies were not *my* patients. After my pontifical pronouncement, I would turn and walk away. I didn't know (or care) what happened to the corpse, let alone

1

the shocked adults beside it. The death had occurred outside the hospital, therefore, "someone else would look after matters; it wasn't *my* responsibility." It was to be several years before I learned that my performance was standard for the entire medical profession—*no one took responsibility.*

PREVALENCE OF "SUFFOCATION"

"It," as evidenced by the biblical quote above, has been present since antiquity, posing under a variety of appellations. Even until the 1950s physicians commonly thought that infants dying suddenly and unexpectedly either had smothered in their bedding, or an adult had "overlayed" them. This assumption was supported by noting the common practice, especially among the poor, of having infants sleep in the bed of their mother or wet nurse.

Garrison's *History of Pediatrics* (1923) mentions a German placard dating from 1291 recognizing the danger of suffocating infants by overlaying, and forbidding mothers from taking babies under age three to bed with them.

Savitt states:

> Infant mortality in ante-bellum Virginia was extremely high. During the 1850's between 16 and 20 percent of all deaths in the state occurred among children under the age of one year. The major causes of death included croup (diphtheria), diarrhea and dysentery, whooping cough, pneumonia and other types of fever, and suffocation (also referred to as smothering and overlaying). With regard to the latter, there is strong evidence to indicate that many deaths which physicians and planters of the 1850's ascribed to suffocation, smothering and overlaying (almost all slaves) were actually cases of the disease presently known as SIDS or crib death. (1975)

Tempelman, the police-surgeon of Dundee, carefully described the picture of what we now know as SIDS in the *Edinburgh Medical Journal* of 1893. Being a dour Scot, he ascribed the cause to intoxicated and neglectful parents suffocating their children, and advocated prison terms for the parents as a means of deterring future miscreants.

An occasional humanitarian voice rose up to challenge the prevailing temper. The following letter appeared in the October 19, 1834, issue of the prestigious British medical journal, *Lancet*:

SUDDEN AND UNEXPLAINED DEATH OF CHILDREN

To the Editor:

Sir, I have lately been called upon to examine two children, who, without having been previously indisposed, were found dead in bed.

In the first case the child was about six months old, and was lying in bed with its mother, who discovered in the middle of the night that it was dead. An inquest was held upon the body, and I was directed, in the absence of anything like testimony as to the cause of its dissolution, to make a post-mortem investigation. I should mention that the mother stated positively that the child had not lain near her, and that it was impossible it could have been suffocated, either from its mouth having been applied to any part of her person or to the bed linen.

I found nothing unusual in the cavity of the skull,—no engorgement of the vessels—no sanguinous or serous effusion. The viscera of the belly were in every respect of healthy appearance, and there was nothing in the stomach to indicate that it had come by its death unfairly. In the chest, however, I found, upon the surface of the thymus gland, numerous spots of extravasated blood, similar spots upon the surface of the lower and back parts of each lung, and many patches of ecchymosis upon the margin of the right ventricle of the heart, and along the course of the trunk of the coronary vein. There was no engorgement, however, of the pulmonary vessels, of the coronaries, or of the vessels of the thymus.

In the second case the child was five months old. It had been pretty well, had been suckled by its mother, and laid in bed upon its side, and in about an hour and a half afterwards was discovered to be dead. There was some frothy matter in and about the mouth, and its hands were firmly clenched. From the position in which it was found it was impossible it could have been smothered.

The appearances exhibited in the autopsy were strikingly the same as in the first case. The contents of the skull and belly were in a perfectly natural condition. The extravasated spots upon the thymus gland were more numerous than in the first case, and those upon the heart and surface of the lungs were fewer in number. There was about half an ounce of serous fluid in the pericardium.

In these cases one naturally asks,—what was the cause of death? The similarity of the post-mortem appearances would lead one to suppose that the cause must in each case have been the same. In the first case I was strongly disposed to think, in spite of the evidence of the mother, that the child must have been destroyed by overlaying it; but after the occurrence of the last case, where, from all the testimony that could be obtained, it seemed impossible that the child could have been suffocated, as it was lying in bed by itself, and was not obstructed in its breathing by the bed clothes, I confess that the opinion I had formed was a good deal shaken, and that I became almost entirely at a loss how to account for death in either. In both cases there seems to have been, from some cause or other, a sudden and violent action of the heart,—and numerous small vessels, from the increased force of its contraction, appear as a consequence to have given way. But so trifling a lesion could hardly, in either instance, be supposed to be of itself sufficient to produce death, and it is with the hope that some of your correspondents who may have seen similar cases, and who may be better able to offer an explanation of the phenomena they present than I am, will take the trouble of enlightening me upon the subject, that I am induced to forward you this communication.

At all events the cases may, I think, be considered of some interest, as well in a pathological as a medico-legal point of view. I have the honour to be, Sir, your obliged servant,

Saml. W. Fearn

Derby, October 19, 1834

THE THYMUS THEORY

High on the humanitarian but low on the scientific scale, as it turned out, was the emergence of the thymus theory, mainly in the German literature of the nineteenth century. The logic of this theory is interesting. Large thymus glands were found on crib death victims in comparison to babies dying of other diseases, leading to the view that death was caused by a large thymus compressing the heart and great vessels. This theory led to the practice among avant-garde pediatricians in the 1920s and 1930s of checking thymus size by X ray of all normal infants, and shrinking the "big" glands by irradiation. All too many of those children treated to "prevent" crib death later turned up with cancer of the thyroid, the price of "modern" medicine. The thymus theory fell into disrepute when the glands of crib death victims were compared with thymuses of babies dying *suddenly* from other causes such as accidents, and were found to be normal. This lymphoid structure atrophies in the course of any severe disease process lasting over a week. So the "small" glands previously considered normal and found on victims of such diseases as chronic infection and malnutrition were actually the result of the disease process. But rather than sneering at those physicians who were doing the best job possible with available knowledge, we should be humble. Who knows what exotic maladies will turn up as a result of our "modern" practices?

The end of the suffocation theory should have come with the publication of Paul Wooley's paper in the *Journal of Pediatrics* in 1945, but alas it was never given the attention it deserved. Wooley, who later served as chief of pediatrics at Children's Hospital in Detroit, was a young pediatrician at the time, teaching at the University of Oregon Medical School in Portland. He conducted a study that would never be allowed by our human subjects committee vigilantes of today. He attached to the ear lobes of infants a photoelectric cell that measures oxygen concentration in the blood (ear oximeter). He then covered their heads with blankets. The oxygen concentration in the blood did not drop; the bedding was porous enough to admit air. Thus Wooley proved it was impossible for normal infants to smother in their bedclothes. One article in a medical journal, however, could not overcome a belief held for centuries.

Some research on crib death was taking place in the 1940s and 1950s, not in prestigious teaching hospitals or research institutes, but in understaffed and underfunded morgues. If the scientific community was unaware of the existence of crib death, coroners and medical examiners had their fill of it.

The "modern era" of SIDS research might be said to have begun in the early 1940s in the unpretentious office of the medical examiner for the borough of Queens, New York. There, in a series of beautifully documented studies, pathologists Jacob Werne and Irene Garrow showed that natural inflammatory processes were involved in most cases of crib death, and ruled out mechanical suffocation (1947, 1953).

Not only was the work of this husband and wife team ignored, but in 1955 they were discharged from their jobs when Werne was charged with neglecting his medical examiner duties. Other coroner's pathologists such as Lester Adelson in Cleveland (1956) and Clara Raven in Detroit (1967) were also pursuing the theory of respiratory infection instead of suffocation, but on their own time in the midst of carrying out their heavy service duties.

DEATH OF MARK ADDISON ROE

In 1958, then, there were a handful of pathologists interested in the problem of crib death, but there was no organized research effort, and no prospect of one in sight. That was the year Mark Addison Roe died in Greenwich, Connecticut. On an October morning the six-month-old boy was found dead in his crib. At the insistence of his pediatrician an autopsy was performed. Cause of death: acute bronchial pneumonia. Case closed.

However, for Mark's parents the case was only beginning. Jed and Louise Roe had no reason to expect the tragedy that disrupted their comfortable life in the summer of 1958. Jed worked in an investment house in New York City and Louise spent her days tending their two sons in the affluent Connecticut suburb. Everything was just as they had hoped it would be.

Two weeks before his death, Mark had been pronounced normal by his pediatrician on a well-baby examination. He had been a full-term baby and received the best of care. There was no indication of future "problems." Why then did he die?

This question obsessed the Roes for the next three years. For Louise there was also the fear that Mark would be a small memory to her, alone. For Jed there was the desire to try to prevent other deaths such as Mark's from occurring. The first few months after Mark's death were spent trying to sort out the isolation and guilt. It was all so inexplicable and no one could even begin to give them an answer. What had they done wrong?

It was during these months that they began to hear of others who had lost babies in the same mysterious way. Friends and acquaintances told them of their own losses. They became aware of newspaper obituaries mentioning other infants found dead in their cribs. Slowly, the isolation lifted and the sense that Mark's death was not a solitary incident led Jed to begin the search for a foundation or a research project to which he might contribute the substantial insurance policy given to Mark at birth by his grandfather. He was persistent and not dissuaded by the not-always-polite suggestions of some physicians that laymen should not meddle in scientific matters.

By early 1962 Jed's quest had led him to every physician who had done any scientific research into sudden, unexpected infant deaths. They were few, they were scattered, and there were but a few minor facts on which they all agreed. But he did not find any foundation or project in which he and Louise could participate or establish a memorial to Mark. He then began to investigate the possibilities of forming a foundation himself, one which would serve as a clearinghouse for physicians and families, organize and support research. One that would "help solve the problem."

At the same time, a comprehensive epidemiological study on "crib death" was being carried out in the offices of Dr. Milton Helpern, chief medical examiner of New York City. Under the direction of Dr. Renate Dische, the investigators hoped to investigate every case of sudden, unexpected, and unexplained infant death occurring in New York City with home visits, parent-physician interviews, and thorough postmortem examinations. After talking to Dr. Dische, Jed was convinced of the importance of his "cause" as well as the necessity of forming a foundation to further research and understanding.

In August of 1962 the Mark Addison Roe Foundation was incorporated in the State of Connecticut. It had as its trustees, Jed and Louise, Dr. Dische, Mark Roe's pediatrician, Dr. J. Frederick Lee, and a young Greenwich attorney, Lowell Weicker, Jr., a close friend of the

Roes, who is now a U.S. senator. (Fate was to also involve another Connecticut senator, Abraham Ribicoff, who lost a grandchild to SIDS.) It had as its medical advisers Doctors Rustin McIntosh and William Silverman of the College of Physicians and Surgeons at Columbia University in New York. The most important recruit, however, was Dr. Marie A. Valdes-Dapena, a pediatric pathologist who then worked at St. Christopher's Hospital in Philadelphia. Dr. Dapena had started her work on "crib death," studying infants brought to the medical examiners office in Philadelphia. She was at the time, and remains to this day, the most eminent authority in the world on sudden unexpected infant death.

There was no office and no staff. It was funded by the insurance policy, and by contributions from friends and relatives and the Roes themselves. The Foundation would be small and "every cent would be put to work on the problem." Before describing the work of the Foundation, I digress briefly to describe what is known and not known about the disease entity, SIDS.

2

WHAT IS SIDS?

It is not the purpose of this book to extensively examine the disease entity, sudden infant death syndrome (SIDS). The reader interested in medical and scientific aspects is referred to other publications, some of which are listed at the end of the book. Some orientation, however, seems appropriate. As mentioned in the previous chapter, SIDS has been with us, masquerading under a variety of names, since biblical times. The term *SIDS*, and its acceptance as a disease entity, however, was not established until 1969.

A signal event in the history of SIDS was the first international conference on the causes of sudden death of infants, which took place in Seattle, Washington, in 1963. (Why Seattle is a question that will be answered shortly.) As the editors of the conference proceedings noted:

> In the summer of 1963 we began reviewing intensively the experiences of those scientists who had recently made significant contributions in this (sudden infant death) field. We found that while much of the information had been recorded, there was a great deal which had not, and which was known only by hearsay and not by published works. It then became our aim to bring together from various parts of the United States and Europe investigators who had been actively engaged in research in this area, and who we felt had a great deal to contribute, as well as others who had more specific interests in the problem. (Wedgwood and Benditt, 1963, p. vii)

The biggest unknown was whether the bulk of infants dying suddenly and unexpectedly were victims of a distinct disease entity or were dying coincidentally from a number of known diseases. Estimates on the incidence of "crib death" in the United States varied between 5,000 and 25,000 per year. There was no agreement on how "crib death" could be diagnosed. Numerous causative theories were put forward; few could be dismissed with confidence. The most important contribution of that conference of experts was to chart the research pathways that needed to be followed if answers to the mystery were to be uncovered.

The second international conference on causes of sudden death in infants was held at Eastsound, Washington, near Seattle in 1969. More knowledge about "crib death" was amassed in the six years between the two international conferences than in the previous 6,000 years. The term *sudden infant death syndrome* was proposed to describe a distinct disease entity with characteristic epidemiological, clinical, and pathological findings. Several commonly held etiologic theories were buried, among them allergic, traumatic, endocrine, and toxic causes. Common cold viruses were generally recognized as playing some role in the majority of cases of SIDS (Bergman et al. 1970).

Although we can now describe SIDS and have limited knowledge about the mechanisms that produce the end result, our state of knowledge is still limited. Like the diseases leukemia, Reye's Syndrome, or juvenile rheumatoid arthritis, the diagnosis can be made, but the cause or causes and means of prevention remain elusive.

EPIDEMIOLOGY OF SIDS

The incidence of SIDS, between two and three cases per thousand live births, is remarkably constant throughout the world wherever the disease has been studied. SIDS cannot be studied in an authoritative fashion without postmortem examinations performed on the victims. That's because other conditions such as bloodstream infections, viral infections of the heart, bleeding into the brain, and certain derangements of body chemistry might also cause an infant to die suddenly and unexpectedly. These other conditions can be excluded only by an autopsy. Because of their expense—currently running between $600 and $800 in the United States—and the shortage of trained pathologists, autopsies for deaths occurring outside a hospital must be considered a luxury item for all but medical-legal purposes, even in affluent countries. Medical-legal generally means that either the police or insurance companies need to know about the cause of death. In developing countries, which tend to have high infant mortality rates, autopsies for infant deaths are virtually unheard of. Therefore our knowledge about SIDS must perforce be derived from developed nations that possess the resources to conduct postmortem examinations. Good epidemiologic studies of sudden infant death have been carried on in such diverse locations as Australia, New Zealand, Canada, Great Britain, Belgium, Czechoslovakia, and Israel. The features to be described below are remarkably constant wherever studies have been conducted.

As mentioned before, the overall incidence appears to range between 2 and 3 per 1,000 live births, or 1 in every 350 babies. A number of risk factors have been identified as making an infant more likely to succumb to SIDS. Chief among them are low birth weight, the presence of a cold, and being born to a family that is poor. These factors, especially poverty, affect the health of infants in general. The rate of SIDS parallels overall infant mortality. Countries with very low infant mortality rates like Denmark and Holland, also see relatively little "crib death." Conversely, other countries, and areas of the United States with relatively high infant mortality rates also see much SIDS. Thus the odds of an infant born to an affluent family living in a nice neighborhood succumbing to SIDS may be 1 out of 600, whereas the odds of death for an infant in an urban ghetto might be as high as 1 in 80.

When I started my research on "crib death" in 1965, we estimated that there were about 10,000 victims a year in the United States. We now estimate the annual toll to be between 6,000 and 7,000. Does that mean that research progress has been translated into saved lives? Unfortunately not. The reason is twofold. First, there is a lower birth rate, and fewer births in the United States; 3,760,000 in 1965 (birth rate 19.4 per 1,000 population) compared to 3,614,000 in 1983 (birth rate 15.5 per 1,000 population). Second, the overall infant mortality rate in the United States has also dropped from 24.7 per 1,000 live births in 1965 to 10.9 per 1,000 live births in 1983 (National Center for Health Statistics 1984). Unfortunately, the infant mortality rate for nonwhites remains almost twice that for white infants, a situation that also pertains to SIDS. The culture of poverty in which teenage pregnancy and premature births run rampant also breeds more than its share of "crib death" victims.

The most remarkable epidemiologic feature of SIDS is its age distribution. SIDS does not claim the tiniest, most fragile, immature victims. It is not a phenomenon of the newborn period. Instead SIDS begins to strike around the third week of life, claims most of its victims between the second and fourth months of life, and then begins to wane. After the sixth month, SIDS is unusual, and though cases have been reported in the second year of life, they are exceedingly rare (Bergman et al. 1972).

The epidemiologic features of SIDS mentioned above are of great interest to the scientist, for they establish a matrix on which etiologic theories must either fit or founder. In other words any theory put forth must take into account the connection to low birth weight, socioeconomic class, and the unique age distribution. Epidemiology looks at bunches of depersonalized cases providing clues that must be followed up rather than definitive answers. The discipline is of no value to an individual family who has lost a treasured baby. In fact, knowledge of the epidemiologic data may cause personal hurt. That's because individual babies rarely fit averages. A 3-month-old infant from a poor family born prematurely is at relatively high risk for succumbing to SIDS. However, a 13-month-old full-term baby born to a middle-class family also may succumb; but not as frequently. The pain for the family of the second child is, of course, just as devastating. By dwelling on statistical averages, families run the risk of thinking of themselves and their baby as some sort of freaks.

There are several clinical features of SIDS that are distinctive. The most important is that death occurs during a period of sleep. The sleep period can be long, like during the night, or very short, like dozing in a car seat during travel. Infants have even died while being held by their parents during feeding. Though it is conceivable that death could occur during wakefulness (never say never in medicine!), if a baby is observed to take its last breaths while awake, a cause of death other than SIDS should be carefully sought.

Another notable feature is the apparent silent nature of death. Even babies sleeping in the same room as their parents are not reported to have uttered any sounds. About half the victims are reported to have minor cold symptoms in the week prior to death. (This means that half the victims do not have colds.) Viral studies do not show any strange or particularly virulent organisms, but rather the same viruses that cause common colds (Ray et al. 1970).

PATHOLOGY FINDINGS

Death in SIDS is thought to be instantaneous. Since the infants are asleep, they pass on peacefully and suffer no pain. Yet, the death scene and appearance of the body may be so unusual that shocked parents gain just the opposite impression. The death scene is often one of disarray. The infant may be found squeezed into one corner of the bed, often with the blanket covering the head, giving the false impression of suffocation. At the time of death, when blood ceases to flow through the body, several alterations take place that may appear grotesque to the uninitiated. These changes are so frightening that most parents won't mention them unless prodded. They include bloody froth emanating from the nose which stains the bedding. The froth is actually edema fluid that fills the lungs, and not actual blood. Purple bruises sometimes are present, which may be mistaken for traumatic injuries. They are in fact due to the settling of the blood to the dependent portions of the body after death; the scientific term is *livor mortis*. Finally, since the body loses its muscle tone at the time of death, soft tissues like the nose and cheeks appear to be pushed in just from the pressure of lying on a bed. I mention these distasteful details to emphasize how the concept of parents harming their own children may have been perpetuated and, more importantly, how parents themselves could be tormented by guilt for the rest of their lives.

STATUS OF RESEARCH

SIDS has rightfully been called "the disease of theories." That's because up until very recently very little organized scientific research was conducted on infants dying suddenly and unexpectedly, so that countless theories could be put forth by "armchair scientists" without fear of contradiction. The sudden and mysterious nature of the deaths lent itself to speculation, some of it interesting, but most of it cruel.

I suspect that most laymen still think of scientific research as a process whereby inspiration suddenly strikes fertile minds. The picture of Isaac Newton being struck on the head by an apple is fairly well fixed in the public's consciousness. In reality, scientific research is an *organized* search for knowledge involving mostly repetitive, laborious work. As mentioned above, such work did not commence in the "crib death" field until the late 1940s and early 1950s with the labors of coroner's pathologists like Werne and Garrow, Raven, and Adelson. Their collective achievement was to dispel the generally held notion of suffocation and infanticide in favor of some infectious process being involved.

A whole host of theories were in the running at the 1963 international conference. Some favorites were allergy (especially allergy to cow's milk, a theory popular in England for a time), endocrine and/or metabolic derangements, immunologic defects, some neurologic dysfunction, and overwhelming infection.

The major accomplishment of the 1960s was to define SIDS as a disease entity with distinct clinical, epidemiological, and pathological characteristics. I'm highly prejudiced, of course, but, to my mind, the most significant contribution to "crib death" research to date was made by my friend and colleague, J. Bruce Beckwith. He had no fancy equipment nor squadrons of helpers. He was taking a residency in pediatric pathology at the Children's Hospital in Los Angeles in the early 1960s. Resident stipends were paltry at the time, and he had a wife and three children to support, so "moonlighting" was a necessity. He took a job with the Los Angeles County Coroner's Office, covering nights and weekends. Because of his interest in pediatric pathology, the autopsies of infants and children were saved for Beckwith to perform. In the course of two years, he was able to perform postmortem examinations on over 200 cases of "crib death."

Prevailing knowledge at the time was that there were no specific pathological findings in "crib death" victims; the purpose of the autopsy being only to exclude other conditions. Beckwith looked more closely at the tiny victims, however, and made a startling observation. Tiny bleeding points, called petechiae, were present in great abundance, but only in the chest cavity. The petechiae were especially prominent over the portion of the thymus gland located in the chest, but not in the portion of the gland that extends into the neck. (In infants the thymus is an important structure involved in development of the immune system. Its relative size and importance diminish in later life.) The presence of petechiae in "crib death" victims had been noted previously, but not in any specific location, hence no significance was placed on the observation.

Beckwith reasoned that the only way these petechiae could be produced was by the infant attempting to take deep breaths against some obstruction *in* the airway (Beckwith 1970). (The phrase "*in* the airway" is used advisedly. No responsible scientist believes anymore that external obstruction, i.e., suffocation, is involved.)

The negative pressure produced by these respiratory efforts produces the tiny bleeding points within the chest cavity. Beckwith could not determine the location of the respiratory obstruction by his postmortem examinations. That question has still not been answered. Speculation, however, centers on a sudden closure of the vocal cords (laryngospasm) or occlusion of the airway by the muscles of the pharynx.

The significance of Beckwith's work was in identifying a "final common pathway" for SIDS. The mechanism of death was shown to be respiratory obstruction. This says nothing about what initiates the fatal process. Some of the other popular theories of the time, such as allergy and overwhelming infection, quickly fell by the wayside. From the time of the 1969 international conference, where Beckwith presented his findings, all possible explanations for SIDS have had to take into account not only the special epidemiologic features, but the characteristic pathological findings.

While research in the 1960s primarily dealt with defining the characteristics of SIDS, scientists in the 1970s turned their attention to searching for any signs or symptoms in infants that would predict whether or not they were susceptible to "crib death." It is not enough to know which groups of infants are more susceptible. Tests must be devised to identify the individual baby who might succumb. To this end, two notable studies were published. The first, in 1972, by Alfred Steinschneider, then of Syracuse, proposed the possibility of a relationship between temporary cessation of breathing, called apnea, and SIDS. The other, in 1973, by Richard Naeye, a pediatric pathologist from Hershey, proposed that "crib death" victims were not otherwise normal at the time of death, as previously believed, but they in fact had structural abnormalities indicative of chronic oxygen deprivation.

The fallout from these two studies was profound. Virtually all SIDS research papers in the next decade led off with the assumption that "near-miss SIDS" or "aborted SIDS," as infantile apnea rapidly came to be called, was closely related to SIDS, and that "crib death" victims suffered from chronic oxygen lack from the time of birth. The "apnea monitor business," as Beckwith, Ray, and Bergman called it (1975), swept the land, understandably, as fearful parents sought electronic babysitters to protect their infants from the scourge of "crib death."

An interesting sidelight was the effect of this work on the omnipresent herd mentality in science. The credence paid to an article is directly related to the supposed prestige of the scientific journal that publishes it. Naeye's important paper on "tissue markers" in SIDS was first published in the *New England Journal of Medicine* (1973), as was an early paper by a group of vigorous apnea monitor advocates at the Massachusetts General Hospital in Boston (Shannon et al. 1977).

The *New England Journal of Medicine* is prestigious, as wire service stories remind us every week while proclaiming new advances. It is also the best general medical journal in the United States, perhaps the world. Nevertheless, as its editors would be the first to point out, not all that appears between the journal's imposing white covers should immediately be etched in stone. In the cases of abnormal tissues in

SIDS victims prior to death, and kinship of infantile apnea to SIDS, the notoriety seems to have been misplaced. Naeye's so-called "tissue markers" of chronic oxygen lack in SIDS victims have not been corroborated by other investigators. Steinschneider himself now says, "there are no scientifically valid data that show an electronic monitoring system is effective in preventing SIDS" (in Tildon et al. 1983, p. 725).

A huge dilemma in biomedical research is the issue of controls. In the last chapter I described how the thymus glands of SIDS victims were assumed to be enlarged until they were compared with a comparable control group who died suddenly and unexpectedly from something other than SIDS. If any abnormality is noted in SIDS, it is crucial to know to what extent it exists in babies who don't die. For example there are periodic scare stories proclaiming that 50 percent of "crib death" victims receive immunizations in the month prior to death. The fact that 50 percent of all babies in that age group also receive immunizations never gains as much notoriety.

In the case of Naeye's work involving the lumping of large numbers of autopsied infants, comparable controls are extremely hard to come by. It is not enough simply to compare autopsy findings in infants of the same age who die of conditions other than SIDS—of which there are few enough. Since premature infants have a higher than average SIDS death rate, truly comparable controls would have to include premature infants who die of conditions other than SIDS, a minute number. The only solution is pooling data from large-scale cooperative studies involving a number of medical centers.

The most recent international research conference on sudden infant death was held in June 1982, in Baltimore (Tildon et al. 1983). If there was a single overriding theme that emerged from the Baltimore conference, it was a challenge to the concepts that SIDS babies were chronically deprived of adequate oxygen before death, and that prolonged and repeated bouts of apnea preceded the majority of SIDS events. One can now speak of "apnea babies" on the one hand, and "SIDS babies" on the other, with the likelihood that there is little overlap between the two populations.

RESEARCH IN THE 1980s

Research in the 1980s still centers on whether there are means that might identify infants susceptible to SIDS before the dread event occurs. For better or worse, clues must be derived from the study of thousands of normal infants. What does that entail? It entails electronic monitoring of the vital functions of infants during wakefulness and sleep, and while they have colds. Such studies are only slightly less complicated and expensive than monitoring the bodily functions of astronauts in space, and much less glamorous. A relatively sizable amount of research has been conducted on the normal functions of newborn babies. Newborns, after all, are congregated in hospital nurseries where research workers can readily subject them to testing. SIDS, however, is not a newborn phenomenon. Normal infants between two and four months old must be studied to see what makes them tick, a prodigious logistical problem.

A number of "sleep physiology" laboratories have tackled the problem in such places as Stanford, California, Los Angeles, and New York. The most ambitious project thus far is presently being conducted under the direction of David Southall of London. Southall and his colleagues are performing the monumental task of collecting and analyzing 24-hour continuous recordings of the heart and lung functions of literally thousands of British infants. It was the Southall group that was able to determine that none of the 29 SIDS victims who had been studied prior to death demonstrated any evidence of abnormal breathing patterns compared to the more than 9,000 infants who survived (1983). In a more recent study, the British research group found no significant differences in either heart rate or breathing patterns in 16 infants who subsequently died of SIDS, compared to a control group of 324 infants selected at random from the rest of the population (Wilson et al. 1985).

SPECULATION

So what is the answer? When will the mystery of "crib death" be solved? When will we know the cause or causes? Most importantly, when will we be able to prevent these horrible tragedies? Being that I am but a mortal, I naturally possess no definitive answers to these questions. The following represents personal speculation.

The "final common pathway" in SIDS is obstruction of the airway during sleep, probably at the level of the vocal cords. The defect is not one that can be seen visually either before or after death, but rather a "functional defect" akin to an electrical short circuit. There is something wrong with the "thermostat" in the brain that controls the workings of the airway. The control centers of the nervous system must be reset after a baby is born to accommodate the change from the fetal environment to life outside the womb. The changes in these control centers generally take place between the second and fourth month of life. For instance, there are distinct differences in the brain waves, heart rate acceleration, sleeping patterns, and breathing mechanisms between a newborn and a five-month-old. The "gears shift" between those time periods. It is my view that SIDS is a "developmental phenomenon" stemming from a failure in the normal maturation of nervous system control centers.

To make matters even more complicated, I don't think any particular baby has a fixed abnormality that destines it for SIDS. SIDS is like a nuclear explosion where a "critical mass" must be attained for the event to occur. An easier analogy is that of an electrical short circuit. If the toaster, vacuum cleaner, radio, and mixer are on the same circuit that blows a fuse, it's impossible to say which individual appliance was responsible. The combination of all turned on at the same instant produced the malfunction. All the "eligibility factors" mentioned previously, like prematurity, age, socioeconomic disadvantage, and the presence of a common-cold increase an infant's odds of succumbing to SIDS. Something must happen, however, during sleep to tip the scale. The something could be an event as trivial as a change in head position. We simply don't know.

The research efforts must continue to be directed toward identifying factors that would predict whether a particular infant is at unusually high risk for SIDS. As mentioned above, large numbers of normal infants must be studied in order to pick out patterns of abnormality. SIDS first must be predicted before a means of prevention can be devised. This type of research is expensive and enormously time-consuming. Though I devoutly hope otherwise, I suspect we are looking at decades instead of years before we have definitive answers.

On a more hopeful note, numerous brilliant scientific minds are presently at work on the SIDS problem. The research arena has moved from the coroner's office to the sophisticated laboratory. Even though we don't have the answer, an enormous amount of knowledge about "crib death" has been amassed. Physicians and other health professionals, as well as the lay public, now know that SIDS exists. Families are no longer being thrown in jail when their babies die of SIDS. Let's return to the narrative of how all this came about.

3

DISTURBING
THE PEACE

Colman McCarthy is a curious and inspiring anomaly. He was both a Trappist monk and professional golfer, though not at the same time. He now is an editorial page writer for the *Washington Post*. I'm certain that McCarthy is the only employee of that famous newspaper who is totally disinterested in the power games that obsess most Washingtonians. Instead he concerns himself with the affairs of "little people." In 1973 he wrote an elegant book called *Disturbers of the Peace*. Since the book dealt neither with sex nor scandal, it predictably plummeted into obscurity. *Disturbers* is about "infamous" individuals who serve as "change agents." McCarthy writes, "Theirs is a 'vocation of paradox' because in upsetting the adjustment patterns of the community, an immense personal peace is gained. You gain peace by risking it."

It was not until 1975 that any semblance of an organized research effort got started to find the cause and seek possible preventive measures against SIDS. It would have been 1995 before research was underway had it not been for the efforts of Mary Dore. Mary qualifies on all counts as a "disturber of the peace." She is smart, dedicated, and drives people crazy. I cringe every time I pick up the phone to find Mary at the end of the line. It's not her single-mindedness that bothers me when she's locked onto a cause. It's that she's invariably right. Her arrows are impossible to duck.

Fred and Mary Dore of Seattle lost their fourth child, a three-month-old daughter Christine, on September 8, 1961. The case was "classic." The otherwise well infant was "fussy" the night before and Mary had been up several times in the night tending to her. She was

18

discovered lifeless in her crib the next morning and rushed to the county hospital where she was pronounced dead. An autopsy was performed: "acute pneumonitis" was listed as the cause on the death certificate. The coroner, Leo Sowers, spent some time explaining "acute pneumonitis" to the Dores, telling them it was a catch-all phrase to include the sudden and unexpected deaths of previously healthy infants. In the course of their conversation, Sowers mentioned that he saw between 30 and 50 such cases every year in the Seattle-King County area.

Fred and Mary had heard vaguely of "crib death" before, but were shocked to learn of its prevalence in their own community. They worried about the term *pneumonitis* on the death certificate. Pneumonia, of course, is a recognizable illness for which treatment should be sought. How could conscientious parents neglect signs of pneumonia in their baby? Sowers explained that the baby didn't really have pneumonia, but it was applied by physicians and coroners for lack of a better term.

As the months passed, Mary purused the newspaper obituary columns and learned of eight other families who had lost their babies in a similar manner. She wrote or called the parents and began collecting newspaper and magazine articles, as well as names and addresses of other parents. She became a one-person support group for the parents of "crib death" victims.

Blessedly there were two features that set the Dores apart from other SIDS parents. Fred was a veteran state senator who served as chairman of the Appropriations Committee (he now is a justice of the Washington State Supreme Court) and Mary, a "disturber of the peace." Like most parents, they asked their pediatrician, Robert Polley, about the cause of "crib death." "It's just one of those things," he responded, "we don't know the answer." The Dores, however, like the Roes in Connecticut, took it one step further. "If you don't know," they said, "is there any research going on anywhere to find the answer?" Fortunately, Dr. Polley took their enquiry seriously.

At the behest of Dr. Polley and the Dores, the Washington State Medical Association set up a special committee under the chairmanship of a local pediatrician, Sherrod Billington, to study the problem of sudden and unexpected death in infancy. After several months they reported back to the Dores that, just as Jed Roe had learned, no organized research was taking place in the United States or anywhere else for that matter. The committee proposed that, if research were to be undertaken, the first step should entail having all crib death victims autopsied in one central location. That was no small issue. Death investigation throughout the United States is carried out under the jurisdiction of individual counties. Practices vary enormously. The cost of performing autopsies and transporting bodies were also barriers. The figure of $20,000 a year was projected by the committee for initiation of a pilot study in Washington State. The Dores went to work.

WASHINGTON STATE LAW

Senate Bill 180 was introduced in 1963 into the Washington State legislature by Senator Dore. It provided that all cases of sudden and unexpected death in children under the age of three years old be studied at the University of Washington Hospital. The lobbying was done by Mary Dore, a Democrat, assisted by Coroner Sowers, a Republican. The Sowers, it turned out, had also lost a baby to "crib death" several years earlier. Several other SIDS parents wrote or called their legislators.

Mary was a pro. She went straight to the wives of the other legislators. On March 11, 1963, the day before the Dores' next child was born, SB-180 passed the Washington State Legislature (see Appendix I for text of law). The bill as originally passed directed that "all babies under three years of age 'dying suddenly' when in apparent good health, without medical attendance, within 36 hours preceding death, be autopsied through the facilities of the University of Washington School of Medicine." The $20,000 appropriation passed as requested in the original bill, and was to cover the costs of the program.

Some of the high priests of the medical school were less than enthusiastic when confronted with an edict from the legislature to conduct research on a problem of which they had never heard. Scientists, after all, set research priorities, not politicians. Fortunately, their protestations did not take the form of returning the money, a beachhead was established.

Mary Dore did not confine her lobbying to legislators. Even before the bill was introduced, she descended on the University of Washington Medical School. Her pleas fell on receptive ears. Warren Guntheroth, a pediatric cardiologist and Donald Peterson, the epidemiologist for the Seattle/King County Health Department, who also taught at the school, began studies which have continued to the present day.

Fred and Mary Dore then nailed their most important convert, Robert Aldrich, who was then chairman of the Pediatric Department.

Early in 1963 Aldrich was tapped by President John F. Kennedy to be the first director of the newly created National Institute of Child Health and Human Development (NICHD). When Aldrich moved to Washington, D.C. he took with him another Seattle pediatrician, Gerald LaVeck, who was to succeed Aldrich as institute director.

One of Aldrich's first actions was to award a contract to the University of Washington to conduct the "First International Conference on the Causes of Sudden Death in Infancy." This seminal event, which took place in the fall of 1963, and the productive activities that followed were described in the previous chapter.

RESEARCH PROJECT AT CHILDREN'S ORTHOPEDIC HOSPITAL

J. Bruce Beckwith has already been introduced. He and I both joined the staff of Children's Orthopedic Hospital and Medical Center in 1964. (Despite the name *Orthopedic*, the hospital is a general children's medical center affiliated with the University of Washington.) I've never seen a mind more brilliant than Beckwith's. He was born and raised in a tiny hamlet in Montana, nestled in the foothills of the Rocky Mountains, called Saint Ignatius. He says that he came from the town's upper crust because their family home had wooden instead of dirt floors. He was the only member of his high school class to attend college.

Beckwith reveres the medical scholars of old. He learned Latin, German, and Italian in order to understand their manuscripts. Luxury for Beckwith is immersion in the ancient manuscript room of the British Museum. One year when he was commuting to and from work on the bus, he studied Chinese to while away the time. Linked to his remarkable brain is an extraordinarily sensitive soul. The most difficult job in "crib death" counseling is contacting the parents right after the postmortem examination. Such a grief-laden encounter would tax the spirit of most experienced clinicians, let alone a pathologist. Beckwith, on the other hand, has counseled literally thousands of families who have lost babies. He perceives his role as a pediatric pathologist as much to help families accept death, as to learn why babies die.

Desiring to continue his research in SIDS after coming to Seattle from Los Angeles, Beckwith found, to his delight, the small pot of money that had been appropriated by the legislature, and intelligently set aside by the university's Department of Pathology until a motivated investigator came along. He gave a talk on "crib death" one day at a hospital conference. It was my second exposure to the subject; the first being Lester Adelson's talk in Cleveland ten years previously. Beckwith proposed conducting a research project whereby all infants dying suddenly and unexpectedly would be studied at our hospital. He needed someone to help with epidemiologic studies. I had some experience in the field, was intrigued with the subject, and offered to participate. Little did I know what I was getting into. We began our study on January 1, 1965. A year later Beckwith and I were joined by C. George Ray, a pediatrician with special training in virology. No colleagues on a research team could have had more intellectual respect and personal fondness for each other than the three of us. Though Beckwith, Ray, and I have all departed from Children's Orthopedic Hospital, the study of all cases of sudden, unexpected infant death in King County continues under the capable direction of Joel Haas and Denis Benjamin. By the end of 1984, approximately 1,000 infants had been studied.

A VISIT TO THE STATE LEGISLATURE

The original $20,000 appropriated by the Washington State legislature got us started on our research but did not last long. We needed a long-term commitment from NICHD, but the application and review process took a year. Some interim funding was required to tide us over. We decided to tackle the legislature, hat in hand, my maiden effort in lobbying.

Accompanied by the lobbyist of the Washington State Medical Association, and with Fred Dore hovering discreetly in the background, Beckwith and I showed up bright and early one morning to testify before the senate committee. I could scarcely believe my eyes. The chairman of the committee had been in the legislature for many years. He was a dentist who gained fame in his hometown of Spokane by advertising on the radio with catchy jingles. His attention to our testimony was less than rapt. Except for an occasional grunt when he felt that the procedure was taking too long, his face was buried in the sports page of the local newspaper during our entire testimony. The senator with the most interest in our case turned out to be a physician from the eastern part of the state, who took a dim view of public funds being spent for any purpose other than laying concrete roads in his district.

I've always been fascinated how legislators, at both the state and national levels, defer to physician-colleagues on medical or scientific matters. It matters not if the colleague hasn't held a stethoscope or scientific journal in his hands for decades. It's, "hey, Doc, what do you think about this?" Such was the case with the sharp-tongued physician-senator that faced us across the table. It was obvious that he held the cards. Fortunately he was a better politician than physician. It was not our mellifluous words that turned the tide. As chairman of the Appropriations Committee, Fred Dore had considerable say about road projects in the gentleman's district. After extracting a promise that we would never again return to the state trough for research monies, the venerable senator agreed to our request, and the rest of the committee members that were awake grunted assent.

In my fuzzy-cheeked innocence, I had not yet become familiar with the legislative tactic of "reprogramming" funds. The Washington legislature did not actually appropriate any new funds for SIDS research. Instead they just took the money "out of the hide" of an existing appropriation. In our case it was the budget of the University of Washington. The Appropriations Bill for 1965 read that "$85,594,690 was appropriated for the University of Washington" *provided* that $20,000 "shall be made available to carry out the provisions of Chapter 178, Laws of 1963, related to infant autopsy to be performed by the medical school."

Beckwith and I had a moment of childish exultation at our seeming power. We pictured the dismay of the university moguls over a project of which they had never heard, with the fantasy of bringing the entire university to its knees if we were not treated right. The state money did manage to tide us over until we received a three-year grant from NICHD for $144,000. It was the first research grant ever awarded by the federal government on the subject of SIDS. Simultaneously NICHD contracted with the Children's Hospital of the District of Columbia to search for viral agents in SIDS.

Announcement of our grant award was made on September 10, 1965, by Senator Warren G. Magnuson of Washington, who also inserted some remarks about our work into the *Congressional Record*. The senator, of course, wasn't involved in the review and awarding of funds for our grant. He was simply following the custom that the illusion of feeding pork to constituents somehow enhances a politician's image. Unless a senator or representative is in disfavor with the administration, legislative offices are notified of all grant awards in their districts a day in advance of the grantee. In this first instance, Senator Magnuson's help was only symbolic. It did not stay that way for long.

Few of the words contained in the daily *Congressional Record* are ever actually uttered in the halls of Congress. Material such as commemoration of the crowning of the marigold princess in Aurora, Illinois, is given in printed form to the clerk of the House or Senate and printed in the *Record* as if the speech had been delivered. Reproductions of the "speech" are then distributed to happy constituents, grateful that their legislator has seen fit to draw national attention to their local event. Magnuson's "speech," which contained a fact sheet about SIDS composed by Beckwith and me, served a more important purpose. Our local parent group had no money to print educational material. Senator Magnuson was only too happy to oblige. Mary Dore arranged for several hundred copies of the *Congressional Record* speech to be printed at government expense. The fact that a United States senator in an official government publication took cognizance of "crib death" as a real entity, and absolved parents from blame, seemed to give comfort to many families.

EXPOSURE TO ACUTE GRIEF

Our research involved a visit to the home of each SIDS victim a few days after the autopsy to gather detailed information about the child, the family, and the environment in which the child lived. It took no longer than my first home interview to recognize that I had not embarked on any ordinary research project. As soon as I had finished taking my medical history, I experienced what was to become a repetitive pattern—stunned parents asking, "why did my baby die?" Behind the spoken question was the unspoken one, "was I responsible for my baby's death?" We had unwittingly stumbled upon another research question; what happens to families who suffer the sudden and unexpected loss of a loved baby? I likened this "natural experiment" to the Cocoanut Grove fire that occurred in Boston in 1943. The after-effects of that terrible tragedy led to significant improvements in fire safety, management of large-scale civil disasters, and a classic paper on acute grief by Lindemann (1944), who, as chief of psychiatry at the Massachusetts General Hospital, had to deal with the families of the fire victims.

At first Beckwith, Ray, and I were reluctant to have any words about our research project appear in the lay press. "Crib death" is ideal grist for the mill of journalists bent on creating a sensational story. Every normal parent who lays the infant down to sleep thinks, however fleetingly, about whether the baby will wake up. Publicity about "crib death" could cause mass hysteria. We soon came to realize, however, that the needs of the victimized families who thirsted for authoritative information outweighed the possible benefits of a medical news embargo. Even were information about SIDS available in the medical literature, which it was not, the lay press was the only medium by which it could be transmitted to those who needed the information the most.

It was during this period when I grew to appreciate the talents of responsible science writers, as opposed to journalists who would exploit scientific information only for the purpose of creating sensation. One such person is Edward Brecher, whose story about our work appeared in the July 1968 issue of *Redbook*. Brecher managed to convey the facts as known without engendering undue anxiety. It was in response to the *Redbook* and similar articles that we received scores of poignant letters such as those quoted in the preface.

THE SEATTLE SIDS MANAGEMENT PROGRAM

How were families to obtain the help they so desperately needed? Several approaches were used. Service and educational components were built into our research program. Mary Dore organized the Washington Association for the Study of Sudden Infant Death, an organization made up mostly of SIDS parents devoted to helping "new" parents. Here's how our system worked:

All infants dying suddenly and unexpectedly in King County were brought by the medical examiner's office to Children's Hospital for autopsy. The postmortem examination would be performed by Bruce Beckwith within 24 hours of the child's death. At the conclusion of each autopsy, he would telephone the parents to explain the cause of death. As mentioned above, this was the most difficult and important part of the counseling program. A condolence letter would also be sent. Two points were emphasized: "Your child died of a real disease entity that is neither predictable nor preventable," and "you are in no way responsible for your child's death."

Several days following the phone call, a nurse from our project would visit the family for a "home study." During the visit she would also provide information about SIDS and counseling about the characteristic grief reactions. She would also leave literature about SIDS. These written words were helpful to the family both in assimilating the death themselves, and also in explaining it to others. The family would be asked if they wished another SIDS parent to call on them, and were invited to participate in the local parent organization. Our nurses, who also started out in "pure research," also got "hooked." Joyce Miller, our first nurse, moved to the San Francisco Bay Area after a year and helped organize its local NSIDSF chapter. Margaret Pomeroy, her successor, organized the public health nurses of the Seattle-King County Health Department to continue the visitation program to SIDS families after the home visit phase of our project was completed. She later served as president of the Washington State Chapter of the Foundation.

THE CHICAGO PARENT–MEDICAL CONFERENCE

By 1971 my scientific involvement with SIDS had diminished. The epidemiological studies were completed and a number of papers were published. With a boost from this published research, I was duly promoted in the university from assistant to associate professor of pediatrics, academe's award for "scholarly productivity." A humane and medically sound SIDS management system had been established in Seattle that did not require my further active participation. And, frankly, so much work with death and grief was wearing. I was suffering from "burnout" and wanted to pursue other interests. The NSIDSF organized the first parent-medical conference on SIDS in Chicago in 1971. Beckwith, Ray, and I were among the speakers; I looked on it as my "swan song." I hadn't counted on two things: the outpouring of grief and guilt from parents throughout the country seeking help, and meeting Judie Choate.

A teary-eyed young woman stopped me in the lobby of the Marriott Hotel saying, "Can you tell me why my baby died?" We sat down to talk. It turned out that she was the wife of a young surgeon in Chicago. She pulled a crumpled piece of paper out of her purse, the death certificate, and handed it to me. On it were the meaningless words, "tracheo-bronchitis: staph aureus." The story she told me was classic. I told her, "It sounds like your baby died of sudden infant death syndrome." "Why didn't anybody tell me, and why did I have to be subjected to a coroner's inquest?" she burst out. I said, "What does your husband say?" Her face turned away and she quietly said, "He can't talk about it."

That episode grabbed my conscience. "If such things happen to physicians' families," I thought, "what happens to the others?" The answer wasn't hard to figure out after the encounters of the next several days. There were all-too-many shocked looks and hurting people.

JUDIE CHOATE

Judie Choate, executive director of the Foundation, had already been through her personal shock and was ready to fight. Here's what she said:

I was a young, rather inexperienced New York housewife with little interest in medicine except as it insured the well-being of my two sons, Michael, 3 years, and Robert, 5 months. On a March morning in 1965 my life changed with a jolt and part of medicine became an all-consuming interest. My five month old son was discovered lifeless in his crib. No warning sickness, no struggle, no cry. Another tiny victim of 'crib death.' Like all cases of sudden, unexpected and unattended deaths in our city, Robbie was a Medical Examiner's case. His body was left in the apartment, in a closed bedroom with a policeman in attendance until mid-afternoon when a medical investigator (from the Medical Examiner's office) observed the body and interviewed us. Questions such as, 'How many times did you hit the baby?', 'Did your other child choke or in any way abuse the baby?' provoked a commitment to see that no family would ever have to endure the agony of responsibility for their child's death. I can remember thinking, as they took the baby to the morgue, what happens to families who don't speak English, who have never heard of crib death, who don't have private medical care. I suppose it was, in part, easier to think about abstracts than to face my own terror. I spent a manic day trying to track down a foundation concerned with crib deaths. I had read about it; I knew it was in Connecticut. I knew it was a child's name and I knew I had to help. I called every medical school, library and hospital in New York with no results. No one knew what I was talking about. I finally started calling the major women's magazines. At the moment they took the baby's body from the apartment, I was given the name of the Mark Addison Roe Foundation by the editor of a national magazine.

I had enough knowledge about crib death to know that the Foundation could not tell me why Robby died, but that was not my need. I just wanted to help in any way I could; thus, one week later when I began to correspond with other parents across the country, I had no idea that my involvement would be long-term nor did I suspect the horror stories I would come to know well. I guess I have kept going with the thought that although I could never save a baby's life, I could help insure that someone would try. Also I could try to save families from the anguish and misery of holding themselves responsible for the death of their child (Bergman and Choate 1975, pp. 4-5).

Judy and I clicked. She was a magnetic speaker, competitive as hell, and pragmatic in her politics. Though I did not know it at the time, she needed a doctor to join her in the battle. She offered up a very large turf, the United States, an underdog position, and much virtue to the winner. My competitive and idealistic instincts were aroused. I jumped aboard!

4

THE BATTLE PLAN

There were two separate but related aspects of the SIDS problem. First and foremost a research effort had to be launched. Research support had been the exclusive interest of the tiny Roe Foundation. A few small grants were awarded, but the Foundation lacked the capacity for any sort of substantial campaign. Money was not the only problem. Few scientists with potential talent even knew of the existence of "crib death"; they had to be recruited to work in the field.

The other dimension was the fate of families losing children to SIDS. The veil of mystery covering both health professionals and the lay public had to be dispelled. We thus were required to put together a multifaceted campaign consisting of promoting research, professional and public education, and support services for bereaved families. It was a tall order!

A common mistake made by political amateurs is failure to identify an end point. Caught up in the excitement of the crowd noise, they run around in circles, and never head toward the goal line. Headlines, television stories, petitions, resolutions, and protest marches are perceived as goals in themselves, rather than as means toward the desired end. Our first task was to mobilize our own troops, and provide them with specific strategies for achieving our objectives. From the perspective of a militant SIDS parent who had been brutalized, Judie Choate drafted a manifesto entitled "No Longer Can We Accept." In this document she spelled out the practices thought to be intolerable, such as unavailability of autopsies, cruel inquests, delays in transmitting a diagnosis to families, outdated and cruel terminology (e.g., suffocation, aspiration, etc.), lack of education of health professionals about SIDS, lack of support services for families, and lack of research on sudden infant death. She then proclaimed our battle plan. We would not accept anything less than a substantial research effort at NICHD, and humane handling of families throughout the United States. (The text of Judie Choate's battle plan is contained in Appendix II.)

SEEKING HELP AT HEW

What resources were available to effect this ambitious program? The Department of Health, Education and Welfare (HEW), of course, was the logical place to look for help. (The name of the Department was changed to Health and Human Services [HHS] in 1980 when a separate Department of Education was created. For simplicity, the old term, HEW, is used throughout this book.)

Though the U.S. Public Health Service had been involved in limited infectious disease research, it was not until after World War II that the federal government came to be a major sponsor of biomedical research. The first National Institute of Health was established in 1937 specifically to conduct research in cancer. In 1948 the second institute was created to combat heart disease. The campus in Bethesda across the street from the Naval Hospital then began to spawn a host of new research enterprises and became known as the National Institutes of Health (NIH). The particular disease targeted for attack depended on how much political power could be mobilized by its victims and their friends and families. (The creation of the National Institutes of Health has been well described by Strickland 1972 and Drew 1967.)

The interest of the Kennedy family in mental retardation brought the NICHD into being. From its inception, with Robert Aldrich as director, NICHD placed research on sudden, unexpected infant death at a high priority level. (Aldrich spent only a year as director of NICHD before turning the job over to his handpicked successor Gerald LaVeck in 1964.) The two international conferences were sponsored by NICHD, and several small research grants on SIDS received NICHD support. The total effort, however, was paltry. For instance, in 1971, the institute supported but a single SIDS grant (to our Seattle group) to the annual tune of $46,000. I must mention again that the paucity of SIDS research had more to do with the lack of meritorious proposals from qualified investigators than from lack of funds or interest from

NICHD. Note should be made of the devoted efforts of Dwain Walcher, who served under LaVeck as associate director for program planning and evaluation. He assiduously encouraged pediatric investigators to tackle SIDS research; the response was underwhelming.

GERALD LaVECK

Gerry LaVeck and I grew up in the same Seattle neighborhood. Though not close friends—he's a few years older than I—we played touch football in the streets together, which establishes a certain kinship. Our paths crossed in later years when he was a pediatric resident, and I a visiting medical student at Children's Orthopedic Hospital in Seattle. Gerry was an outstanding resident headed for a career in infectious disease research. He achieved legendary status among his fellow residents for diagnosing an acutely ill child with diphtheria, the first and last case seen in Seattle in ages. He turned instead to a career in mental retardation when he saw that there were no capable pediatricians working in the state institution housing his own profoundly disabled daughter.

As NICHD director, LaVeck was an excellent bureaucrat in a good sense of the word. He knew what he could and could not do, and did not make extravagant promises or try to impress others with his power. In the "corridors of power," it seems that a person's true clout is inversely proportional to the amount of publicity he or she receives. Initially I hoped my past friendship with LaVeck would result in the magic opening of doors. That did not happen, mostly because he did not possess the requisite powers. Instead he imparted the precious gift of frankness, a quality I was subsequently to learn was in short supply with government officials.

An appropriate SIDS research effort, LaVeck explained, would only occur by setting a pot of gold in front of the scientific community. He was not about to fill that pot by diverting existing NICHD resources from other meritorious programs. On the other hand, if the United States Congress, in its wisdom, were to provide extra gold for SIDS research, he promised to administer an excellent research program. When it came to helping bereaved families, LaVeck demurred. "The mission of the National Institutes of Health," he explained, "is to conduct biomedical research. There are other parts of HEW that are supposed to help families." There were no offers to intercede with those other offices on my behalf. LaVeck knew, and I later learned, that such "interference" would be fruitless.

OFFICE OF MATERNAL AND CHILD HEALTH

There was in fact an HEW office specifically charged with improving health services for families, called the Office of Maternal and Child Health (OMCH). It is the direct descendant of the once-proud Children's Bureau. The Children's Bureau was founded in 1912 to safeguard the welfare of children in the United States. A specific health mission was added in 1935 with passage of the Social Security Act, which, among other things, directed the Children's Bureau to "improve the health status of mothers and children in areas of greatest need through a program of assistance to the States." In one of HEW's periodic sweeping reorganizations, the Children's Bureau was dismembered in 1967, with the health functions lodged in OMCH, and other functions dispersed and submerged within the bowels of the huge HEW establishment. (With multiple missions, i.e., health, welfare, nutrition, special education, etc., children's services within the federal government were effectively downgraded and have still not received the attention they deserve.) (See Report of the Select Panel for the Promotion of Child Health, 1981.)

Presiding over OMCH was Dr. Arthur Lesser, a veteran from the Children's Bureau days, whose administrative style was 180 degrees opposed to that of Dwain Walcher at NICHD. Walcher, who literally saw himself as a servant of the public, made it clear to prospective grantees that the money he administered belonged to taxpayers, and therefore any taxpayer had the right to know exactly how decisions for spending that money were made. Lesser, on the other hand, made one feel that the funds he administered belonged in his personal stash, and that questions about how it was spent were impertinent. (Unfortunately too many "public servants" hew more closely to Lesser's than Walcher's style.)

Clearly the management of SIDS in the United States fell into the prescribed mission of the Office of Maternal and Child Health. Lesser, however, was totally occupied with maintaining existing programs and evinced no empathy, let alone interest in the "crib death" issue. "Get us some money and we'll help," he said. "What kind of program would you run if you had the money?" said I. "Don't know," he said, "no point in worrying until we get funds." Over and out! The message was clear. No one within the Department of Health, Education and Welfare was going to take the initiative either in augmenting the research effort or in tackling the humane aspects of SIDS. At NICHD, at least, we had knowledgeable persons who were committed to administering a quality research program if we could get the funds allocated. At the

Office of Maternal and Child Health, however, we perceived only sullen hostility toward "outsiders" who dared to promote new missions. Sadly, this attitude never disappeared even after funds from Congress were provided.

WHERE WERE THE TROOPS?

What about health professional organizations? After all, in response to prodding by Mary Dore, the Washington State Medical Association formed a special committee to study SIDS. Their example was not emulated elsewhere. Logically, pediatricians would be expected to take the lead in addressing child health problems. Our "union," the American Academy of Pediatrics, turned out to be supportive, but not about to take any initiative. Groups like the American Medical Association and the American Public Health Association were silent, as were the professional societies of pathologists. Medical examiners and coroners who had it within their power to "humanize" their handling of "crib death" were to be the targets of our campaign. It was left then to SIDS parents and their supporters to mount the barricades. For practical purposes in 1971 this meant two organizations, the National SIDS Foundation and the Guild for Infant Survival.

The Guild for Infant Survival (GIS) was founded by Saul and Sylvia Goldberg of Baltimore in November 1964. The Goldbergs' two-month-old daughter, Suzanne, died of SIDS in December of 1963. Their story is similar to those of the Roes and Dores. They were insistent that something be done about the malady that had taken their child. There were abortive attempts to get together with the Roes, but the styles did not mix, and the Goldbergs formed their own organization. By design, the guild never had a strong central organization; they believed in confederacy with individual guilds setting their policies for operation. At the time of this writing, they have ceased to function as a national organization. In the 1970s, however, there were several strong chapters centered in the mid-Atlantic states, namely Baltimore, Philadelphia, Washington, D.C., and northern Virginia. Parents who wrote to the Goldbergs expressing interest in their work were immediately chartered as guilds for their local communities. Hence guilds were listed for a number of cities in the United States, and even in other countries, leading to the appellation, *International* Guilds for Infant Survival.

The philosophy of the Goldbergs in battling SIDS is important to understand, though because of my obvious bias, I am far from the best person to describe it. A quotation from the book *Crib Death* by Richard Raring (1975), a Guild mainstay, provides an illustration:

> Our Department of Health, Education and Welfare has long been aware of the extent, the seriousness, and the public ignorance of crib death. It is aware also of the danger of the public's becoming aware and of the reaction that would result if the truth of its neglect became common knowledge. Consequently, the virtually total neglect of crib death research in HEW's vast research budget is top secret, or is privileged information denied common citizens without what HEW deems a "need to know." That is one of the coverup devices used by bureaucrats to withhold, distort, or to falsify information.
>
> With its multimillion-dollar public relations organization, HEW has done an outstanding job of controlling crib death news and of maintaining public ignorance. (p. 126)

Though it may be tempting to dismiss the statement above as baseless paranoia, what were parents like the Goldbergs and Rarings to think after experiencing the apparent apathy of HEW bureaucrats about a malady that killed thousands of infants every year including their own? To their minds, these prominent doctors couldn't possibly be so dumb or uncaring. Thoughts of conspiracy were not outlandish.

Thus, the Goldbergs and their followers were not about to submit to any medical direction of their campaign. When I told the Goldbergs that there were about 10,000 SIDS deaths a year in the United States, rather than 25,000 as stated in their literature, they were both skeptical and uninterested. What was scientific accuracy to me was nitpicking abstraction to them. Their prodigious energy was fueled by indignation. If they shouted loudly enough from the rooftops, help in the form of a research breakthrough might emerge. Thus they provided some money to the excellent medical examiner of Maryland, Russell Fisher, to add a wing to his Baltimore office for the purpose of conducting SIDS research. They also raised money for a project of dubious merit in northern Virginia involving the use of heart-rate monitors.

The Goldbergs scoffed at our attempts to involve public health nurses in counseling visits to SIDS families. They felt that parent-to-parent counseling was more effective, and that by engaging in health professional education, we neglected the more important task of research promotion. I scoffed at their political naivete in thinking that the addition of then-Vice-President Spiro Agnew to their letterhead would result in more research dollars. I worried that their flamboyant aggressiveness might cause some of our congressional allies to turn against all SIDS groups. This fear turned out to be unfounded.

Officials in the Office of Maternal and Child Health tried mightily to turn the Guild and Foundation against each other, of which more will be said later. Nevertheless, though our styles and philosophies were profoundly different, the two organizations were reasonably successful in avoiding public disputes. I also respected the incredible effort put forth by the Goldbergs in helping SIDS families. They were certainly more effective than the vast majority of health professionals in easing the pain of tortured souls.

As mentioned previously, the Foundation was at a crossroads in 1970. In 1967 the Roes moved from Greenwich to Denver. While they had arranged for office space in the basement of a Greenwich law firm, they knew that the organization would have to "go national." Another couple, Arthur and Ann Siegal, offered space in their advertising agency in New York City. Their offer was accepted and the Roe Foundation moved to New York changing its name to the National Foundation for Sudden Infant Death. (There was always discomfort with that name . . . how could our organization be *for* infant death? In 1976 the name was changed again to the National SIDS Foundation. To avoid confusion, the current name is used throughout.) The move and name change did not alter the fact that it was a volunteer operation. The office equipment and telephone were donated by the Siegals, volunteers staffed the office on a rotating basis, and stationers and printers were coralled into donating their products and services. In 1968 the first full-time employee was hired to function as executive secretary and to direct the volunteers in day-to-day operation of the Foundation. The emphasis was on public education. The lay and medical press began to write more frequently about the "mystery killer," resulting in more and more mail to the Foundation office. Almost all the time and money was spent responding to inquiries of "why did my baby die?" The Board of Trustees was mostly composed of old friends and associates of Jed Roe, including the president, Ralph Colin, Jr., of New York, an executive with CBS Incorporated.

Our Washington state group did not immediately affiliate with the NSIDSF. Mary Dore, Beckwith, and I felt that the National Foundation should emulate our local group in supporting education and services to families instead of concentrating exclusively on trying to finance research. Judie Choate felt the same way. In the spring of 1969 she convinced the board to shift gears. I was invited to become a trustee, and Beckwith, a member of the medical board. With the shift in emphasis, the Washington State Association became a chapter of the National SIDS Foundation in May of 1970.

What was the condition of the Foundation at this time? The contributions solicited through a regular newsletter barely kept up with the expenses of answering the mail. One paid staff person, about a dozen dedicated but inexperienced volunteers, and no money. Hardly the ingredients for a campaign to change the way a major health problem is handled in the United States. If our little band did not possess the power to bring about this change we would have to enlist the help of those who did. Judie Choate and I decided to obtain some consultation. Mike Gorman and Mary Lasker were first on the list.

CONSULTING THE PROS

No two persons have had a greater influence on the health programs of the United States government then Mary Lasker and Mike Gorman, but their names remain unknown to all but a few Washington cognoscenti (Drew 1967; Strickland 1972). The reason is that they remain active lobbyists and do not want their covers blown. A lobbyist may conceive and draft a piece of legislation, write all the supporting speeches and committee reports, line up all the votes and arrange for media coverage, but it is a senator's or congressman's name that is attached to the bill. The legislator gets all the credit or blame. Whenever I refer to a Lasker-Gorman bill (such as the Community Mental Health Center Act, the Regional Medical Programs, and the National Cancer Act—there are scores more), Gorman admonishes me, "Always give credit to the politician," he says, "he, not the advocate, is the one who must stand before the voters."

Technically Gorman was employed by Mrs. Lasker to lobby for her health interests in Washington; in fact they operated as partners. He's had several "official" titles. In the early 1970s it was executive director of the National Committee against Mental Illness. The committee, as such, never convened. It was like a CIA front for good causes. Now he heads a group called Citizens for Treatment of High Blood Pressure. Mike, a former newspaperman, is a gruff, tough Irishman who sports a Phi Beta Kappa key from City College of New York. Righteous university presidents and foundation heads who tend to take themselves seriously are put off by this man whose clean to profane speaking ratio is about three-to-one. Gorman cares little, however, about his standing among academic types. He does care about getting research dollars for his causes.

I met Gorman shortly after Senator Magnuson was reelected to his fourth term in 1968. The senator, nicknamed Maggie, replaced the retired Lister Hill of Alabama as chairman of the Appropriations Subcommittee for the Departments of Labor and HEW. Under Hill, the subcommittee staff consisted of one southern gentleman who spent much of his time at the hospital of the NIH being treated for a variety of ailments. This was fortunate for the health concerns of the country. Gorman, the health lobbyist, did all the work. "I hear you advise Maggie on health stuff" he said, "let *me* start advising you." It was true that I had advised Maggie, or more accurately his staff, on some health matters, as did others; his chief health aide was to be Harley Dirks, of whom more will be said later. I wanted to learn about health lobbying, however, and Gorman was willing to teach. Every time we spoke he took pains, in his undiplomatic manner, to emphasize my amateur status, a point which, most of the time, I was willing to cede. When in doubt then on how to throw the next pitch, it was to this grizzled old pro that I turned.

"YOU NEED A DOCTOR AS PRESIDENT"

Judie Choate and I met Gorman for lunch in Washington late in 1971 and laid out our problem. Being a former newspaperman, who gained prominence by exposing the wretched conditions in Oklahoma mental hospitals (snake pits) in the 1940s, Gorman focused on how we might gain media coverage for our cause.

Media attention is an absolute necessity for successful public interest lobbying. The corporations try to get what they want by spending a lot of money. The labor unions also spend money, but also wield power by claiming to control large numbers of votes. "Do-gooders" like you have neither money nor votes; your only chance is to try and mobilize public opinion. Your story is so powerful that you'll get the changes you need if only you reach a wide enough audience.

Gorman had another suggestion besides a national media campaign without money. "Get yourself a doctor as spokesman," he said. "TV and newspapers are suckers for anything that out-of-town doctors have to say. It's automatic free publicity. In fact, you'd better have a doctor as President, that's what the Cancer Society and Heart Association do. Why don't you take the job, Abe?" Mike concluded.

Judie smiled benignly; I later learned that that was precisely what she had in mind. I had joined the NSIDSF Board of Trustees in 1969 but had not anticipated a major time commitment for myself. What

Gorman said, however, could not be denied. Some doctor had to do it; not many were fighting for the job. I consulted my professional colleagues back home in Seattle. Bruce Beckwith said that, if I would work with the National Foundation throughout the country, he would relieve me from any advising responsibilities with the Washington State Chapter. George Ray, who hated to travel anywhere, agreed to take charge of the SIDS research project. As usual, my boss at Children's Orthopedic Hospital, Dr. Jack Docter, was supportive. In December 1971 Ralph Colin became chairman of the board, and I was elected president of the National SIDS Foundation.

I owe aspiring public interest advocates a personal note at this point. Though I consulted with plenty of professional colleagues about taking on the presidency of the Foundation, I did not consult with my wife or children. It was always assumed around our house that Daddy was off riding a big white horse on behalf of little children and that any sacrifice that wife and kids had to make was always for the greater good. By no means was my work with the Foundation the major cause of my marriage dissolution in 1977, but my physical absence and, more importantly, my emotional involvement in the intense struggle placed substantial strains on our family life. Had I been off drinking and gambling, I could have been criticized with impunity. That my distance was on behalf of such a worthy cause, stifled protest, and thus heightened tensions. A decade having passed, and with new wife and additional children acquired, it's now readily apparent that if one wants to maintain a good family life, spouse and children must have the opportunity to give "informed consent" to activities that so significantly affect them.

That brings me to another cardinal ordinance of public interest lobbying. We guys with the white hats do not possess the money or control enough votes to achieve power. To be successful, therefore, we must expend tremendous amounts of personal time and energy, for which a psychic price is exacted. One hopes the results are worth the price.

MARY LASKER'S ADVICE

A few months later Judie and I visited the elegant townhouse of Mary Lasker in New York. Mary, truly one of the most remarkable women in America, was then in her seventies. She has three main loves: impressionist art, fresh flowers, and improving the nation's health. She also has energy, money, and brains, the combination of which is responsible for her success. Politicians who vote for health get a financial contribution from Mrs. Lasker. I know of no other health advocate who lays it on the line in such a fashion. Money alone, however, is not the secret. Several times a year Mary makes the rounds of Capitol Hill offices to urge support for health legislation and appropriations. She is tenacious. If a congressman is delayed, she will patiently sit in the waiting room for hours, if need be, to deliver her persuasive message. Interestingly, the most distinguished health lobbyists I know, like Mary Lasker and Michael DeBakey, the heart surgeon, are also the most patient. Others, who achieve less success, huff and puff about their busy schedules as if they are doing the congressman a favor to testify or visit with him. In lobbying it is well to remember who is the supplicant.

Mrs. Lasker abhors publicity about herself, not because she is shy, but for the pragmatic reason that it would reduce her effectiveness. It was first lady Lady Bird Johnson who presided over a national beautification program, not her flower-loving friend Mary Lasker. It was Senator Lister Hill of Alabama and Congressman John Fogarty of Rhode Island who built the National Institutes of Health, not Mary Lasker who with her trusted aide Mike Gorman, set them up, along with NIH Director James Shannon. (Drew, 1967).

Our visit to Mrs. Lasker had two objectives: we wanted her to serve on our Board of Trustees, as well as her advice on how we could raise money. I was frank with Mary (it does not pay not to be) in saying that we wanted her name on our letterhead for the prestige it would lend. I knew that Mrs. Lasker had long ago staked out her major health interests; cancer, heart disease, mental health, and universal health insurance. Though supportive of other "disease campaigns," she does not spread herself too thin. Mary agreed to serve on our board as long as she did not have to attend any meetings. Gorman later said she assented because she liked my political activities, and did not want me to get discouraged.

Mrs. Lasker's ideas about raising money were blunt and fascinating. "If you're thinking that your foundation can ever raise enough money to support an adequate SIDS research effort, forget it," she said. "By tremendous effort you may be able to scrape up a few pennies, but SIDS can never be a cause that will attract big dollars."

The youthful-appearing septuagenarian who was instrumental in founding the American Cancer Society went on to explain: "Basically, people give money to fight a disease either because they've had personal experience or because they fear it might strike them. Why do you think the Cancer Society and Heart Association are so successful?

SIDS hits young families and poor families. Older people who have money to give aren't afraid of dying of SIDS."

Mrs. Lasker did not intend to discourage us; she was just being realistic. Providing a glimpse into her political philosophy, she went on: "The federal government has the responsibility of dealing with health problems of the poor. We all pay taxes; a certain proportion of those dollars should go to improve our health. You'll have a much better chance of reaching your goals if you push HEW than if you try to do the job yourselves."

"Abe," she said, turning to me, "you've been successful working on 'the Hill' and you've already got the most powerful legislator [Magnuson] as your friend. Get *him* to work for you."

So those were our marching orders from the individual who has been more successful than anyone in the country mobilizing both private and public funds for health. Her advice made sense.

5

THE POWER OF
WARREN MAGNUSON

At the time of his unsuccessful effort in 1980 to win a seventh term, Warren G. Magnuson, who loved to call himself a "workhorse," (as opposed to a "showhorse") was president *pro tempore* of the U.S. Senate, having served longer than any other member. Yet, in 1980, the senior senator from Washington probably ranked near the bottom of a name-recognition list of American politicians. When Eric Redman, a former aide, offered to do a piece on him for the *New York Times Magazine*, he was told that few readers would know of or care about the senator's existence.

Magnuson, orphaned in infancy, grew up in Fargo, North Dakota. At the age of 19 he literally "rode the rails" out to Seattle where he worked his way through the University of Washington by carrying ice on his back. He was elected to the House of Representatives in 1937 at the age of 31. Virtually the first bill to carry Magnuson's name as sponsor was the authorizing legislation creating the National Cancer Institute. He was elected to the Senate in 1944 and routinely reelected until 1962 when he barely survived the challenge of a political unknown. Senator Magnuson is prominently mentioned in Eric Redman's *Dance of Legislation* (1974), the best single account of how the U.S. Congress functions. Here is what Redman says of Magnuson's career:

> The 1962 election formed the watershed of Magnuson's career, even though that career was already thirty years old and the Senator in his late fifties. Had he been defeated, or simply reelected without difficulty, he might have been remembered almost solely for billions of dollars'

41

worth of capital improvements in Washington State, a handful of major bills like the National Cancer Institute and the National Science Foundation, and an important but arcane mass of transportation legislation he had moved through his Commerce Committee. From the ashes of near defeat, however, Magnuson's career rose in what can only be termed a phoenix-like transformation. It was not that he stopped bringing Federal dollars home to Washington State, or that he backed away from expressing his liberal views. He simply began to use his accumulated power systematically in behalf of more social legislation with national significance. With a new staff of young lawyers, headed by Gerry Grinstein, he began to produce consumer-protection legislation—first in a trickle, then in a torrent. The Senate Commerce Committee, once the staid guardian of business interests, changed almost overnight into the "consumer's panel" on Capitol Hill (it was as if the Armed Services Committee were suddenly to take up the citizen's cause against the Pentagon). Old cronies and lobbyists spluttered in disbelief, Ralph Nader had easy access to the Senator's office, reporters wrote of a "rekindled" Magnuson, and back home, Republican officials with eyes on a Senate seat became more and more dispirited as Magnuson's image began to change. (pp. 194-95)

I came to know Senator Magnuson in 1966. I had completed a survey of power lawn mower injuries and came to the conclusion that their number and severity could be markedly reduced by some basic changes in product design. I mentioned the work at lunch one day to an old high school classmate, Stan Sender, a young attorney then employed by Magnuson's Senate Commerce Committee. Sender asked, "what are you going to do with that study, publish it in a medical journal?" "Of course," I responded, "I'm just starting up the academic ladder and publish all my research." "That's just like you doctors," he said, "you're always talking to each other instead of to people who can do something about problems." Continuing on the "straight-man" line, I said, "what do you suggest?" "Just give me the paper," he said. Indeed my precious manuscript eventually was published in a medical journal (Bergman 1965), but not before I saw a wire-service story headlined: "Magnuson Warns Power Mower Industry." His Senate floor speech, drafted by a student summer intern, threatened regulatory legislation unless the industry corrected the unsafe design features.

That was my introduction to the practice of what I call "political medicine," which is employment of the political system to achieve improvements in health. It seemed that the power mower industry paid more attention to the chairman of the Senate Commerce Committee than to an obscure baby doctor in Seattle. I was promptly invited to speak at the industry's convention about lawn mower injuries and was impressed by the many protestations of concern and resolutions to produce safer mowers. Infinitely more skeptical was an attendee at my talk, Mike Pertschuk, a buddy of Ralph Nader, who had been appointed counsel of the Consumer Subcommittee of the Senate Commerce Committee. (Pertschuk later became chairman of the Federal Trade Commission under President Carter.) He and Stan Sender introduced me to Magnuson's administrative assistant, Gerry Grinstein, who became a close personal friend, as well as my "political guru." The power mower industry's failure to promulgate meaningful safety standards led directly to Magnuson legislation creating first, the National Commission on Product Safety, and, later, the Consumer Product Safety Commission.

WORK AS A CRYPTIC STAFF PERSON

Awed by the alacrity with which my power lawn mower study had been adopted by the Magnuson staff, I threw a few more proposals into the pipeline that ended up as the Flammable Fabric Act Amendments of 1967 and the Poison Prevention Packaging Act of 1970. To be accepted by the Magnuson team I had to contribute more than grand concepts. They were in need of unbiased technical advice, drafts of speeches, reports, etc. When I did not have the information, which was frequent, I was able to call on others at the University of Washington who were honored to help. For example, in the flammable fabrics legislation, the advice of a mechanical engineer and a home economist were invaluable. I also learned the importance of swallowing hard when my advice was not taken or when my speech drafts were not delivered. For example, during the 1968 campaign, Magnuson was asked to speak to a convention of health insurance executives. I drafted what I thought was a stupendous speech containing some very innovative proposals. Grinstein very calmly tore it up and substituted some warmed-over palaver. "We don't go making big waves when we're ahead in the polls," he explained.

The 1968 campaign was run almost wholly on the consumer issue. Great emphasis was placed on Magnuson's legislative efforts in child safety. "I've got kids, I'm for Maggie" was a campaign slogan displayed prominently on billboards throughout the state. Because of or in spite of his campaign, Magnuson won an overwhelming victory. There is no better way to gain the trust of a politician than to assist him during a political campaign. Because I had "earned my spurs," Senator Magnuson was not averse to listening to my recommendations.

One such recommendation was that the Senator take on the chairmanship of the Appropriations Subcommittee, which held the purse strings for the Department of HEW. Given his seniority, Maggie had his choice of any of the subcommittees. Most of his staff wanted him to oversee funds for the new Department of Housing and Urban Development. The nation was in the midst of the "war on poverty," and they felt that the most "action" (e.g., political influence) was to be had in affairs of the cities. Health lobbyists, however, like Mike Gorman, were desperate for a sympathetic and powerful senator to fill the shoes of the just-retired Lister Hill. I spoke to the senator several times about how much personal pride he would gain by activities in the health field. I did not fail to mention how much he would be able to help his beloved "baby," the National Cancer Institute. His wife was being successfully treated for bladder cancer at the time. Far more important than my recommendation was that of his chief aide Grinstein, who also urged him to chair the HEW Subcommittee. Who knows what finally tipped the scales? Magnuson waited until the day before Congress organized in January 1969 to announce that he would assume chairmanship of the HEW Appropriations Subcommittee.

WORKINGS OF THE HEW APPROPRIATIONS SUBCOMMITTEE

Before 1975 when Congress created its Budget Committees, members of the Appropriations Committees in both Houses, especially the subcommittee chairmen, held unrivaled power over policies of "their" departments. (The final results of the turf battle between the traditional Appropriations Committees and the upstart Budget Committees are not in at the time of writing, but it is possible to say that significant incursions have been made into the Appropriation's bastions.)

Department witnesses appear before the Appropriations Subcommittees starting off with the secretary, then going on down to the program directors to "defend" the budget submitted by the President through the Office of Management and Budget (OMB). It is a phony exercise, because everyone knows that the administration witnesses all have fought with OMB for a larger slice of the pie but are obliged to support the president. The sessions can be a love feast or a grilling depending on the personalities involved and the political currents of the time.

After hearing department witnesses, public witnesses then appear. This consists of a parade of advocates requesting that funds for their particular program or disease be increased. Since department officials cannot themselves plead for more money, they arrange for grant recipients to come in on their knees. A favorite ploy is to get constituents of members, especially the chairman, to do the pleading. As soon as Magnuson took over the subcommittee, a host of witnesses from the State of Washington, including me, began trekking across the country.

At the completion of the hearings, the subcommittee meets to decide on budget allocations, which is called a "mark-up." The committee also issues a report ostensibly to explain its decisions. It serves as a report card from Congress on the performance of the agency. The report may applaud or criticize operations. New "initiatives" may be called for, or "unsuccessful" programs may be axed. Wording nuances such as suggest, recommend, strongly urge, or demand do not carry the force of law, but they are ignored only at the agency's peril.

The subcommittees have a lot of money to work with. For example, the total budget for the fiscal year 1984 for the Department of Health and Human Services was $318.5 billion, which includes entitlement programs like Medicare, Medicaid, and Social Security. The members of the subcommittee cannot possibly keep tabs on the details of the budget, let alone concern themselves with the details of the committee report. Members do concern themselves with the total figure, or more accurately, how closely the budget conforms to the president's request. They also concern themselves with pet projects in their districts. Getting reelected is still priority number one for any self-respecting legislator. Otherwise, the details are left to staff members. By details, I mean influence over millions rather than billions of dollars, and total responsibility for the committee report. It is said with accuracy that a senior staff member of an appropriations subcommittee has more power than a junior representative or senator. Among congressional staffers, few were as influential, or as little known (to the public), as Harley M. Dirks, who bore the inauspicious title of "professional staff member" of the Labor-HEW Subcommittee of the Senate Committee on Appropriations.

HARLEY DIRKS

Harley Dirks comes from a small farming community in the eastern part of Washington state, called Othello. He has never been accused of lacking enterprise. During World War II he was stationed on an isolated naval base in the Aleutian Islands. To pass time, the brash 19-year-old published a successful newspaper widely distributed throughout

Alaska. After the war he simultaneously operated several successful businesses in Othello, including mercantile, shoe, and liquor stores. He also dabbled in Democratic politics.

In 1964 he ran Lyndon Johnson's presidential campaign in the eastern part of the state. The Democrats did unexpectedly well in that traditionally Republican area. Dirks's work came to the attention of Senator Magnuson, who invited him to come to Washington, D.C., to be his staff person on the Appropriations Committee. With his bright colored shirts and ties, and "home-spun" manner of speech, Harley loved to play the role of the "rural rustic." The more pompous his visitor, a frequent happening, the more "laid back" became Dirks. Woe to the unsuspecting dude who underestimated Harley. It was his job to be familiar with every decimal point of the massive budget.

Why the talk about Harley Dirks in a discussion about SIDS? It's simply that well-intentioned advocates will continue to beat their heads against the wall until they find the Harley Dirks of the world. *To effect change, one must either possess power oneself or find someone with power willing to "push the button."* Warren Magnuson was favorably inclined toward helping with SIDS, just as he was willing to help with many other worthy causes. SIDS, however, was not an issue that consumed much of his attention. Dirks was the person who actually pushed the button.

Some described me as a good friend of Warren Magnuson. It was not true in the usual sense of social relationships. However, since the notion imbued me with a degree of clout, I did not run around denying it. I dropped by to see Magnuson when in Washington, but rarely discussed business. I learned that, when I came to him with a shopping list of requests, he would quickly "turn off." On the other hand, when he knew I was not going to "bug" him, he would relax and become sociable. Magnuson liked to get his information and make decisions in an orderly fashion. He hired good staff and expected them to sift through the myriad of requests and consult him at an appropriate time. Many big moguls think that a successful trip to Washington means laughing and scratching with the "big man" and do not demean themselves by visiting with lowly staff assistants. They are the losers. The successful advocate is one with a scent for the person who can do the job.

NO LUCK IN THE HOUSE

Try as we might, we could not locate a Warren Magnuson or Harley Dirks on the House side. I tried testifying twice before their Appropriations Subcommittee, presided over by Daniel Flood, from Wilkes-Barre, Pennsylvania, one of the most colorful figures in Congress. At one time Flood is said to have been a Shakespearean actor, and he played the part perfectly. He strode through the halls of Congress with a long cape, sporting a thin waxed mustache. In contrast to the gregarious Magnuson, who enjoyed chatting with the "public witnesses," Flood gave the appearance of scarcely being able to put up with the ordeal. He gave a courtly greeting and dismissal to every witness. While I testified he slowly and meticulously tapped his pencil as if it were a metronome. No questions were asked. I did not succeed in moving the committee; they did not mention a word about SIDS in their report, let alone appropriate any funds. Judie Choate testified another year but succeeded only in drawing the ire of Congressman Paton of New Jersey who had read somewhere that the prevention of "crib death" had already been discovered. Ann Barr of our Massachusetts chapter and their medical adviser, Dr. Fred Mandell, from Boston Children's Hospital, worked hard to cultivate Representative Silvio Conte of Massachusetts, a member of the subcommittee. Whether their efforts had anything to do with it or not, SIDS was at last mentioned in the House Subcommittee reports starting in 1974, but no additional funds were recommended.

EARMARKING FUNDS FOR SIDS RESEARCH

Beginning in 1970, I appeared every year as a witness before the Senate Appropriations Subcommittee to plead that funds be earmarked for SIDS research. Much more importantly, I prepared appropriate language urging such support, which Dirks inserted into the committee report. At first, no specific sum was mentioned; the committee urged that NICHD utilize a proportion of its already appropriated funds for SIDS. This was a difficult proposition for NICHD, never one of the favored institutes (compared to cancer and heart disease) and already committed to such important problems as research in mental retardation and aging. To help matters at the other end, the NICHD director, Gerry LaVeck, convened a meeting of prominent scientists in August 1971 to designate important target areas for SIDS research "should funds be made available." This was a ploy to demonstrate that the institute had a definite "battle plan" and was prepared to launch a SIDS research program if and when funds were appropriated.

Here is a reasonable facsimile of the pirouette danced by Chairman Magnuson and NICHD Director LaVeck during the appropriations hearings in 1973:

Chm: "Is SIDS an important health problem?"

L: "Yes sir, SIDS kills about 10,000 babies a year in the United States."

Chm: "Then why aren't you asking for any money for SIDS research?"

L: "Well sir, this Administration is very concerned about inflation and is attempting to exercise fiscal constraint in regard to new budget initiatives."

Chm: "Look doctor, this committee knows something about inflation, but we are asking you for your professional opinion as to whether money should be spent on SIDS research?"

L: "My professional opinion is that more research on SIDS is needed."

Chm: "Does the Institute have a plan for spending money on SIDS research if we make it available."

L: "I am not authorized to request any new monies for SIDS research, but if the Committee sees fit to provide additional funds, we do in fact have a plan for supporting SIDS research."

Chm: "Thank you doctor."

It quickly followed that in 1973 the Senate Appropriations Committee recommended that $8 million be earmarked for SIDS research. How was that figure arrived at? Institute officials estimated that $4 million would fund an appropriate research effort. The administration, as usual, requested no money; neither did the House of Representatives. Since differences between the more generous Senate and more miserly House were usually split in half, Magnuson allowed $8 million to go into the Senate bill. The script went as predicted. Despite a Nixon veto of the HEW Appropriations Bill in 1973, $4 million became available and a significant SIDS program finally got underway.

THE NICHD RESEARCH INITIATIVE

It was quite evident that Warren Magnuson's power reached the NIH campus at Bethesda. When NICHD officials finally were sure that there would be additional funds for SIDS research, they proceeded to develop an impressive research program. Dwain Walcher never got to participate in allocating the extra funds provided by Congress; he had left NICHD by that time. The SIDS research program was administered by Eileen Hasselmeyer, a pediatric nurse with a Ph.D. in physiology, who headed the Perinatal Biology and Infant Mortality Branch, and Jehu Hunter, originally trained as a chemist, who was assistant director of the Office of Program Planning and Evaluation.

As mentioned previously, the problem in SIDS research was not only paucity of money but a lack of trained scientists willing to turn their attention to the problem. NICHD used two approaches to cultivate the scientists. First, they simply took out full-page advertisements in scientific journals that funds for SIDS research were available for proposals in a selected number of subject areas, an example of which can be seen in Appendix III. The scientific community, reeling from the cutbacks of a Republican administration, responded to the bait. The other strategy was to invite selected investigators to SIDS research seminars focusing on such aspects as neurophysiology, immunology, and epidemiology. Most of the attendees knew nothing about SIDS, which was the idea. They had to learn about the problem in order to discuss it intelligently. Some of the most promising research work has been conducted by scientists who were solicited to attend those NICHD workshops. (I have harassed NICHD officials for over a decade to follow the same tack in sponsoring research in childhood injury prevention. Injuries are the greatest killer of children and young adults, and only a handful of scientists have interested themselves in the problem. To date I have been totally unsuccessful.)

For a problem like SIDS, where there was much speculation and few established investigators, a large number of proposals were received by NICHD that can only be described as license-seeking to chase wild geese. The institute was under much pressure, especially from the Guild for Infant Survival to fund any kind of research that was labeled as being related to SIDS. I commended them at the time, and still do today for insisting that the dollars spent for research only be given to projects rated by peers as being of high quality. Though there are flaws in the NIH peer review system of awarding grants and contracts, no one has yet come up with a better procedure. Note should be taken of my praise for this HEW agency. It is the last time in this book that I will have any good words for "the feds."

Getting a research initiative going was relatively easy. There was one target, NICHD, that could be moved by congressional pressure. Seeing that SIDS families were dealt with in a compassionate manner was far more difficult. There were so many different bases that had to be touched.

6

SENSITIZING
PROFESSIONALS

A basic premise of our "humanization" campaign was that SIDS parents were treated badly because of ignorance rather than malice. In the early 1970s most laymen had never even heard of "crib death." Health professionals fell into two general categories. Either they knew nothing or, if they had heard of the entity, held the belief that, "since nothing was known about 'crib death,' there was nothing that could be done about it." Our educational mission was aimed at making two main points: SIDS was a distinct disease entity that could be identified through a postmortem examination; and that something *could* be done, alleviation of guilt.

Our educational technique consisted of simple consciousness raising. When the plight of SIDS parents could be graphically illustrated, we could invariably count on a compassionate response from both laymen and health professionals. Our task was to cast out a large net and draw in as many "converts" as possible. Given our limited resources, we had to be selective about our targets. Highest priority was placed on educating those most likely to come in contact with SIDS, namely physicians, nurses, social workers, firemen, policemen, clergymen, and morticians. Our NSIDSF chapters understandably wanted to "get the word out" to any ears that were listening. Judie Choate and I were constantly urging them to direct their educational efforts toward these target groups, rather than passing out pamphlets at state fairs.

REACHING PHYSICIANS

Physicians were the most important and most difficult targets. Important because, whether we physicians know anything or not, the public thinks we do, and thus we set the style on health matters. Difficult, because we are trained to act "professional," which all-too-often results in our being perceived as cold and inhumane.

How are physicians influenced? Many parties are interested in this question, none more than drug companies who have millions of dollars at stake. Physicians are inundated with propaganda of all sorts urging some change in practice. A most challenging task for those of us involved in medical education is to teach young doctors how to sort the wheat from the chaff. We constantly stress the difference between information that has been reviewed and criticized by colleagues supposedly expert in the subject, and unreviewed material tending to reflect some personal or organizational bias. With justification, physicians are especially skeptical when subjected to onslaughts by zealous laypersons about medical practices. As is apparent, despite protestations by many segments of society, I happen to believe that the public is best served by this traditional and admittedly elitist approach.

With the above philosophy in mind, we knew that our appeals to physicians would be more effective if buttressed by papers in respectable medical journals and presentations at prestigious medical meetings. In 1969 Beckwith, our project nurse, Margaret Pomeroy, and I prepared a manuscript called, "The Psychiatric Toll of Sudden Infant Death Syndrome." It was the first description of the characteristic grief and guilt reactions in SIDS. We decided to submit the paper to the *American Journal of Psychiatry*. It seemed obvious to us that psychiatrists would want to be among the first to learn about this hitherto undescribed entity. Another less lofty motive was Beckwith's desire to be the first pathologist to have an article published in a psychiatric journal. Despite our logic, the manuscript was summarily rejected on the grounds that SIDS was not deemed appropriate subject material for the journal's readership. We next tried a journal with a wide readership, *General Practice* (now called the *American Journal of Family Practice*) that did not feel so snooty and published the paper (1969).

SUPPORT OF PEDIATRICIANS

From the beginning we knew that our main source of medical support would have to come from pediatricians. Besides being the lowest paid of all medical specialists, pediatricians also have tended to be more involved than their colleagues in community health activities. In inspiring contrast to any other group of medical specialists, the American Academy of Pediatrics calls on pediatricians to be concerned with the health and welfare of *all* children, not just those under one's personal care. A fact not well known to those who rail against the "medical establishment" is the relatively progressive political posture of the academy. For example, they have been at the forefront of the battles for Project Headstart, expanded and improved day care, maternal and child health appropriations, family planning, banning of lead from paint, and many forms of consumer safety legislation. It was not difficult, then, to enlist the resources of the academy for our cause. It did not hurt that I had worked on other academy activities in the past and was known to their leadership.

To digress a moment, I've found it advantageous to work whenever possible within the structure of organized medicine. Despite the fact that my political philosophy is to the left of that of most of my colleagues, I'm accepted in my local and state medical associations as well as the Academy of Pediatrics. The tangible support of these organizations (e.g., access to their paid lobbyists) has helped bring several of my advocacy projects to fruition. An exception is the American Medical Association, to which I do not belong. The AMA's political stances are too far removed from my own.

A key determinant of the success of a local NSIDSF chapter was the presence of a committed pediatrician serving as medical adviser. These individuals, all of whom had busy practices, like Fred Mandell of Boston, Norman Lewak of Oakland, Wayne Marsh of Omaha, and many others, rank high on my personal honor roll. Countless hours were devoted to counseling individual families, interpreting confusing autopsy reports, explaining the welter of sensational stories in the lay press, and interceding with local physicians, coroners, and health department officials. It is virtually impossible for laymen, no matter how energetic, to bring about changes in the health system without participation of physicians. Whether it is right or wrong, doctors listen to other doctors before they listen to anyone else. To ignore this precept is to invite failure.

The American Academy of Pediatrics helped in three ways: First, by allowing me to present papers on SIDS at their annual conventions in 1968 and 1974. The academy meetings are well covered by the medical and lay press. Scores of reports on my talks went out all over the country. Second, the academy's legislative office in Washington, headed at the time by George Degnon, helped all our efforts on Capitol Hill. Lastly, the academy periodically issues position papers on child health care that are important in establishing "standard procedures." After I submitted written and oral testimony, the academy's Committee on the Infant and Pre-school Child adopted the Foundation's four-point program for managing sudden and unexpected infant death. The academy's statement was published in the December 1972 issue of their official journal, *Pediatrics*. Armed with that statement we could then visit recalcitrant physicians, health departments, or coroner's offices and not be dismissed as emotional kooks.

MEDICAL EXAMINERS

The National Association of Medical Examiners was another story. This organization of forensic pathologists had the power to demonstrably improve the management of SIDS throughout the country. Some medical examiners such as Larry Lewman in Portland, John Coe in Minneapolis, Lawrence Harris in Vermont, and Russell Fisher in Baltimore, among others, were already doing a good job and needed no pressure from us. The majority of the group, however did not see that counseling families was a responsibility of forensic pathologists. Our chief targets were big-city medical examiners such as James Luongo in Boston, Milton Helpern in New York, and Thomas Noguchi in Los Angeles. They were already the objects of considerable criticism from SIDS parents in their local communities and thus were not exactly in a receptive frame of mind.

In 1972 Helpern was considered the dean of American forensic pathologists. He had been a founder of their association. When Judie Choate bravely appeared before their group in Atlanta that year to ask for assistance, Helpern took the floor to loudly rebuke her for "telling lies about my office in New York City." Such was his influence within the association that none of his colleagues rose to Judie's defense. But in 1974 Helpern was forced to resign from his post as New York medical examiner after investigators found a prominent socialite's skull in his museum bearing what obviously were bullet holes. Helpern had previously ruled that the cause of death in this case was natural. It was only upon Helpern's departure in 1974 that some of our friends within the association were able to push through a suggested management standard similar to that issued by the Academy of Pediatrics.

Because of the potential for both direct influence and attendant press coverage, we always were trying to wangle speaking engagements at the meetings of national organizations of health professionals, but we achieved only marginal success. The only organizations and publications that on their own accord came to us soliciting speakers and articles were from the nursing profession. Nurses justifiably perceived an important role for themselves in assisting SIDS families.

EDUCATIONAL SEMINARS

Our most effective means of professional education turned out to be multidisciplinary seminars. The format was always the same. Our local chapters, aided by their medical advisers, sent invitations to physicians, public health nurses, mental health professionals, clergymen, policemen, firemen, morticians, and any others apt to have contact with SIDS. An out-of-town guest speaker always boosted attendance. Most hospitals conduct weekly educational conferences called grand rounds, as much to give physicians an opportunity to socialize as to improve their minds. Scheduling the seminars to coincide with pediatric grand rounds helped ensure physician attendance.

The scientific aspects of SIDS were covered first. This was always "safe" and bestirred few emotions. Next came the "grabber": parents giving account of what happened to them. There was no need for embellishment; the stories were real, and it took a hard heart indeed to remain unaffected. Those with experience in dealing with SIDS families would then provide helpful suggestions on appropriate management.

The seminars produced a number of results. First, sensitization of local health professionals invariably led to improvements in the local SIDS management system. Second, local media publicity reached many SIDS parents and their relatives and friends. A single newspaper story proclaiming that parents are not at fault when their babies die can have enormous impact. I encountered numerous parents clutching a tattered newspaper story as if it were a reprieve from the gallows. Finally, each seminar seemed to inspire one or two "converts" who would involve themselves in the cause by participating actively in the work of our local chapters.

I should mention a fascinating phenomenon that frequently occurred when I gave talks on SIDS to physicians. After the question period, a doctor would hesitatingly move toward me, not sure whether or not to make contact. He would then say something like: "you know, 12 years ago I had a baby in my practice who died of 'crib death.' I'd just examined the kid two days before, and he seemed fine. I've always wondered what I missed." The same thing happened with Beckwith. Before long we began to anticipate the parade of guilty doctors wanting to confess their guilt. It was not only parents who were unnecessarily guilty about losing babies to SIDS. Though theirs were not as heavy, physicians too were bearing crosses.

GETTING A MOVIE PRODUCED

Soon after we launched our national consciousness-raising campaign, we became aware of our acute lack of troops. There were few physicians who knew anything about SIDS, fewer still who could integrate the scientific with the human aspects, and there were none willing and able to travel around the country. In fact, up until 1974 our national physician-speaking engagements were filled exclusively by Molly Dapena, Bruce Beckwith, and myself. Judie Choate and Carolyn Szybist of Chicago were more effective speakers than we physicians, but they too had many responsibilities, not the least of which were families with small children.

There was no way that our tiny band could reach audiences around the country that needed to be "saved." We had not even begun to bring our message to medical, nursing, and other health professional schools. How could we multiply our efforts? An educational movie seemed the answer, but the NSIDSF lacked the $30,000 that was the minimum amount for a "bare-bones," black-and-white product.

Remembering Mary Lasker's words about pressing the feds, Judie Choate and I decided to drop into Harley Dirks' cluttered office. We explained that we had run up against a stone wall in trying to evince any interest from the Office of Maternal and Child Health (OMCH) in assisting our educational campaign. Harley mused for a few moments, puffing on his ever-present pipe. He then picked up the phone and called Dr. Lesser, the OMCH director. "Doc," (Harley's form of addressing all physicians) he said, "I've got two people in my office who are having some difficulties trying to educate doctors and nurses about that disease that kills little babies—crib death, I think it's called. I wonder if you would be able to help them?" That was all. No threats, no cajoling, no yelling; just a polite request for assistance. Lesser told Harley that he would look around to see if he could find some extra money.

Back in Seattle a few days later, I was not too surprised to get a phone call from Lesser, who sounded ever-so-much more cordial than in our previous meeting. Without once alluding to Dirks, he said that by some prodigious effort, he had somehow come up with $30,000 produce a movie and $5,000 to conduct regional seminars. OMCH could not give the money directly to the NSIDSF, however, because we did not have a formal mechanism for receiving grants, and the funds could only be given to an institution affiliated with a university. George Stone, the administrator of my hospital, agreed to have Children's Orthopedic Hospital and Medical Center in Seattle serve as a conduit for the NSIDSF, and in a few weeks the money was awarded.

The $5,000 allowed us to conduct ten regional seminars. With the $30,000 we were able to contract with New York filmmaker Peter Robinson to produce a black-and-white movie that we called *One in 350*. The film was very simple. There were interviews with Bruce Beckwith and Molly Dapena on the current state of knowledge about SIDS, along with sensitive interviews with four families who had lost children. The family interviews were gut wrenching. I've seen *One in 350* over 50 times and still get tears in my eyes when a nine-year-old girl describes how she felt when taunted by her classmates after her baby brother died.

Our contract covered the costs of making ten prints of the film. These ten prints were kept in constant use by our chapters. We had hoped that OMCH would reproduce enough prints to send to hospitals, and to medical and nursing schools around the country. They demurred. There were technical imperfections that kept the film from "coming up to government standards." Also, they felt that by reproducing and distributing a film produced by the Foundation, they would antagonize our "competitors," the Guild for Infant Survival. The Office of Maternal and Child Health would contract for production of an "independent" film about SIDS. It took two years, and three times as much money for that film, *After Our Baby Died*, to be made and distributed. (It turned out to be a fine movie.)

By spending $30,000 on a movie and $5,000 for a series of seminars, the Department of Health, Education and Welfare had finally become involved in the human aspects of SIDS. This miniscule step was taken, not because the department perceived the dimensions of the problem, but because Harley Dirks turned their heads in the right direction. This was an important victory for us, not easily won. The pace of progress, however, was far too slow. We needed a big break. That came in the form of an announcement of a Senate hearing on SIDS.

7

THE MONDALE
HEARINGS

On January 25, 1972, the Subcommittee on Children and Youth, of the Senate Committee on Labor and Public Welfare held a hearing on "the problem of sudden infant death in the United States." It was "part of the subcommittee's continuing examination of the rights of children—1972" or so read the official announcement, as if congressional hearings allow for scholarly systematic examination of anything.

Of all the complex operations of Congress, hearings probably are the most misunderstood. Our legislators go to great lengths to keep it that way. Most people look upon hearings as judicial proceedings where evidence is presented, received, and passed upon in a dispassionate manner. This perception is far from the truth. No congressional hearing ever is convened without some predetermined political end in mind. Invariably that end benefits the committee chairman, who holds almost absolute control over the agenda and the list of witnesses. To keep the legislative machinery greased, the ranking minority member is usually "consulted," but the chairman runs the show. Aside from having a minimum term of six years instead of just two, the biggest attraction of holding a Senate seat as opposed to a position in the House is the chance for each senator to chair some committee. Just about every member of the Senate, no matter how junior, gets to be a chairman or ranking minority member (depending on one's party) of some subcommittee. Not so in the House where there's a long waiting list for every chairmanship.

At the time of this writing, former Vice-President Walter Mondale is still recovering following his defeat by Ronald Reagan in the presidential election of 1984. Indeed, Mondale vows never to seek public office again. In 1972, though, Mondale, a bright, handsome, articulate Democratic senator from Minnesota, was looking for some turf he could call his own. Throughout the 1970s it was his fate to find himself constantly overshadowed by other liberal Democrats, Hubert Humphrey and Edward (Ted) Kennedy. After 1972, when Humphrey, for a time, renounced his own presidential ambitions, he tried to push those of his protege Mondale. Kennedy was not so self-effacing. When Mondale finally did make a run for the brass ring in 1975, Kennedy simply refused to yield ground as the leading liberal spokesman on a variety of issues (i.e., social welfare, foreign affairs, finance), thus depriving Mondale of a substantial constituency. The senator from Minnesota eventually withdrew from the 1976 presidential sweepstakes, stating, at the time, that he lacked the superhuman ambition required to maintain the grueling pace of a presidential campaign. But we're getting ahead of our story; in 1972 Walter Fritz Mondale was positioning himself for a presidential bid.

It is unfortunate that the health and welfare of mothers and children are not an issue over which politicians grapple for attention. Mondale thus was not treading on anyone's turf by assuming the chairmanship of the Subcommittee on Children and Youth. In 1971 the major focus of the subcommittee was proposed legislation to provide federal assistance for day care. The legislation passed swiftly through Congress before the conservative community became aware of its existence. When the word got out, however, the alarms were sounded, and the legislation was vetoed by President Nixon. Nixon characterized this much-needed program as "destructive to American family life." Coming on the heels of the bruising day-care battle, SIDS was a noncontroversial lark, and Mondale took up the cudgels.

It would be unfair of me to suggest that Fritz Mondale adopted the cause of SIDS just for his own political gain. SIDS was a minor issue carrying with it little potential for significant political gain or risk. Nevertheless, there were political stakes, or else Mondale would not have wasted his time. *A simple truth that often fails to affect the behavior of many "do-gooders" is that even the most idealistic politicians have to win elections. There's a fine line between a "courageous stand" on a controversial issue and political suicide.* Senators Wayne Morse of Oregon and Ernest Gruening of Alaska will long be remembered as the only two senators who voted nay on the Gulf of Tonkin resolution that "legitimized" U.S. involvement in Vietnam. Less well remembered is that both men were defeated the next time they ran for office due in large measure because of their "courageous" votes. Advocates of a cause will get farthest if they keep in mind the potential political consequences, as well as the intrinsic merits, of their viewpoint. This does not mean advocacy only of popular views will be successful. It does mean that, in urging a politician to take up a potentially controversial issue, morally righteous browbeating is usually counterproductive.

INSTIGATING THE HEARINGS

Neither I nor anyone else from NSIDSF had much to do with initiating the Mondale hearings. Most of the credit belongs to the Guild for Infant Survival (GIS). As mentioned before, it is hard for me to be objective about the guild. They desperately wanted to do something about SIDS, but their enthusiasm was often tinged with suspicion. Nevertheless, their approach worked in late 1971, as guild members bombarded legislators with letters urging a congressional investigation into why the Department of HEW was ignoring SIDS.

The mere suggestion of a purposeful conspiracy in the executive branch attracts the attention of legislators like a shark to blood. The quickest way to get the attention of an executive department is to send a letter of complaint to a congressman. All such letters are quickly shipped over to the suspected offender. Congressional inquiries receive top priority; the department is obliged to answer each one within a few days. Most of the time the legislator does not wish to get actively involved but merely expects that his constituent will receive some information. In such cases, the letter to the constituent actually is drafted by a department functionary and then signed by the congressman or, more accurately, signed by the congressman's automatic letter-signing machine. Dr. LaVeck told me that in 1971 the task of answering critical letters written to Congressmen by members of the Guild for Infant Survival consumed almost half the time of NICHD personnel involved in the SIDS program.

So the interest of Congress was piqued by the guild. Who would take the lead? Enter Ellen Hoffman, professional staff member of the Senate Subcommittee on Children and Youth. She had been an education writer for the *Washington Post* before joining the Mondale subcommittee. Congressional staffers can be described as feudal knights serving their lords. Almost as much of their effort goes into jousting within their own castle grounds for the master's attention as into forays against other armies. All legislators assign staff members to the various committees on which they serve. These staff members are forever pulling at the master's sleeve for more attention to their committee. It was no small feat, then, for Hoffman to gain Mondale's assent to devote a whole half-day to hearings on SIDS.

PLANNING THE HEARINGS

Both the NSIDSF and GIS were officially notified in the beginning of January 1972 that the Senate Subcommittee on Children and Youth would hold a hearing on SIDS later in the month. Suggestions for witnesses were solicited. The guild dutifully complied and requested that Saul and Sylvia Goldberg be heard. I, on the other hand, was out of the starting block like a shot and instantly tried to take over the whole show. Descending on Ellen Hoffman's cubbyhole office, deep within the recesses of a converted apartment building known as the Senate Office Building Annex, I did not know if she would give me a welcome embrace or throw me out the door. With supreme arrogance, I made sure that she understood that while *she* had been in the Senate (a term loosely used by Senate staffers) for less than a year, *I* had been on the scene since 1966 and was intimately familiar with each and every detail of conducting Senate hearings. In every other sentence I bandied about the names of Warren Magnuson and Harley Dirks, both guaranteed to create awe from anyone interested in HEW appropriations.

It may have been true at that stage that I had more experience than Hoffman in stage-managing hearings. I was also aware that selection of the right witnesses was crucial in assuring that the hearing had maximal impact. I suspect, however, that the reason Hoffman allowed me to select the witnesses had more to do with her desire to share some of the workload than with my alleged superior wisdom. The format for the hearing was the same as that used for our presentations all over the country, namely, the combination of authoritative scientific information with the emotion of SIDS parents telling their own stories. The message had to be clearly portrayed. The federal government was doing absolutely nothing about a tragic disease that was killing 10,000 American babies a year. It was, in effect, to be a morality play.

A coup was getting Dr. Jay Arena, the president of the American Academy of Pediatrics (AAP) to testify on our behalf. This was arranged through the ever-cooperative director of the Washington AAP office, George Degnon. Dr. Arena's presence lent credibility, showing that SIDS was not just an issue for a small group of emotional parents. Rather, it was the concern of *the* major child health organization in the United States.

Which parents would testify? "New parents" who had just recently lost their baby could have the most dramatic impact. On the other hand, if they had no previous experience in public speaking, there was a danger that they would be overawed by the setting and retire into embarrassed silence. We decided on known quantities—SIDS parents who were experienced in telling their stories.

MEDIA COVERAGE

The impact of a congressional hearing is directly related to the coverage it receives. The media have to be constantly massaged, which involves several basic techniques. First, they have to be induced to cover the event. There are usually about 20 congressional hearings every day on Capitol Hill. TV can cover, at most, two or three. Newspapers and wire service reporters may cover a few more, but the event has to have some special appeal.

Senator Mondale's press secretary sent routine notices of the hearing to all the media contacts. If publicity efforts had been restricted to that action, the hearing would have played to an empty house. Judie Choate and I therefore followed up with letters and telephone calls to TV and newspaper assignment editors stressing the unusual (i.e., sensational) nature of the upcoming hearing. We were aided immeasurably by a magnificent feature story on "The Sudden Infant Death Mystery," written by Colman McCarthy, that appeared on December 31, 1971, in the editorial pages of the *Washington Post* (Appendix IV). To the Washington power structure, the importance of an issue often is defined by whether it is covered by the *Washington Post* or *New York Times*. The December 31 article, aside from eloquently stating our case, was our best possible calling card as we sought to obtain media coverage for the hearing.

A second technique is to "press the flesh" of reporters covering the hearing. Like other human beings, reporters are much more apt to respond to personal contact. A brief orientation to the subject matter at hand is appreciated.

Third, the chances of media coverage are greatly enhanced if a witness provides written testimony beforehand. Because of deadlines and the necessity of covering various events, reporters rarely stay throughout a hearing. More often they wander into a hearing, pick up copies of testimony lying on the press table, and leave. Likewise, television directors cannot keep their camera and lights on witnesses during the entire hearing. They try to identify "sexy" passages beforehand. The sequences of witnesses is also related to media coverage. Anything that happens after 11:00 A.M. will not make the evening newspapers. The "newsworthy" witnesses therefore must come first. All Congressmen are acutely conscious of "deadline time." If a sensational bombshell is to be dropped, there is a crucial time both in the morning and afternoon that will ensure maximum coverage.

The same game is played by the administration. Traditionally, in congressional hearings, the chief administration witness, usually a cabinet officer or an assistant secretary, comes first. If they wish to keep news out of the media, they will filibuster with long boring statements, thus putting off the appearance of critical witnesses beyond deadline time. This byplay for media attention is a fascinating process to observe.

THE HEARING COMES TO ORDER

Because of, or in spite of, our beating of the bushes, four television cameras (three major networks and a local D.C. channel) were in position, along with a full press table, when the hearing opened on the morning of January 25. Quite incidental to our overall purpose, the hearing room was also packed, mostly with SIDS parents. Normally, at routine Senate hearings, only the chairman of the committee and perhaps a minority member are present. Nothing attracts the senators to a hearing room, however, as much as the word that TV cameras are around. All of seven senators made the scene, which is remarkable for a hearing on a "minor" issue. The senators themselves were obviously surprised at the attention. We were later able to obtain a thoroughly unauthorized video tape ("out-take") of the proceedings through a contact at ABC News. Turning to Senator Allan Cranston, Senator Mondale observed, "Look at all those cameras; we'll get a lot more mileage out of this than I expected." The chairman, of course, did not realize that the microphones were already turned on and that his irreverent words were preserved for posterity.

Assuming his senatorial demeanor, Mondale banged down the gavel at 9:30 A.M. He proceeded to read a moving opening statement that had been drafted by Ellen Hoffman. The purpose in holding the hearing, Mondale said, was "to learn about past and present research efforts; to explore the prospects for discovering the cause and preventing future occurrences of SIDS; to understand the scope of activity within HEW; to inform the public and professions about this disease; and to learn from government officials, medical experts, and parents what more we can do to determine both the cause and provide assistance to those families who have been the victims of this deadly disease" (Hearing record, p. 2). He then called the first witness, Dr. Merlin K. DuVal, assistant secretary for health and scientific affairs of the Department of Health, Education and Welfare. DuVal was flanked by Dr. Arthur Lesser, director of the Office of Maternal and Child Health, and Dr. Gerald LaVeck, director of the National Institute of Child Health and Human Development.

THE WITNESS PARADE

Monte DuVal was a professor of surgery at the University of Arizona Medical School before coming to HEW. His knowledge about SIDS was doubtless gained the evening before the hearing when he was being briefed by his underlings. He had a large black notebook before him which he hoped contained answers to any questions that might be put forth.

DuVal's statement was relatively brief and straightforward. He outlined what the department was doing in SIDS, described some of the research but mentioned nothing about assistance to families. He testified:

> During FY 1971, 43 grants relating to SIDS and totaling 1.8 million dollars were supported by the NICHD. Of these, one is directed specifically to the cause of SIDS and is funded at a level of $46,258. The other grants are in areas of research which have been identified by scientists working in the field as being relevant to the sudden infant death syndrome. (Ibid., pp. 3-7)

Mondale, who also had been well briefed by Ellen Hoffman, took over the questioning. (Just in case, I had provided Ellen with a briefing memo for the senator along with a list of proposed questions.) He knew the points he wanted to bring out and proceeded quickly. Mondale's theme was the lack of any initiative at HEW in dealing with a disease that kills 10,000 babies a year. He elicited the information that HEW was doing nothing about soliciting research proposals, providing professional or public information, or caring about services to families. The factual portion of the hearing could have ended right there. The department's deficiencies had been brought out into the open. All the rest of the witnesses amplified on the enormity of the SIDS problem and the absence of government effort to deal with it.

Next came the medical testimony. Dr. Arena of the Academy of Pediatrics performed ably. Gray-haired southerners (Arena is from North Carolina) tend to make excellent Senate witnesses. Their chemistry blends even with senators from the North. I was up next, with Judie Choate joining me at the witness table. We were introduced with a warm, supportive statement by Senator Weicker, who had been called by his old friend Jed Roe. I had considered asking the more influential Senator Magnuson to introduce me but discarded the notion. Magnuson disliked introducing home-state witnesses before legislative committees, both because he considered such ceremonies a waste of time, and because the other senators often ended up "putting the touch" on him for money to fund their pet projects. Harley Dirks was in the back of the room, however, when I testified, a fact that was respectfully noted by Senator Mondale.

My testimony consisted of my standard recitation for medical audiences. The words were redundant, for what followed was heart-wrenching drama of a sort rarely heard within the walls of the U.S. Senate. Judie Choate, Frank Hennigan, and Arthur Siegal each spoke for less than five minutes, telling of their experiences when their babies died. There were few dry eyes, including my own. For those moments, I forgot about political stage managing, experiencing a combination of sadness that my friends had been forced to suffer so, and anger that the suffering was so needless.

Hennigan, then executive vice-president of the American Meat Packing Corporation in Chicago, literally shook with indignation as he said:

> The cruelest part of this whole nightmare was the inquest. I asked that my wife be spared this additional assault to her emotional stability and, mercifully, she was excused. The supposition is that a panel of experts, forming a jury, is to listen to all the facts associated with the death of the child and then decide whether the evidence warrants prosecution. In actual fact, the coroner's jury consists of aging political appointees who are neither expert in law nor medicine and who rubber-stamp the conclusions made by the State attorney's office.
> I stood tearfully as the official read the facts: "Caucasian male, 2 feet, 4 inches long, 28 pounds; no social security number—cerebral spinal fluid negative for arsenic—evidence of healed fractured rib probably sustained at delivery—." His conclusion, following the statement of all the facts, was that there was no evidence of foul play. The jury retired to their deliberation room and returned within five minutes to report their agreement that indeed no crime had been committed.

My feeling is that it is a crime to subject loving parents, grieving for their child who had been stricken by crib death, to such treatment. Sudden, unexpected death in children should not be handled by the intern on duty in the hospital emergency room and the disposition of the body left to clerical aides. (Ibid., pp. 64-66)

Because he was a prominent businessman, the Chicago newspapers "covered" the "unexplained" death of Frank Hennigan's baby. The implications of guilt were clear. It was ironic justice, therefore, that the Chicago newspapers and television stations gave prominent coverage to his Senate testimony.

The three parents had made a powerful impact. They were seen and heard by millions that evening as all three television networks carried the story. The same was true for newspapers and radio. The Mondale hearing was a success. We had reached an audience far beyond the few senators sitting on the dais.

The remainder of the hearing was anticlimactic. What was there to say after the words of these three eloquent parents? It was nearly noon and all the senators except Mondale had left, along with the reporters. The last witness was Saul Goldberg of the Guild, and he was understandably furious. The Foundation witnesses had come first and had gotten all the attention. I would have felt sorry for Saul except for the knowledge that, had he testified earlier, we might have lost the attention of the press and the senators. With his wife, Sylvia, and an assistant medical examiner for the state of Maryland at his side, Saul proceeded to read a very long statement, much of which was a description of the Guild for Infant Survival and none of which provided new information. It was as if he had not been present for the previous testimony. Goldberg made the mistake of many witnesses who concentrate more on reading their own statements than in attracting the sympathy of the legislators. As Saul continued to read his long statement, Mondale grew more impatient and interjected to ask if he would summarize. Saul could not do it. Mondale was trapped until the entire statement was completed. Even as Mondale was making his closing statement, Sylvia Goldberg interrupted to show him a scrapbook with pictures of dead babies. By then thoroughly exasperated, Mondale banged the gavel and recessed the hearing 25 minutes after he had intended, at 12:55.

EFFECTS OF THE HEARING

What were the effects of the Mondale hearing? I already mentioned the widespread publicity. I was able to get on such major network television programs, as NBC's "Today Show," ABC's "Good Morning America," and the "Phil Donohue Show." These network appearances immeasurably eased our entree to local stations all over the country. "Crib death" was no longer just a subject for women's magazines.

On February 17, 1972, Senator Mondale introduced Senate Joint Resolution 206 "relating to sudden infant death syndrome," (Appendix V) which in essence directed HEW to expand research and provide assistance to SIDS families. What good is a resolution? It expresses the will of Congress but does not have the force of law. Publicity is generated by its passage and pressure is put on the administration. Resolutions, of course, are also much easier to pass than legislation. They do not have to go through the same tortuous committee routes. SJR 206 passed the Senate by a vote of 72-0. The point had been made and we did not try to push a similar resolution through the House of Representatives. We would save our guns for another day.

Of great practical assistance was the printing of the hearing record. Besides the testimony and letters received by the committee, Hoffman included all the most important articles on SIDS. The transcript of the Mondale hearing thus became the most authoritative piece of literature available on SIDS. It was also free. The Foundation did not have to be the sole source of information about SIDS, and thus we saved some printing and mailing expenses. We recommended to our chapter members and other interested parties to write their own senator for a copy of the hearing record, which was also a means of registering interest in SIDS. So many requests were received that Senator Mondale had to make a *pro forma* request of the Senate Rules Committee to have more copies printed.

AWARD FOR MONDALE

How does one demonstrate appreciation to a politician for assistance he has provided? Campaign contributions are obvious. Securing publicity for his accomplishments is another. Public interest lobbyists would be much more successful if they called more attention to the accomplishments of their politician-helpers than to themselves. Mary Lasker, whose accomplishments to improve the public's health are second to none, is distraught whenever her name is mentioned, instead of the politician who "carried her mail."

Fritz Mondale did not know much about SIDS at the time Ellen Hoffman urged him to hold the hearing. He knew a great deal about the subject, however, after listening to the testimony of the parents, and the "waffling" of the HEW brass. He became an important ally in our campaign.

When Senator Mondale ran for reelection in the fall of 1972, it would have been illegal for the Foundation to contribute to his campaign, even if we had the money. We did the next best thing. I flew to Minneapolis to present the senator with a large (but inexpensive) plaque at a luncheon well covered by newspapers and television. He was gracious and grateful.

The congressional hearings and national publicity were all very heady and certainly raised the morale of our chapters. Our goal, however, remained humane treatment of individual families losing infants. The battles in this war had to be fought in local communities around the country.

8

CAMPAIGNING ON
THE LOCAL LEVEL

Indignation without action is froth.
                    Speech given by Wm. Gladstone, Liverpool, 1896.

A frequent shortcoming of well-meaning social change agents is their failure to study the battlefield before marching into action. Anyone who works for social change must first know where the power to effect change lies. Speeches, petitions, mass meetings, newspaper headlines, are all totally useless unless they result in some tangible action. Thus our efforts to change the fate of families losing children to SIDS could not rely on announcements by government officials in Washington, D.C., famous scientists, or medical organizations. We knew that it was the local coroner or medical examiner who called the shots.

The death investigation system in the United States is a county responsibility lodged in either an elected coroner (usually not a physician) or an appointed medical examiner, usually a forensic pathologist. Though there are significant differences between them, for convenience's sake I shall refer to coroners and medical examiners interchangeably. In all cases of sudden and unexpected death, coroners or medical examiners claim the bodies of all those who die suddenly and unexpectedly in order to conduct an examination and render a verdict. Their legal obligation is to judge whether or not a crime has been committed. Any activities beyond legal duties are optional (Cleveland 1975).

The extent to which an individual coroner perceived his or her role to include providing help and support determined how SIDS families would be handled in his or her locality. An example is Robert Creason, the elected coroner of San Diego County. As a driver and investigator in the office, he had frequently come in contact with crib death cases. Saddened by the repeated tragedies and indignant that the families were provided no assistance, Creason, on being elected coroner, and with the aid of Dr. Sidney and Sally Salzstein, who had lost a child to SIDS, prepared a personal letter to send to all SIDS families, explaining why the death occurred and absolving them of guilt. Medical examiners like John Coe of Minneapolis and Lester Adelson of Cleveland brought parents in for a personal conference. Our task was to persuade every coroner and medical examiner to establish a standardized, humane system.

In some communities, where the coroner or medical examiner was already sympathetic, the task was easy. All that was needed was an offer of help from a local NSIDSF chapter. In New Orleans, the chapter president, Jane Adams, met with the coroner, Dr. Carl Rabin, the chief pathologist, Dr. Monroe Samuels, and the health department director, Dr. Doris Thompson, all of whom agreed to work together. Immediately an excellent system evolved. The same occurred in Omaha, Baltimore, St. Louis County, and Portland, Oregon. We always tried conciliation and gentle persuasion first. This strategy did not always work. If the attitude of the local coroner or medical examiner could not be changed by the dictates of his own heart, external pressures were applied.

PLOTTING ON THE MAP

Since only a handful of communities had an adequate SIDS management system in place, we had virtually an unlimited choice of cities on which to target our efforts. Judie Choate and I sat down one day with a big map to choose among them. Our criteria for "invasion" were (1) a large population area, (2) a recalcitrant coroner or medical examiner, and (3) the presence of a local NSIDSF chapter. We then hit the road in separate directions.

The format was invariably the same. I would arrive in the early evening for a briefing and pep talk to our local chapter. Early the next morning—always early—I would stagger into a television studio for "the morning show." Morning shows are the same everywhere. News, entertainment, and out-of-town guests. That was me. Then a scientific talk at a children's hospital or medical school. Such sessions were important to establish my credibility with the medical community and to gain some physician converts. Then either a press conference or sit-down interviews with local newspaper reporters were held. Finally, if they were receptive, meetings with the coroner or medical examiner, and health department director. Each of these events had a different strategic objective, which will be described, but first a couple of truisms. Anyone blowing into a town from the outside with the title of doctor in front of his name is considered a celebrity. Another is that, unless a Boeing 747 has crashed nearby, newspapers and television and radio stations are always parched for news to report. They are obliged to disgorge reams of copy every day. Finally, medical subjects captivate the public, as is evident from the contents of daytime television shows or of the best-selling newspaper in the United States, the *National Enquirer*. It follows, therefore, that "Doctor Anybody from Elsewheresville" has a ready-made forum.

USING THE MEDIA

Large corporations have one big thing going for them in pursuit of their interests: money. They can hire competent staff and advertise. The major tool of "public interest advocates" is attempting to mobilize public opinion, and thereby votes, mobilized through stories in the media. Ralph Nader has mastered this art to the ultimate degree. Reporters have been my hidden partners too, in all my public health advocacy projects. The relationship has to be a two-way street. I alert them to potential stories in the medical community and steer them to experts who can verify their facts. They reciprocate by covering stories important to me.

In working with representatives of the media, it is important to respect their professional pride. Point them in the direction of a story but never tell them what to write or film. Good reporters must also report both sides of a story. That was fine in the case of SIDS; there was no need for gimmicks. The straight story was powerful enough. All we needed was exposure.

Gerry Grinstein's skills at orchestrating political campaigns are legendary among the pros. He has a whole book of precepts contained in his head. I consulted him frequently during the course of our campaign, especially on how to obtain free publicity, a goal of all politicians. "Find a villain [he used a grosser term] to attack in every town" was his advice. "The media are much more apt to carry attacks than accolades."

PARENTS OUT FRONT

The one theme that ran through my visits with the media and medical community was outrage. Outrage was not hard to summon after meeting with local SIDS parents. I quickly became bored talking about the current scientific theories of SIDS. It was a necessary chore, however, particularly with the physicians who must feel intellectually satisfied before allowing their hearts to open up. I exploded once at the venerable chairman of the Pediatric Department at Mt. Sinai Medical School in New York, who persisted in asking questions on the significance of immunoglobulins in "crib death." "If you want to know more about that subject, read the paper written by George Ray," I said. "I've come here today to talk about why you New York pediatricians sat on your hands when a young black couple in the Bronx were thrown in jail for six months after their baby died of crib death." The sanctified halls of Mt. Sinai were not used to such talk. The pediatric resident who had arranged for my visit was reprimanded and told "never bring that crazy guy back here again."

I remained in constant awe of the brave and powerless SIDS parents who had been hurt so badly but yet were willing to struggle so that future parents would not have to endure the same agony. Our chapter members were never the socially prominent in any community. They were little people with lots of guts. Judy Smith had a job delivering newspapers starting at 4:00 A.M. in Houston. The medical examiner, Dr. Joseph Jachimzyk, persistently refused to meet with her (he refused to meet with me also), but she kept plugging along and counseled other families that came to her attention. Donna Gimeno worked in a plastics factory in Denver. She organized the press conference when I visited and with great dignity and eloquence introduced all those present, including the governor's wife, whom she had gotten to come as a guest. There were many more like them.

I always insisted on having a SIDS parent with me at any appearance, knowing full well that they would "steal" the show by a simple recitation of their own story. This was particularly effective with physician audiences, who were used to hearing other physicians but sat up and listened to the simple eloquence of parents.

Judie Choate's experiences were similar to mine. Since she was not a physician, it was not as easy for her to schedule appearances before medical groups and the media. When she did appear, however, no listener was unmoved.

TV EXPERIENCES

I rapidly became a connoisseur of television studios. I was ever so grateful for reporters who bothered to read the explanatory material about SIDS beforehand and contemptuous of those who were simply looking for a sensational story. There was a constant tug of war between me and the interviewers. They invariably dug for exciting new research breakthroughs and I doggedly kept talking about the inhumane handling of families. Like most politicians, I got so I could give my own spiel, no matter what questions were asked. Though it is hard to generalize, older reporters in smaller towns tended to be more sensitive; young "mod" reporters with blow-dried hair, anxious to up the ratings, asked the most superficial questions. My best TV interview was at the NBC affiliate in Rochester, New York, with an old-time radio announcer who had turned to television, a rarity. My worst was at an NBC affiliate in Portland, Oregon. The reporter called me a few days in advance of my appearance to tell me that he was considered "controversial." True to his word, he said, "You say the babies do not suffer when they die, doctor. Why then do you find blanket fibers wedged under their fingernails?" I did not know whether to slug him, walk off the set, or finesse the question. I thought very quickly why I was there, and stuck it out.

One of my most bizarre experiences occurred on the "Today Show" at the NBC studios in New York. We had tried for over a year to get on the "Today Show"; it reaches a tremendous and influential audience. Judie Choate convinced a friend of hers, who was also an acquaintance of "Today's" producer Stuart Schulberg, to try. The woman reported that Schulberg turned her down flat and seemed not to want even to discuss the subject.

As mentioned previously, our break came just after the highly publicized congressional hearings on SIDS in January 1972. All three national networks had carried excerpts of the hearings on their news shows, which qualified us for a bid. The interviewer, the late Frank McGee, was dreadful. He had done no preparation, kept getting my name wrong, and mechanically read his questions off the prompter. I paid little attention to McGee's questions, however, and managed to make my emotional hard-sell.

As I was walking off the set, a man wandered toward me as if in a daze. He kept mumbling "that was really something, that was really something . . . . I'm Stuart Schulberg," he said as a few people gathered around. "About 15 years ago while I was in Germany we had a baby who died like that—we've never talked about it . . ." and his voice trailed off. A lifetime of tragedy was etched on his face, and I wanted to pull him off into a quiet corner and provide some help. Such was not to be. Television is a frenetic world, however, and we passed like two ships in the night.

Besides reaching a large viewing audience, my "Today Show" appearance opened the doors of local NBC affiliate stations. In the spring of 1972, I cynically exploited this situation during the presidential primary campaign. I spent three weeks campaigning for the late Senator Henry Jackson in the unfriendly snows of Wisconsin. About a hundred Jackson boosters from the state of Washington descended on Wisconsin in a chartered plane to gain support for our senator. There were businessmen, labor leaders, physicians, priests, rabbis, blacks, Indians, and so on all primed to enlist the support of our counterparts in the dairy state. Since the Jackson campaign organization was virtually nonexistent in Wisconsin, we had to fend for ourselves and create engagements. I made the rounds of the TV stations in Milwaukee and Madison, introducing myself as the president of the National SIDS Foundation who had just appeared on the "Today Show," which automatically conferred celebrity status. Naturally they would not give me air time to pitch for votes, but we worked out a deal that, as long as I talked about SIDS, they would give me an opportunity to say that I was visiting Wisconsin on behalf of "that great guy Jackson." The Jackson campaign people were awed that I was able to finagle myself onto the TV screen. Most of them had not actually viewed the programs and thought I had used my television appearances to extol the senator's virtues rather than pontificate about SIDS. My partisan political efforts notwithstanding, Henry Jackson attracted few votes in the Wisconsin primary.

My favorite medium is radio. The pressure and gloss of TV are absent. It is possible to communicate one's message without having to put on a show. On late night call-in programs, I invariably reached grieving families who had never received reliable information about SIDS.

Newspaper stories had tremendous beneficial impact. Sensitizing medical reporters to our cause resulted in long-term dividends. Our local chapters could usually count on them for subsequent stories long after I departed. A poignant indication of the great authority of the printed word is brought home to me every time I see parents clutching newspaper stories like a golden treasure, as if the articles represent official documentation that they were blameless in their child's death.

APPEALS TO LOCAL PRIDE

Appeals to local pride have more effect than appeals for human decency. "Since we've done it in Seattle, I do not know why you cannot do it in this town," I would say. That statement would cause a lot of bristling but it was always printed. Exploiting more close-at-home civic rivalries was even more effective. When Fort Worth parents told me that the local coroner refused to meet with them, I said on their TV station, "Dallas seems to have worked this problem out; I do not understand why it cannot be done in Fort Worth." The TV reporter had to get a response from the Fort Worth coroner. With a microphone thrust in front of him, the gentleman was the picture of sweetness and light, probably wishing he could put a time bomb in my suitcase as I left town.

The most powerful weapons in our public relations arsenal were TV documentaries or a series of newspaper articles. The longest TV news spot is about three minutes; most are less than that. It is easy for public officials to dodge and weave in response to a single news story. A series of follow-up stories can usually be expected to hit the mark.

Our Cincinnati chapter, despite being headed by a pediatrician, could not even get through the door of the local coroner's office. His attitude changed remarkably, however, after a series of articles by Frank Denton of the *Cincinnati Enquirer* in November 1974. How did Denton get interested in our cause? He met Kathryn Patterson. Kathryn is a nurse who worked with me in injury prevention for three years before coming to work as a field representative for the NSIDSF. Her job was to assist local communities in developing management programs. She is an attractive, vivacious blonde who cared deeply about the plight of SIDS parents. Sometimes she had to play the stereotype role, which occurred in Cincinnati when the reporter took her out to dinner. A series of newspaper articles, and subsequent "capitulation" of the coroner followed.

CHICAGO

Because there were so many "contenders," it would be hard to pick out the city where SIDS families fared the worst, but Chicago had to rank near the top of the list. If an infant in Chicago died suddenly and unexpectedly and the family had a knowledgeable and concerned personal physician and was also able and willing to shell out $250, it was possible to get a proper autopsy performed by a private pathologist. Otherwise, there was no autopsy and the terminology on the death certificate depended on the bias of the particular deputy coroner on duty at the time. Naturally, poor people suffered the most. They were given no information on why their babies died. Every bureaucratic procedure like the coroner's inquest conveyed the implication of parental fault. As was illustrated by the treatment of the physician's wife I described earlier, brutalization was not confined to the lower socioeconomic classes. Onto this scene came Carolyn Szybist.

Carolyn, an Irishwoman with bright red hair, was raised in the metropolis of Grand Ledge, Michigan. She received her diploma from a hospital nursing school in Lansing in 1959 and, after marrying Tony Szybist, moved to Chicago in 1960. In order to care for two-year-old Lori, and support Tony while he was going to school, Carolyn worked the night shift in the emergency room of Skokie Valley Community Hospital. In the early hours of the morning of July 10, 1965, she re-returned home from work to find her three-month-old son, Lawrence Anthony, dead in his crib. The Chicago "system" worked in its usual cruel manner, and the Szybists were left to fend for themselves. Like Judie Choate in New York, Carolyn somehow found strength and courage amidst the horror and was galvanized to become a "disturber of the peace." With Judie Choate's encouragement, she founded a Foundation chapter in Chicago in 1968 and struggled mightily to bring about reforms.

Carolyn Szybist became one of the most articulate spokesmen of the National SIDS Foundation and eventually succeeded Judie Choate as executive director in 1976. She wrote a humorous and sensitive piece on the tribulations of raising a "subsequent (following SIDS) child," which is widely quoted (Szybist 1976). Success, however, came very hard until Dr. John Connelly came to Chicago to head the pediatric department at Stritch-Loyola University School of Medicine, and a hard-hitting television documentary was aired. We were always begging TV stations to make documentaries; our subject was made to order for good TV ratings, e.g., medicine, pathos, heartless bureaucrats, and so forth. Everyone involved in the production side of television loves documentaries, but the auditors with the green eyeshades prevail. Documentaries are rarely produced because they cost too much to make and don't bring in enough revenue. Hence it was a real coup when the NBC affiliate in Chicago agreed to put on a half-hour documentary on SIDS. The skilled hand of Gerry Grinstein was involved. The program director of the Chicago station had previously worked in Seattle and was a friend of Grinstein. I got in his door with an introduction from our mutual friend; harassment did the rest.

As soon as the TV people came in contact with the first SIDS parent, they couldn't believe that such injustice had never been exposed. The producer, reporters, and even cameramen labored like spirits possessed to put together a story that had a devastating impact. Advocacy journalism is marvelous when one's own point of view is featured.

The program opened at the graveside of a newly deceased infant. With dignified eloquence, the black mother told how she was unable to get an answer from the coroner's office as to why her baby had died. "Doctor why didn't you tell Mrs. _____ why her baby died?" the reporter asked the coroner with poised microphone and whirring camera. The uncomfortable gentleman, Dr. Andrew Stine, a political appointee of the late Mayor Richard Daley, stammered and stuttered, and finally said, "well, we just can't." He was soon to change his mind when John Connelly joined forces with Carolyn Szybist.

JOHN CONNELLY

Before coming to Chicago, Jack Connelly directed the pediatric outpatient clinic at the Massachusetts General Hospital (MGH) in Boston. His move to Chicago was a good one; Connelly was never meant to breathe the rarified atmosphere of the MGH. No matter where he resides, Jack Connelly is the quintessential Boston Irishman, combining blarney and pragmatic toughness. He had started one of the first nurse-practitioner training programs in the country and established a neighborhood health center in Charlestown, which was only a mile away in distance, but a century away in attitude from the MGH. A year before he moved to Chicago, Connelly's first grandchild died of SIDS.

Soon after Connelly arrived in Chicago, he induced Loyola Medical School to announce that henceforth all infant autopsies in Cook County could be performed at that institution free of charge. Next came a visit to the legendary Mayor Daley. It was a meeting of two professionals; the mayor agreed to cooperate. As if by magic, the hitherto recalcitrant coroner became meek as a lamb. Chicago was on its way to an acceptable SIDS management system.

Jack Connelly gave me a good lesson on how to discover the true sources of power when I visited Chicago late in 1974. He took me to meet the two persons in the city who he said were the most influential in making the system work. The first was the coroner's secretary, who worked in a tiny office whose walls were adorned with pictures of her hero, John F. Kennedy. She lit up when Connelly came into the room. She could not get over that he was from Boston and had personally met the Kennedys.

The other important personage was the chief diener (attendant) at the Cook County morgue, who presided over a vast roomful of corpses. Connelly had sent him a case of scotch the previous Christmas. That was not all. The man pulled me aside for some words worth recording: "There are six medical schools in this town, but Dr. Connelly is the only chairman I know who's ever been down to the morgue."

ATROCITY STORIES

We did not always win. Success in New York City took the longest time coming. I lay most of the blame at the doors of newspaper and television editors who played the tough New York stereotype to the hilt and could not be bothered to deal with the "crib death" issue. Frank Field, science editor of WNBC, did several good reports on SIDS but stuck pretty well to the scientific aspects. He dared not attack the medical examiner's office presided over by the mercurial "crime doctor," Milton Helpern. Judy Klemensrud of the *New York Times* joined me one evening at a meeting of our New Jersey chapter and wrote a sensitive story based on parent interviews that appeared on the "women's page." The *Times* editors turned a deaf ear to our pleas for news coverage of the medieval medical examiner practices.

The story of Roy and Evelyn Williams illustrates the frustrations of our battle in New York. The *New England Journal of Medicine* published the following letter from me on August 3, 1972.

UNEXPLAINED SUDDEN INFANT DEATH

To the Editor: Recently, I was called to testify on behalf of a young black couple, who were on trial in the Bronx Supreme Court for 'criminal neglect' resulting in the death of their two-month-old son. Specifically, they were accused of withholding food and water from the infant for three days.

The infant, who was discovered lifeless in his crib by the father, was the second child of the young couple, having been born by caesarean section. The mother was undergoing outpatient psychiatric treatment at Lincoln Hospital for post-partum depression. The father was caring for both children. The infant had a cold during the last week of life.

After discovery of the body, the parents were distraught and delayed three hours before calling the police. The body was removed, and the parents were taken to a precinct station and questioned separately for several hours by a detective. The detective apparently understood the father to say that the baby had not been fed for three days; the father claims to have said no such thing.

At autopsy, performed by the Deputy Chief Medical Examiner for the City of New York, the anatomic diagnosis was listed as "congestion of the viscera" and the cause of death "pending further study." There were no bruises. The thymus was of normal weight, and the liver was normal. The medical examiner wrote on the autopsy report the words "abandonment and neglect." He testified at the trial that he did so on the basis of his conversation with the detective and *not* as the result of his autopsy findings. He further stated in court that his anatomic findings were "consistent with crib death."

On the basis of the detective's conclusion and the medical examiner's report, the couple were indicted by a grand jury for "criminal neglect" and were jailed, because of inability to post a $1,000 bond. The father remained in jail for five months, and the mother for six months before bail was finally posted. The older child was placed with a grandmother. Though I was present to testify, I did not have to. The judge dismissed the charges at the end of the prosecution's case. The parents were free— free to live with their memories of spending half a year inside a New York City jail mourning for a baby who in all probability died of sudden infant death syndrome.

We, as physicians, probably cannot have much influence on a criminal-justice system, but we can do something about our colleagues who participate in that system as instruments of the police instead of using their independent medical judgment.

The National Foundation for Sudden Infant Death has launched a campaign to "humanize" the handling of infant death cases in the United States. Too many American parents who lose children to "crib death" are forced to face callous investigative procedures that suggest some wrongdoing.

Cases of sudden unexpected death should be properly investigated. Our organization insists, however, that such investigations be carried out by persons whose knowledge about sudden infant death syndrome is coupled with an attitude of compassion toward parents who have just lost a treasured infant.

(signed) Abraham B. Bergman, M.D.,
President, National Foundation for Sudden
Infant Death, Inc.

Before going up to the trial, I stopped by the press room in the Bronx courthouse to try and interest the resident reporters to cover the case. It was a scene straight out of a 1930s gangster movie. A cynical reporter leaned back in his chair and said, "What, another black family in the Bronx being f----d over? That's not news." Being an innocent little boy from the West, I gave an earnest speech saying, "Maybe these people wouldn't be f----d over if you guys would do some investigative reporting." Derisive laughter filled the room. When the judge dismissed the case (he confided to me that he had lost a grandchild to crib death many years ago), I rushed back to the press room to see if a story would be filed about the miscarriage of justice. The reporters from the three metropolitan papers, who had never left their desks, smiled. One said, "Yeah, I'll file the story, but I doubt whether my editor will run it."

I called Judy Klemensrud and asked if she could get the *Times* city desk to cover the Williams case. She tried but was unsuccessful. In a rage I somehow managed to get through on the phone to the editor of the *New York Daily News*, Mike O'Neil. Mike Gorman, who knew him when he was a medical reporter in Washington, had given me his name. O'Neil was very civil, especially considering the fact that he had never heard of the distraught nut at the other end of the line. He said the story sounded interesting, and he would check it out with his courthouse reporter. Elated, I had visions of New York's largest paper crusading against the devil. I called O'Neil a few hours later to see if he was going to run the story. "I'm sorry," he said, "you don't seem to have your facts straight. My reporter, who was at the trial, tells me that this probably was a case of child abuse but that the judge let the parents off on a technicality." "Jesus Christ," I screamed, "I know your goddamned reporter was sitting on his ass in the press room the whole time and never even set foot in the court. How could he even have heard that crap." "Sorry," O'Neil said, "I've got to go with my own man."

For me, this episode was the nadir of our entire campaign. I was exhausted and depressed. "What in hell was I doing running around in the Bronx, and fighting with New York newspaper editors," I wondered. I longed to be back in my cluttered office at Children's Orthopedic Hospital, talking with pediatric residents about the treatment of children with recurrent abdominal pain. The "paralysis" was temporary. I continued to think about Roy Williams telling me how he came close to hanging himself three times in Rikers Island Prison, and concluded that the fight had to be pursued.

Mike Gorman took me out to dinner in Washington the next evening and restored my spirits by scoffing, as usual, at my naivete. The gruff former newsman from New York explained the facts of life about police reporters: "What kind of guys do you think are sent to cover the Bronx courthouse? They're third stringers trying to hang on to their jobs," he said. "You can't expect them to file stories about the District Attorney throwing innocent parents in jail when that man is their lifeline for stories."

9

OUR
"NADER REPORT"

When the list of the most important Americans of the twentieth century is compiled, Ralph Nader should surely rank high. By word and deed he has shown how citizens without money or position can alter the status quo. Any citizen lobbyist who does not study Nader's techniques is foolish. Our SIDS campaign drew heavily on Nader's lesson book, especially on the chapter that describes the now famous "Nader report."

A "Nader report" is developed from a detailed study of an organization or practice considered detrimental to the public's interest. The research is conducted by committed students who work hard and are paid little. A key component in the effectiveness of a "Nader study" is that the data presented are totally accurate and verifiable, however idealistic and biased the investigators might be. Since the entrenched powers always fight back, absolute credibility is essential.

The impact of a "Nader report" is generally felt in two ways. First, the very process of gathering data sometimes results in beneficial changes. Corporate or government officials, few of whom are inherently wicked, sometimes are spurred to reform their practices simply by being forced to defend them. Second, the final report is publicized in a manner timed to gain maximum attention and produce the desired reforms. In the months following the Mondale hearings it was apparent that HEW would still take no action to assist our "humanization" campaign.

In addition to its political value, there was another reason to conduct a systematic national survey of SIDS management. We genuinely needed better information on which to base recommendations for public policy. Besides exposing the bad, we wanted to identify communities that were doing a good job, so that their techniques could be adopted elsewhere.

Where to get funds for the management study? I had accepted the NICHD premise that they could not fund service programs, but a study of SIDS management was research. I called on my old friend, Gerry LaVeck, who, as always, was understanding, but who nevertheless turned me down flat. LaVeck explained that all NIH grants had to be reviewed by study sections and councils, and that my concept of research did not coincide with that held by the members of those bodies. On the other hand, he told me that a request from Senator Magnuson for a certain study might be viewed differently than a request from Abe Bergman. I got the message and promptly activated the "Dirks machine." The call from Harley to LaVeck was placed the following day conveying the chairman's interest. Shortly thereafter I received a call from an NICHD official who said the institute wanted to offer a contract to Children's Orthopedic Hospital for a study on SIDS management. Political interference in the scientific process? And how!

INSULT TO ACADEMIA

Something interesting then happened at the Seattle end; the dragon of academe reared its hoary head. At the time I wore several hats. My paycheck came from Children's Hospital for running their outpatient department. My teaching and research activities, however, were conducted under the aegis of the University of Washington, where I held faculty appointments both in the department of pediatrics of the medical school and in the department of health services in the School of Public Health and Community Medicine. I was exceedingly fortunate in that my immediate boss, Jack Docter, the medical director of Children's Orthopedic Hospital and Medical Center (COHMC) allowed me to range freely in the field of child health as long as the outpatient services were functioning smoothly. In particular, he supported my child-advocacy activities, in the belief that they were consistent with the hospital's mission. A number of these activities, of course, were "controversial." Docter, jokingly, but accurately, said that part of his job was serving as "Abe Bergman's shield." I remain eternally in his debt. Even though he did not have to pay my salary, the dean of the School of Public Health and Community Medicine, Robert Day, was likewise supportive. When I told him about the NICHD contract and asked if I could hire 20 graduate students through the school as summer research fellows, he readily agreed. Donovan Thompson, professor of biostatistics, and Donald Peterson, professor of epidemiology, immediately pitched in to help design a scientifically credible study.

The chairman of the medical school's pediatric department, Ralph Wedgwood, was not so obliging. He was incensed that I had been "free-wheeling" with the National Institutes of Health without consulting him or going through the established university review process. He even threatened to have my faculty appointment taken away if I did not return the money to NIH. When I told him that a delay would result in us having to wait a whole year to conduct the study, he countered by citing the importance of "maintaining the integrity of the academic review process." When I said I did not give a damn about my academic appointment, he acted as if I had cast my lot with the devil.

Would I have been so bold if Wedgwood had controlled my paycheck? I do not know. I have abiding contempt for academics who wrap themselves in priestly robes and maintain themselves above the fray in an aura of moral superiority. So, despite the misgivings of the pediatric chairman, the study proceeded onward, and I retained my academic titles.

Every summer when money was available, the U.W. School of Public Health offered a three-month fellowship program for students throughout the country. It was from this pool that our field investigators were recruited. Twenty students participated, half from Seattle, and half from elsewhere. There were 14 medical students, 4 law students, a social work student, and an undergraduate who was a communications major. They all gathered in Seattle for one week of training. This consisted of learning about the scientific aspects of SIDS, some basic epidemiology, and improving their interviewing skills. Ten teams, each consisting of a pair of students, then spread out across the country.

THE STUDY

The sample consisted of 148 counties and towns included in the 243 Standard Metropolitan Statistical Areas (SMSAs). Every state, with the exception of Hawaii and Alaska, was visited. The county was chosen as a unit of study since coroners and medical examiners, who have jurisdiction over cases of sudden unexpected death, are all county officials. The counties included were all of the 33 SMSAs with populations over 1 million persons. A 1/6 sample was then chosen randomly from the rest of the 210 SMSAs, stratified by four geographical regions as defined by the Bureau of the Census. A community profile was compiled for the handling of SIDS cases derived from interviews with the coroner or medical examiner, a sample of local physicians, and, most important, parents who had recently lost children to "crib death." County and state health department officials were also interviewed on the extent of their involvement in the SIDS problem.

Out of a possible 157 coroners or medical examiners (ME), 145 were contacted and interviewed (92 percent). A total of 421 parent interviews were conducted. Because the parents were not chosen in a statistically valid sampling plan, they cannot be said to be representative of all families who lost children to SIDS. Also, because standardized autopsies were not performed on the infants in the study sample, there was no way of being sure that all of them died of SIDS.

Autopsy Procedures

In only 25 percent of communities studied were autopsies routinely performed on all sudden, unexpected infant deaths. These tended to be larger cities with well-staffed coroner or medical examiner offices. In 20 percent autopsies were performed only if a crime was suspected. In the remaining 55 percent, the performance of an autopsy depended on the personal inclination of the coroner or medical examiner, available funds, and whether the family and private physicians pushed hard enough.

The official who certified the cause of death was a pathologist in 27 percent, a physician who was not a pathologist in 30 percent, and a nonphysician in 43 percent of communities. Included in the latter group were a whole host of individuals such as morticians, ambulance drivers, sheriffs, and others who were high on political, but low on medical, qualifications.

Terminology

An incredible variety of terms were found on death certificates to describe presumed "crib death." Among them were SIDS, SUDI (sudden unexpected death in infancy), SUID (sudden unexpected infant death), pneumonia, interstitial pneumonitis, respiratory infection, acute necrotizing laryngitis, crib suffocation, anoxia due to un-determined cause, aspiration of vomitus, suffocation under bed-clothes, acute tracheobronchitis, and pulmonary edema. Some coroners and medical examiners felt that SIDS was caused by another disease (e.g., pneumonia, upper respiratory infection) and preferred to use that term on the death certificate in the belief that it was more scientifically correct and that parents needed to be told something "more definite" than SIDS.

From the families' view, 52 percent were told that their baby died of SIDS or "crib death," 15 percent pneumonia, 15 percent were given no explanation, 4 percent suffocation or strangulation, and 16 percent were given other assorted diagnoses. Eighty-three percent of families said that the verbal explanation provided at the time of death varied with the death certificate diagnosis, understandably leading to much confusion and bitterness.

Time in Reaching Diagnosis and Issuing Death Certificate

Where autopsies were not performed, a death certificate listing cause of death was issued immediately. In communities where autopsies were performed, 37 percent of the jurisdictions issued a death certificate immediately after the gross autopsy. In 28 percent of the jurisdictions, the certificate was issued immediately, but the diagnosis was listed as "pending." In 25 percent of the offices, the diagnosis was not entered until all studies (gross, microscopics, bacteriology, toxicology, etc.) were complete. Because the microscopic results could take from one to three months to complete, families often had to wait weeks and months to learn the cause of their child's death.

Notification of Parents

Sixty percent of coroners or medical examiners interviewed said they routinely notified parents of the cause of death, usually by tele-phone. This finding was not corroborated by the parents. What it usually meant was that if the parents would take the initiative and call, someone would speak to them. Even were it true, 40 percent of officials admitted that they had no routine notification system.

Thirty-nine percent of families learned the autopsy results in under one week after their child's death; 13 percent learned the results in under a month; 10 percent in under three months; and 3 percent after three months. A very sad 9 percent of parents *never* heard the results of their child's autopsy.

Assistance Received

Policemen and firemen were usually the first officials on the scene after a lifeless infant was discovered. Though some distasteful episodes were reported, the families generally were laudatory of the efforts of these officials. "They tried so hard" was the comment often expressed. This was in contrast to the general attitude expressed toward physicians and nurses in hospital emergency rooms, where 77 percent of infants were rushed. "They seemed so cold and seemed to resent us bringing our baby there" was a typical comment.

Racial and Social Class Differences in Treatment of Families

Marked racial and social class discrimination was found in the management of SIDS throughout the country. This was primarily an indicator of whether a family had a knowledgeable private physician to intercede on their behalf. If not, families were left to the vagaries of "the system"; sometimes it was good, most of the time it was awful.

For example, half as many blacks as whites were given SIDS as an explanation of death; four times as many were told that their baby suffocated, and three times more blacks than whites were never told why their baby died. Seventy-five percent of upper class families had heard of SIDS before their baby died, and 92 percent received information afterward. Only 48 percent of lower class families had ever heard of SIDS before their baby died, and, appallingly, only 40 percent received information about SIDS after their baby died.

We were not surprised to find some serpents under the rocks, like a coroner in rural Alabama. He classified white crib death victims as "pneumonia"; black ones were called "suffocation," because "those folks do not know how to take care of their babies."

Community Rankings

The primary county in each SMSA was ranked using four criteria as a basis for judgment: autopsy practices, death certificate terminology, notification procedures, and the follow-up and referral practices of the coroner or medical examiner. Four groupings were devised: excellent, good, fair, and poor. Seventy-four primary counties were ranked; 9 (12 percent) were given excellent rankings, another 9 (12 percent) were rated good, 21 (29 percent) were given a fair ranking, and 35 (47 percent) were considered poor. (The complete community ranking is shown in Appendix VI.)

In 1972, then, only nine communities were judged to do an excellent job in handling SIDS. The situation is, of course, much better now. The most important single factor in determining how parents are treated is the personal sensitivity of the local coroner or medical examiner to the human aspects of SIDS.

At the time of the study, only two local health departments (King County, Washington, and Orleans Parish, Louisiana) and *no* state health departments were actively involved with the SIDS problem. Likewise, SIDS was found to be a matter of profound unconcern to medical schools and pediatric centers. For instance, in Boston, where there are three medical schools and in Chicago, where there are six, less than a third of possible SIDS babies were even autopsied.

THE PRICE CASE

Two University of Washington medical students, Charlie French and Jim Merrill, came across a real atrocity while they were traveling in Tennessee. They caught a small item in a local newspaper about a young couple in South Carolina charged with the murder of their infant. They immediately set off to investigate. Here is the story of the Price case as it appeared in the July 22, 1972, issue of North Carolina's *Charlotte Observer*:

DEATH OF TOT RULED 'NATURAL'

The Mecklenberg County medical examiner has ruled that a York County, South Carolina, infant whose parents were jailed Sunday on charges of assault and battery with intent to kill, died of natural causes. Despite the ruling, John Junior Price, 20, father of the six-month old baby girl, was still in jail in York Friday on the same charge. The child's mother, Mrs. Billie Ann Price, 19, was released Wednesday.

A spokesman for the York County Sheriff's Department said Friday that Mrs. Price was not home when police believe the baby died, apparently while sleeping in a bed at the couple's mobile home near Fort Mill. Captain William Thomas said that at first, Mrs. Price had said she was home, but that investigation showed she was not.

A spokesman for Dr. Hobart Wood, the medical examiner, said that there were no marks or bruises on the baby's body. The cause of death would not be known for several days, the spokesman said, until tests were completed.

The parents were jailed Sunday by York County sheriffs deputies after the couple had taken the baby to Charlotte Memorial Hospital, where she was dead on arrival.

Thomas said Sunday that a hospital doctor had reported the death to York County authorities and that an investigator was sent to the hospital. The Prices were taken to Rock Hill, where an arrest warrant was issued. The Prices were then put in the York County jail in York.

Thomas said Friday that Price was still in jail, in lieu of $1,500 bond. Thomas' office had been given what he said was a telephone report on the baby's death from Mecklenberg medical examiner's office.

"We're going to wait until we get the written report," Thomas said, "then we'll present that, together with the results of our investigation, to the magistrate. We can't withdraw the charge. Only the magistrate can do that."

Charges against Mrs. Price were dropped Wednesday by Rock Hill Magistrate Fletcher Lumpkin, Thomas said.

Charlie and Jim did more than collect information. They kept pressing the sheriff until John Price was released from jail, five days after his daughter died, and two days after her funeral. Price had pleaded to attend the funeral, even in chains, but the authorities "hung tough." The two medical students then went to the editor of the *Charlotte Observer*, who, to his credit, assigned a reporter to find out what went wrong. The resulting story criticized not only of the officials involved, but, with humility uncharacteristic of a newspaper, the press coverage as well.

In contrast to the atrocity stories, we also found numerous examples of sensitive individuals who reached out on their own to help SIDS families.

LACK OF MONEY FOR AUTOPSIES

We knew that ignorance was a strong deterrent to a good SIDS management system. We had not anticipated, though, how little money was available in most communities to pay for autopsies. For a family to know why their baby has died, there must be an autopsy, which in 1972 cost on the average about $250.

Only a handful of communities in the United States have well-funded coroner or medical examiner offices able to perform an autopsy on all cases of sudden, unexpected death. In the vast majority of counties, the limited funds available for autopsies are reserved for cases where criminal liability or substantial insurance claims are involved. We were told repeatedly by coroners or medical examiners that their job was to answer legal questions, not to provide medical diagnoses. Thus, in large cities like Boston and Chicago, prohibitive costs discouraged families from having autopsies performed. The situation was even more difficult in small towns, where autopsies were performed by private pathologists hired on a fee-for-service basis.

I recall vividly a conversation with the sheriff of Helena, Montana, who also acted as the county coroner. He showed me through his jail, which was constructed in the early 1900s. This sincere gentleman said, "I have seen a number of cases of crib deaths, and would certainly like to see autopsies done, but my commissioners allow me $2,000 a year for all autopsies. I simply must reserve that money for investigation of possible crimes, not in cases where the individual died of natural causes." I could not argue with him. It therefore seemed totally unrealistic, to press for development of a SIDS management program in every community. Larger cities like Los Angeles, Chicago, and New York, which have several hundred cases of SIDS per year, could support a local management program. In a state like Montana, however, with but one forensic pathologist and no more than 30 SIDS cases a year, a regional approach seemed most appropriate.

HEALTH DEPARTMENT NONINVOLVEMENT

Traditionally public health departments have been the "fallback" resource for those who cannot afford private medical care. Since fewer than half the SIDS families had private physicians (SIDS occurs more frequently in poorer families), it might have seemed logical for health departments to "pick up the pieces." In Seattle, public health nurses routinely visited all SIDS families to provide information and counseling. It seemed reasonable to expect other health departments to involve themselves in a similar fashion. Such was not the case. Our field investigators were careful to interview a representative of every state health department (except Alaska and Hawaii), usually the director of maternal and child health (MCH). In 1972 not a single one of these individuals was in any way involved with SIDS. Many, like the MCH director of Oregon whom I interviewed, knew nothing about SIDS and thus did not even recognize that a problem existed. More typical was the reaction of the California MCH director who said, "we have problems that are of higher priority than SIDS."

The repetitive refrain was "give us money and we'll do something." This response elicited mixed feelings in me. On the one hand, I was disgusted by their unwillingness even to try using existing resources to meet such a pressing need. The number of nursing hours required to visit SIDS families could not have been a great burden on any health department. On the other hand, I knew that if adequate services were ever going to be available for SIDS families, the pots of the health department decision makers were going to have to be sweetened.

I expected that the management study would provoke controversy, because it called attention to shortcomings of public officials. In fact, there was a minimum of fuss. We had carefully required that each official review the interview form, check the accuracy of the information, and sign a release for publication. There had been a few complaints about the behavior of our youthful field investigators, but there had been many more compliments and expressions of appreciation for bringing an important problem to their attention. A whole lot of consciousness raising occurred in the process of interviewing, which in itself justified the expense of the study.

BUREAUCRACY FIGHTS BACK

It is well to remember that there is always a price to pay for carrying one's torch outside of regular bureaucratic channels. "They" find ways to fight back, usually through zealous scrutiny and interpretation of the rule book. From the moment the contract was awarded, the middle-grade bureaucrats at NICHD were uncomfortable with the management study. That the contract was awarded through the good offices of Dirks, the "impurity" of the research, and above all, its "controversial" nature together caused the institute staff to view the project as some sort of odious time bomb. This spirit was personified in the body of the project monitor, Jehu Hunter, scientist-administrator at the NICHD. A capable individual trained in biochemistry, Hunter's *modus operandi* was never to make waves. Since dissemination of the results of the management study would inevitably ruffle some feathers, Hunter sought to cover the project in a blanket of secrecy. He seemed less troubled by the medical examiners who waited six months to tell anguished parents why their babies had died, than those of us who were attempting to alter the *status quo*.

A standard clause in government contracts requires the contractor to obtain prior clearance for any publicity emanating from the project. In April 1973 I presented a paper on the management study to the Ambulatory Pediatric Association meeting in San Francisco. I did not consider that the publicity restriction pertained to scientific meetings. Hunter did. I received an official letter stating that because I had willfully violated government rules, that the contract funds would be cut off. I felt as if I were accused of spitting on the flag.

By then Gerry LaVeck had left the institute and had been replaced by an acting director, a gentle soul named Gilbert Woodside. I called Gil and did not delete the expletives. He agreed that Hunter might have gone too far. Soon after the contract was restored, but that was not the end of the story. Hunter had a small measure of revenge. Having promised all who participated in the study a copy of the final report, I mimeographed 500 copies. The $450 reproduction cost was disallowed by Hunter, again, because I had failed to obtain prior approval. Hunter claimed that, since NICHD had agreed to print and distribute copies of the final report, I was duplicating their efforts.

TESTING THE "NEW BOY"

When did the institute print and distribute the report? Never! A whole host of "administrative difficulties" managed to "delay" the publication. A final note: In 1974 a new director, Norman Kretchmer, formerly chairman of the pediatric department at Stanford, came to the NICHD. He was the outsider bursting forth on the D.C. scene full of enthusiasm and idealism. With the country in the throes of the Watergate revelations, I wanted to see how far the cleansing spirit extended. I wrote to Kretchmer and innocently asked if he would look into why the report of the SIDS management study had been "covered up." He promptly called me on the phone and said that he would check into the matter and have his administrative assistant call me with a report in a week. I thanked him profusely but requested that, since I wanted to include the story of the cover-up in a book, I would appreciate a response in *writing*. There was a pause at the other end of the phone.

The reader should be aware that nothing chills the marrow of a bureaucrat so much as having to record his actions on paper. An untapped phone is infinitely superior when one might have cause to be ashamed of one's actions. Five *months* later I received Kretchmer's written response explaining why it was impossible to publish the study. From the phraseology I suspected that the letter had been drafted for Kretchmer's signature by Jehu Hunter.

THE CASE FOR REGIONAL CENTERS

So by 1973 we had documented the mismanagement of SIDS in the United States. Consciousness raising had occurred both through the process of gathering information for the management study and through the efforts of local NSIDSF chapters. We learned that, good intentions notwithstanding, lack of money prevented the performance of autopsies in many communities and that, without additional funds, health departments were unlikely to provide public health nursing services. Our conclusion was that a series of *regional* SIDS centers serving defined population areas were the most practical means of providing a minimally acceptable standard of care for all families that had lost children to SIDS.

In 1973 Judie Choate, Carolyn Szybist, and Jack Connelly persuaded the Chicago Community Trust to assist in the establishment of a regional SIDS center located at Loyola Medical School. We pointed to the Loyola Center as an example of how major metropolitan areas should deal with SIDS. Where would the money come from to set up other programs around the country? Federal assistance funneled through HEW seemed to be the only answer. Was an act of Congress necessary to launch such a program? Certainly not. Establishment of the requisite program was well within the existing statutory authority of the Department of HEW. Having the authority was one thing; using it would be quite another.

10

THE SATISFICERS

Why was the Department of Health, Education and Welfare unable or unwilling to respond to the needs of SIDS parents without engaging the United States Congress in the incredibly complex and time-consuming process of passing a brand new law? The department, of course, is not a monolith, but rather, like all large organizations, is a vast collection of individuals, each of whom has an agenda of his or her own. I divide the Tower of Babel, that is, HEW, into three sections: the policy makers who, in theory, chart the course; the middle-level bureaucrats who in theory steer the ship along the charted course; and the support staff who man the engine rooms. (The fuel for the engines, by the way, is paper.) The "top brass" are relatively few in number who come and go at a rapid clip, depending on changing political tides or corporate and academic job markets. (Senator Magnuson used to say that the busiest workers in Washington are the sign painters at HEW.)

The clerical workers at the bottom rungs are no better or worse than their counterparts in any organization. In general I have found that the secretaries throughout HEW tend to be more idealistic and helpful than their managers, when asked to carry out the missions of their respective offices. The middle-level bureaucrats are, however, another story.

TYRANNY OF THE BUREAUCRACY

Successive presidents have been correct in attempting to gain control over the federal bureaucracy that is supposed to execute the policies of our elected officials. Elected officials can always be thrown out of office, but the layers of bureaucrats stay on and work their wills, chief of which is self-preservation.

In 1965 I had attempted to launch a physician assistant training program, which then was considered radical but now is "old hat." A deputy assistant secretary of HEW, George Silver, assured me that the department was committed to funding such innovative programs. Buoyed by encouragement at so high a level, I literally skipped off to the Bureau of Health Manpower expecting to receive a check. My naive enthusiasm was short-lived. An official in that office, whose name I long ago forgot, leaned back in his swivel chair, his hands pursed in a prayerful pose, and solemnly intoned that the department had no authority to fund training programs for physician assistants. "But," I eagerly interjected, "the deputy assistant secretary told me that the department is committed to funding such programs." A faint smile crossed his face. With a lilt of triumph in his voice, the gentleman said, "if the deputy assistant secretary thinks that the department can fund such a program, let him come down to this office and sign the papers."

In my subsequent dealings with HEW, the truth of that official's statement was borne out many times. George Silver, like most top officials of any administration, served only a limited time, and then returned to his teaching job at Yale. The underling, however, remained. Upon that person's retirement, I conjure up a successor who also leans back in the same chair with the same smile on his face, saying "no."

SATISFICERS

The penultimate book about HEW, *The Satisficers*, was written in 1970 by a young pediatrician, Arthur Levin. (He now writes for the *Village Voice* in New York.) Like a number of physicians, including myself, Levin fulfilled his two-year military obligation by serving in the U.S. Public Health Service. He was "stationed" as a "policy analyst" in the office of the assistant secretary for health and scientific affairs. Levin was appalled by what he perceived as the deadly combination of incompetence and inertia among his colleagues in dealing with the nation's pressing health problems. He coined the term "satisfice"—a combination of satisfy and suffice—to describe how the bureaucracy survives by doing as little as possible. "Officials," he says, "do not try for the best of all possible worlds; they try to 'get by,' to 'come out alright,' to 'avoid trouble,' and to 'avoid the worst.' " Further describing his comrades, Levin says:

They [the planners] had no knowledge of real planning—planning that springs from the needs of people, and is geared to meet those needs. They were and are, since many are still in high government positions, men who like to meddle with the lives and futures of others without ever taking the responsibility, not to mention the time, to prepare for doing so. (p. 104)

The above is provided as background for understanding why the department was unable to come to grips with a relatively straightforward problem like SIDS. The top levels are perpetually dealing with huge global issues such as containing the costs of medical care, reforming the welfare system, and (constantly) "reorganizing the department." There is always some alphabet soup simmering, like PSROs, HMOs, and DRGs. Then highly visible brush fires, like the swine flu epidemic, or the latest "cancer-causing" additive are sure to burst forth. (See Neustadt and Fineberg's *Swine Flu Affair* [1978] for a brilliant analysis of HEW's decision-making.) Small finite issues that affect the lives of individuals are finessed.

KNOCKING ON DOORS

We knocked on many different doors at HEW before we took the legislative route. I have already described the dealings with the National Institute of Child Health and Human Development (NICHD) and the Office of Maternal and Child Health (OMCH). Through my "Magnuson connection," I also had access to the higher reaches of HEW, the Office of the Assistant Secretary for Health and Scientific Affairs. I was always graciously received by the incumbent of the moment—Drs. Roger Egeberg, Merlin DuVal, and Charles Edwards. They *all* promised to help but did not. Why not? All of these men were intelligent and sympathetic to the problem I posed. The answer, alas, is that the SIDS issue was too *small*.

I am confident that after each of my visits, orders were issued to "see what can be done to help that fellow." When the orders reached the desks of the midlevel managers, they were either ignored ("procrastinate, this secretary is on his way out"), or a "satisficing" memo was prepared containing a hundred reasons why the requested action was ill-advised, illegal, and immoral. The three well-intentioned assistant secretaries did indeed move on to other jobs, leaving SIDS to fall between the cracks. Congress was our only hope.

LINING UP THE DUCKS

At the conclusion of the SIDS hearings in January 1972 by the Subcommittee on Children and Youth, Ellen Hoffman and her boss,

Senator Mondale, were convinced that legislation would be necessary. The question was only one of form and timing. With the results of the management study in hand, Hoffman and I sat down in early 1973 to discuss legislative strategy. Ego problems immediately ensued, which were to cause problems throughout the course of the legislative campaign. Very simply, I thought that I knew more than Ellen about "moving" health legislation.

The successful advocate must *always* submerge his own ego to the end of achieving the goal. The politician has to run for office; the lobbyist does not. Therefore, the ideas the legislator promotes, the speeches he delivers, or the letters he writes, all of which emanate from another hand, *must* appear to be his alone. The same holds for staff. Even if I did know more legislative ropes than Ellen Hoffman, lording it over her could not help but cause resentment and hurt my cause. She, after all, had been hired to run this part of Mondale's show, and no matter how I saw myself as a political tactician, I was viewed by people on "the Hill" as a doctor who dabbled in politics.

SHOULD RESEARCH BE STRESSED?

Our first disagreement was over the extent to which SIDS research should be stressed. Hoffman was aware that, thanks to Magnuson's appropriations subcommittee, support for SIDS research was steadily increasing and that new legislation was required only to deal with the humane aspects of SIDS. She felt, however, that a bill providing for the education of health professionals and counseling services to SIDS families might not be sexy enough to attract the votes of legislators. She therefore proposed that money for research be used to "carry" the other items. It is true that the riches bestowed on the National Institutes of Health were a response to rhetoric calling for "crusades" to conquer dread diseases. It is also true that in the early 1970s anything that smacked of Great Society antipoverty programs (e.g., social services for the poor) was viewed with great skepticism in Congress. I felt, however, that the SIDS legislation was "small potatoes" and would not be examined on the basis of its content but only on how many bucks were involved and how vigorously it was pushed by its sponsors. (More about this in a moment.) I thus did not feel it necessary to "con" the legislators and preferred a straightforward bill providing only for what we actually needed.

My objections were muted, however, for two reasons: First, since Ellen would be doing the work on the Hill, I could not afford to "turn her off." Second, the language in a bill when it is first introduced is not crucial. All bills must be referred to committees where they are examined and "refined." The draft that *emerges* from a committee is important. Accordingly, Ellen drafted a bill that was labeled S 1745 and introduced into the Senate on May 8, 1973. It was entitled, "a bill to provide financial assistance for research activities for the study of sudden infant death syndrome and for other purposes."

Six companion bills were introduced during the next several weeks in the House of Representatives. How did that happen? Every congressional office has a staff person who reads the *Congressional Record* everyday for matters of interest to bring to the boss's attention. If an interesting, and usually noncontroversial, bill is introduced on the Senate side, an enterprising congressman might "lift" the text and introduce it on the House side the very next day. One's constituents can then be informed that their congressman had taken one more step for mankind.

Constituents are generally impressed when their congressman introduces legislation. Numbers of bills introduced and co-sponsored along with voting records are about the only tangible manner by which congressional activity can be documented. To introduce a bill, a congressman or senator has only to drop a piece of paper into a hopper at the front of the legislative chamber. For the great majority of bills, after the issuance of the obligatory press release, that's the end of the "action." Sometimes a legislator is in fact serious about his bill becoming law. He must then embark on a complicated "dance of legislation." For example, in the two-year period from 1972 to 1974, when the Ninety-third Congress was in session, 4,260 bills were introduced in the Senate and 17,690 bills in the House. Of these 21,950 bills, hearings were held on 4,303 (20 percent). The House passed 829 bills and the Senate passed 995; 697 bills were passed by both houses, or 3 percent of the total introduced. The President signed 649 bills into law, and 7 were passed over his veto. The chances of an introduced bill completing "the dance of legislation" are thus not good.

What are the ingredients of success? In brief, success depends on the power of the sponsors and how hard they want to push. Support from the chairman of the subcommittee to which the bill is referred is imperative; otherwise, the bill will never see the light of day. A subcommittee chairman must not only support a bill, he must also agree to hold hearings. Success is most likely if one can get a subcommittee chairman to sponsor a bill himself. In our case, Mondale, chairman of the Subcommittee on Children and Youth, was the sponsor on the

Senate side. It takes two houses of Congress, however, to make a law. In the House of Representatives, Paul Rogers of Florida was the man to see about health legislation.

PAUL ROGERS

Rogers, a progressive southerner, served in Congress from 1955 to 1979, retiring at the peak of his political power to pursue a law-lobbying career in Washington, D.C. At the time he was chairman of the Health Subcommittee of the House Interstate and Foreign Commerce Committee. Most health lobbyists considered Rogers to be the most knowledgeable legislator on Capitol Hill in the health field.

Rogers is an incredibly hard-driving individual, who still manages to exude southern charm. I came to know him during the campaign for the National Health Service Corps, which he fathered along with Senator Magnuson. Whenever I called at his office, the routine was the same: I would be ushered to a couch, Rogers would draw a chair right up opposite, clamp a hand on my knee, and graciously ask how he could be of assistance. If I mentioned any problem with HEW, which I usually did, he would snatch up a nearby phone and demand to speak to the secretary or the next highest official within telephone range. Rogers could maintain friendly personal relations with HEW officials while "chewing them out" if he disagreed with their policies. Some called this phony showmanship. I called it *effective* politics. Paul Rogers had a remarkable record of achievement in the health field. Since I was not the only person who knew that Rogers held the key to success for health legislation, the line at his door was always long, and his hearing schedule horrendous.

I made it a point to call on Rogers periodically to brief him on the SIDS situation but was careful not to ask for anything. In fact, following the Mondale hearings, when the SIDS resolution was before the Senate, I specifically mentioned to Rogers that since no legislation was at stake I saw no need for House hearings. He was visibly relieved.

When I called on Rogers in the late winter of 1973, I made sure that his chief health aide, Steve Lawton, would be present. If any commitments were to be made, Lawton was the one who would implement them, and I wanted everyone to hear the same marching orders. Rogers quickly got to the point, wanting to know the type of legislation I thought was required. He was totally disinterested in the Senate version of the bill. Members of the House envy the publicity received by senators and the fact that they only have to run for office every six years, but tend to view their legislative talents with disdain. Senators are spread more thinly with several committee assignments, while House members specialize in one, or at the most, two areas. Thus Rogers was confident that if there were to be a SIDS law, *he* would write it. He was correct.

"Okay," he said after I had stated my case, "it should not take more than a half day of hearings. We've got a heavy schedule, but we'll try to fit you in." I skipped out of his office. When Paul Rogers "signed on" I knew that we would have a SIDS law.

Working with Steve Lawton was a pleasure. We had decided when we first met that we liked and trusted each other. It was the jock ethos. . . e.g., keep an ironic sense of humor and, above all, be cool. Steve, who also became a D.C. lawyer-lobbyist when his boss retired from Congress, worked as hard and was as compulsive as anyone on the Hill. He also had a lot of fun playing the game of politics, which helped in the supercharged atmosphere of Washington, where so many people take themselves seriously.

THE FIFTH FLOOR AGAIN

After the visit to Rogers, I had one more call to make—into the camp of the "enemy." Once more I marched down the long fifth floor corridor of the HEW building to see the current incumbent sitting in the assistant secretary's office. It was Charles Edwards. I had met him before when he headed the Food and Drug Administration. The handsome, well-spoken former surgeon always looked like a movie star playing the role of a cabinet officer.

Why visit the "enemy"? First, I wanted to explore the unlikely possibility that HEW might at the last minute implement a SIDS program and thus make it unnecessary to go through the whole "dance of legislation." "You do not need a new law to do the type of thing you want," Edwards said. "You're right," I said, "how about putting together the program and we'll drop the legislation." The secretary smiled wanly and mumbled something about "budgetary constraints." We both knew that all legislative initiatives emanate from the White House and that the administration of President Nixon was not interested in proposing *any* new health programs.

Edwards wished me luck, noting that he would have to testify against any proposed new legislation. I wished him luck in having to appear before Paul Rogers for the umpteenth time to defend a position in which he himself did not believe.

The other reason for the visit was simply to maintain lines of communication. Though the pay-off is not always apparent, I make it a point to talk with political opponents because in politics it never hurts to maintain decent personal relationships. If the legislation passed and was signed by the president, the guys who opposed us, HEW, would then be given the responsibility for carrying out the law. If I expected to have any influence beyond getting a piece of paper through Congress, I did not want to burn the bridges.

After the amiable visit with Edwards, I stopped by an adjacent office to touch base with HEW's health lobbyist, John Zapp. Zapp, a dentist from the state of Oregon, hit the political trail working in the 1968 Nixon campaign and ended up in HEW. (He now works as the chief lobbyist for the American Medical Association.) We had been on opposite sides over the National Health Service Corps, where the political stakes were much higher. Zapp appreciated my briefing and admitted that he would not lose much sleep if the SIDS bill passed.

My visit to the HEW building confirmed my suspicions that no one was going to actively come out and oppose a "motherhood" issue like SIDS. On the other hand, sudden infant death syndrome was not a high priority matter for our congressional sponsors. The greatest threat to successful passage would be inertia. The fires, once lighted, would have to be continually stoked.

11

HOUSE HEARINGS

The bills were in the hopper, the commitments had been obtained, and now we had only to wait for hearings. Since Ellen Hoffman had started off the legislative activity and since Mondale was our original champion, we naturally expected that he would promptly lead off with his hearings on the Senate side. Months went by and nothing happened. I called Hoffman almost weekly until I was certain that she too had been pushing as hard as she could without success. The problem? In the middle of 1973, Ted Kennedy was backing away from the idea of campaigning for the presidency in 1976; Fritz Mondale was trying to pick up the mantle. Priorities in the Mondale office had changed. The senator's travel schedule increased mightily; he had much less time for mundane Senate duties.

That disquieting news was forgotten in a flash, however, when my secretary announced that a Mr. Lawton from Washington was on the phone. "Okay, Bergman," he announced, "we've had a cancellation. Can you put your act together in seven days?" "Hell yes," I said, "it's more notice than I expected." "Fine," said Steve, "line up your witnesses and have them here at 10:00 A.M. next Thursday. Don't worry about written statements in advance; just show up. I told you we'd come through." He had indeed.

I mentioned earlier that congressional hearings are *not* judicial proceedings, where evidence is dispassionately weighed and impartial verdicts rendered. They *are* chairman's choice—serving whatever purpose he has in mind. House hearings tend to be more searching, probably because they receive less publicity. Also, while it is common for a single senator to hold a hearing, House rules demand that members of both the majority and minority parties be present before a hearing can be convened.

Since it may be the only opportunity for members to focus their attention on a particular bill, a hearing can either turn them on or off and can determine how much energy even a sponsor will expend in pushing a bill through the legislative briar patch. Initially, Paul Rogers and Steve Lawton knew little about SIDS; they had agreed to hold hearings mostly as a favor to me. My objective for the hearing was to convince Rogers and Lawton that a serious, substantive issue was at stake which warranted their attention and energy.

THE WITNESSES

Chairman Rogers gaveled the hearing to order promptly at 10:00 A.M. on August 2. Sitting to the right of Rogers was Steve Lawton, the subcommittee counsel, and Richardson Preyer, a congressman from North Carolina. To his left were two Republican members, Tim Lee Carter from Kentucky and William Hudnutt, a clergyman from Indiana, serving his first (and, as it turned out, his only) term. Carter, the ranking minority member, was a small town general practitioner and, though he had not seen a patient for many years, he was deferred to as the medical expert of the subcommittee. His contribution to the hearings consisted of a recitation on his theories about SIDS. Hudnutt took an active interest in the proceedings and seemed genuinely moved by the SIDS parents who testified.

First up to the witness table was the administration witness, Dr. Henry Simmons, acting deputy assistant secretary of HEW, representing Charles Edwards. Central casting could not have provided a better victim for Rogers to cut up. The colorless Simmons scarcely had time to draw a breath before Rogers lit into him with an excoriating cross-examination. Simmons kept his poise, knowing that the attack was not personal and that this was just one of the trials of his job that had to be endured.

I then took the stand to present a synopsis of the 1972 management study. Thanks to Jehu Hunter's "cautiousness," the study had not yet been "cleared" by NICHD. I had prearranged with Lawton, however, that Rogers would ask me to include the entire study in the hearing record. Thus it was that the report of the SIDS Management

Study officially saw the light of day (U.S. Congress, House, 1973, pp. 60-125).

The next witness was Jack Connelly, representing the American Academy of Pediatrics. As mentioned previously, Connelly was in the process of organizing a prototype regional SIDS center in Chicago, located at Loyola Medical School. The "seed money" provided by the Chicago Community Trust was insufficient for full-scale operations, however, so Connelly approached HEW for help, without success. NICHD claimed that they could not use their research funds for such a service-oriented project. Since his program was exactly the type called for in the proposed legislation, Connelly produced his rejected grant proposal to Rogers. True to script, Rogers held the sheaf of papers aloft in his hand thundering that he personally would inquire why HEW felt they had no capacity to fund the project.

Connelly was followed to the stand by Portia Giffin, president of our Indianapolis chapter. Besides being an attractive and articulate witness, Portia also happened to run the Indianapolis field office of a veteran Indiana congressman, William Bray. He accompanied and introduced her at the hearing. The effect of an employee of the U.S. Congress also being a SIDS mother was not lost on the members.

Charles and Anne Barr, who live in a suburb of Boston, next described their moving story. Charles was chairman of the Board of Trustees of the NSIDSF, and Anne, president of our eastern Massachusetts chapter. We purposely chose witnesses who were educated and articulate. As mentioned previously, I feared that less sophisticated witnesses, whose stories might be more compelling, might become mute in the atmosphere of a congressional hearing.

Next up was Larry Lewman, deputy medical examiner for the state of Oregon. In the course of the management study we found that Oregon had one of the best statewide death investigation systems in the country. Lewman, a totally apolitical and sincere human being, had instituted a humane and medically sound system for handling SIDS that could easily be copied elsewhere. People outside the medical profession know little about the important field of forensic pathology, so that the committee members spent considerable time picking Lewman's brain.

The last witnesses of the morning were Saul and Sylvia Goldberg. Saul appeared upset. He had not been involved in plans for the hearing and had, once again, been placed at the bottom of the witness list. I felt a slight twinge of sympathy, but not enough to regret what I had done. The guild still had no clearly articulated program other than "conquering crib death." I continued to fear the Goldbergs might cause us to lose sympathy with the legislators and thus damage our prospects for the legislation.

Congressman Rogers was impatient; the regular noon closing time had long since passed. Courtly as always, he asked the Goldbergs to summarize; they once again persisted in reading their entire statement. Rogers let them finish, and finally gaveled the hearing to a close at 1:30. He announced that he had been impressed by the testimony and committed himself to "moving a SIDS bill through the House."

DRAFTING A "CLEAN BILL"

During the hearing, little was said about specific language for the House bill because, after hearings, Rogers liked to prepare what is called a "clean bill," one that could then be sponsored by all the members of the subcommittee. Rogers assiduously courted the minority members and thus nearly always obtained unanimous support for his health legislation. Often this meant dropping some of his pet ideas, but in the long run the policy paid off handsomely in terms of passed legislation. Legislators who are always enmeshed in controversy may sound virtuous to their constituents, but also sport anemic batting averages in terms of bills that eventually pass.

The major substantive question in the SIDS legislation continued to be whether dollars were to be specifically earmarked for research. I was torn. There was no question that by highlighting a specific research area, more dollars were likely to be spent. Personally I detest battles between diseases. How can anyone say that one sickness is any more important than another. We should attack all diseases and injuries that cause death and discomfort, not just those promoted by a celebrity or around which a political constituency can be mobilized. I did not feel, however, that my personal opinions should determine the outcome of such an important issue.

I sought counsel therefore from three experienced experts whose views I trusted: Mike Gorman, Harley Dirks, and Gilbert Woodside. I put the same question to all three: Would SIDS research be enhanced by specifically earmarking funds through a new authorization bill? The response was a unanimous negative. Gorman, one of the original health "earmarkers" (i.e., heart, cancer, and stroke), and Dirks both felt that the HEW Appropriations Committee might even resent the move, since they were continuing to add funds in their yearly bills for SIDS research. Woodside, who canvassed his colleagues at NICHD before responding, felt that extra money might be wasted in that SIDS research suffered more from lack of qualified investigators than from shortage of funds. I was reassured that we were on the right track in pressing for modest amounts of money rather than "shooting for the moon."

BILL LANGUAGE

Several weeks later I was in San Francisco having dinner at the home of friends. The phone rang at 9:00 P.M. Pacific Time. Steve Lawton had somehow tracked me down. "The subcommittee is meeting tomorrow morning to mark-up the SIDS bill," he announced. "What should it say?" So at midnight Washington time, Lawton was at home drafting what was to become a new law while I offered helpful comments from the kitchen of friends in San Francisco.

"Carrot and stick money for regional centers is the main objective," I said. "Okay," he said, "but let's not use the term '*regional center*.' It sounds too close to regional medical programs, which we're trying to kill." "Make sure there's a provision for money to perform autopsies," I said. "Do we have to use the word 'autopsy'?" said Lawton. "It may offend some sensibilities." "Call it whatever you want," said I, "just make sure there's dough for autopsies." He thought for awhile, and proposed that the act "authorize grants . . . for projects which include both the collection, analysis, and furnishing of information (derived from postmortem examinations and other means) relating to the cause of SIDS, and provision of information and counseling to families affected by SIDS." "A bit vague for my tastes," I responded, "but you know your employers, and it should do the trick." The next morning the members of the subcommittee met and unanimously approved Lawton's midnight draft.

COMMITTEE REPORT

When a subcommittee takes action on a bill, they must both approve specific legislative language and issue a report explaining their reasons. Technically, subcommittee reports are prepared to aid legislators in making up their minds on how to vote once a measure reaches the chamber floor. Perhaps one in a hundred reports are ever read for that purpose. More importantly, committee reports are meant to explain the intentions of Congress to administrative agencies charged with carrying out a law. Though reports do not carry the same weight as bill language, they are crucial when disagreements over interpretation occur. This was especially pertinent in our case, where the administration opposed enactment of the original legislation.

Just as legislators have little time, or in some cases, talent, for writing their own letters, speeches, or reports, neither do their senior aides. No one is more appreciated by an overworked legislative aide than a person who will provide drafts of speeches or reports. To Steve Lawton, Ellen Hoffman, or Harley Dirks, who are called on to churn out reams of these documents, a well-drafted statement is treated like gold. It is difficult for amateurs to accept how eagerly congressional offices accept grist for their never-ending word mills. There are some important qualifying conditions, however, for the anonymous scribe. The author must be willing to allow another name to appear on his work, and must accept that his effort might be altered or never used, without an apology. This does not seem too high a price to pay for seeing one's concept advanced toward actualization, but I am surprised by the number of potential amateur lobbyists who balk at the chance. Professional lobbyists know this very well. They draft a good proportion of the bills, speeches, and reports on Capitol Hill. I composed a draft of a committee report on the SIDS bill, which I sent on to Lawton. As it turned out, little of my prose was used. A student working that summer as an intern in Rogers' office prepared a superior document which found its way into print (U.S. Congress, 1974a).

12

SENATE HEARINGS: SECOND ROUND

I have already pointed out that advocates who intend to advance their aims effectively must use legislative staff in order to reach the ears of their "masters." At times the process is reversed, when congressional staff use advocates to further their agendas. A paid employee has one kind of relationship with his boss. An independent lobbyist or, particularly, an important constituent, has quite another. In dealing with my two steadiest "customers," Senators Magnuson and Jackson, I always worked with their aides. Usually when the boss had to take some action, or permission for a new plot had to be obtained, it was the staff person who did the soliciting. Sometimes, however, the outsider has a better shot, particularly when "the man" has already said no to the staff person. In Magnuson's office, given the senator's inherent cautiousness, the campaign to win him over was often more arduous than any subsequent legislative battle.

As I mentioned in the last chapter, Ellen Hoffman's repeated attempts to persuade Senator Mondale to hold SIDS hearings had been unsuccessful. When I asked if I could take a crack, she readily assented and obtained an appointment for both of us to meet with Mondale. At the time the Senate was engaged in a prolonged debate over the Alaska oil pipeline. Mondale was leading a coalition of Midwest senators trying to gain some advantage for his region. He was opposed by a coalition led by Senator Jackson, who along with Senator Magnuson, considered Alaska to be an extension of the State of Washington. Jackson was already shifting into high gear for his own presidential quest. On the day of my appointment with Mondale, Jackson took me to lunch in the Senate dining room where we ran into the Minnesota senator.

Later that afternoon, when Ellen and I were ushered into Mondale's office, he was clearly exhausted and just wanted to "shoot the bull" for awhile. He longingly talked about a fishing trip he was planning in northern Canada, jokingly saying that it was *my* friend, Scoop Jackson, who was responsible for keeping him from escaping the summer heat of Washington. Though the SIDS hearings were paramount in my mind, I forced myself to relax and relate to Senator Mondale as a fellow human being rather than as an omnipotent target. I had just finished reading Anthony Lewis' marvelous book, *Gideon's Trumpet*, which described the events leading to the Supreme Court's landmark decision that gave indigents in criminal proceedings the right to publically funded counsel (1964). As attorney general of Minnesota, Mondale played a prominent role in the case. He seemed pleased to be remembered in that capacity, as well as to be able to reminisce about matters outside his current political business.

The SIDS hearings came up almost as an afterthought and consumed all of about 15 seconds of our conversation. Mondale, of course, knew why I had come to see him. Virtually everyone a senator meets wants something from him. I waited until he brought the matter up himself. "Of course we'll have hearings," he said, turning to Ellen, "why don't you go ahead and schedule a day as soon as possible." It was as if the two of them had never before discussed the subject. That was all. She had her marching orders, and could proceed to lay claim to a half day of her boss's calendar.

KENNEDY STAKES A CLAIM

The Subcommittee on Children and Youth announced hearings on legislation pertaining to SIDS for September 20. It was then that the "Kennedy gang" decided to make their move. Where previously they had not evinced the slightest interest, the Subcommittee on Health, chaired by Senator Kennedy, suddenly claimed jurisdiction over the SIDS legislation. Both Hoffman and I were furious, for different reasons. Ellen had labored hard to make SIDS Mondale's issue. Here was another example of Kennedy keeping Mondale from having turf of his own. From my perspective it meant more delay. If Kennedy claimed jurisdiction, then his subcommittee, with a calendar fuller than that of the Subcommittee on Children and Youth, would have to hold hearings.

As quickly as I conjured them up, my paranoid interpretations about the effects of Kennedy's intervention proved to be baseless. Lee Goldman, staff director of the Health Subcommittee, met with Ellen Hoffman and made it clear that he did not wish to disrupt her well-laid plans. Two hearings would not be necessary; there would be a single meeting of both subcommittees to be jointly chaired by Senators Mondale and Kennedy. Ellen would continue to be responsible for planning the hearing; the only responsibility of the Kennedy staff would be to produce their boss and write a statement for him. To Hoffman this was a mixed blessing. It meant that, while she did all the work, Kennedy would reap some benefits at the expense of Mondale. At that point, I could care less about who got the political credit. I wanted the train to keep chugging.

In contrast to my role in the House hearings, my role in the Senate hearings was only a minor one. Ellen Hoffman was under much pressure. Besides my persistent efforts to "stage manage" the production, there were the Kennedy staff intrusion and strong efforts by the Guild for Infant Survival (GIS) not to be "aced out" again. Saul Goldberg had never heard of Steve Lawton, but he did know Ellen Hoffman and contacted her frequently. The result was that Ellen opted for an "even-handed" policy between the Foundation and guild, growing increasingly remote and official with me. We would be allowed two witness slots and have no responsibility for publicity.

Judie Choate and I thought hard about appropriate witnesses. As mentioned before, Senate hearings, in contrast to the House, play more to the media. The Mondale hearings the year previously had generated a great deal of publicity. We hoped for the same effect this time. We decided that I should be one of the witnesses. The medical story, and our "Nader Report," had to be presented in a straightforward fashion. For the other slot we took a gamble and recommended the victims of one of the most blatant SIDS atrocities, John and Patricia Smiley.

THE SMILEYS

In the early morning hours of April 11, 1973, John Smiley, age 21, and Patricia Smiley, age 20, of Elsinore, California, put their three-week-old daughter Genya to bed in an extended dresser drawer. They were poor and could not afford a crib. Later in the day, they found the baby lifeless. John, who was a hospital orderly, called the Riverside county sheriff's office for help. Because of the run-down condition of their apartment, the police suspected child neglect. John and

Patricia were taken to jail and charged with "involuntary manslaughter" even before an autopsy had been performed and before they could talk with an attorney. They remained in jail for two days before John's mother posted the $2,000 bail. The *Los Angeles Times* published a small story on the case, which was read by Ovidio Penalver, a student at the University of Southern California Medical School who had worked in our field study the previous summer. (He now is a pediatric practitioner in Puyallup, Washington.) After talking with me on the phone, Ovidio and his wife, Meg, a pediatric nurse, drove to Riverside and conducted their own investigation. They checked the autopsy findings and found them to be totally consistent with SIDS. (We always feared becoming unwittingly involved in a real case of child abuse, which is why we had to be certain of the autopsy findings before intervening on behalf of the parents.) They also spoke with the Smileys, who still had not received any legal assistance.

My first reaction on receiving Penalver's report was dismay at the injustice inflicted on these pathetic parents who had lost an infant to "crib death." I authorized him to retain the best attorney in Riverside that he could find to represent the Smileys, with the promise that the Foundation would pay the bill. I contacted a few members of our Board of Trustees, including Mary Lasker, who generously agreed to cover the legal costs herself. Penalver retained J. David Hennigan, who carefully prepared his case and succeeded in having the charges dropped at the preliminary hearing on April 27. John and Patricia Smiley went on their way, free to live with their memories of time spent behind bars, official accusations, and a legal hearing while grieving over the death of their baby daughter.

My second reaction was exhilaration that we might finally have a *cause celebre* so blatant that, if it received sufficient national attention, our "humanization" campaign might take a huge leap forward. The New York papers had refused to write about the Williams case. Publicity about the Price case had been limited to North Carolina. Our hopes were dashed again, however, when our numerous entreaties failed to persuade the *Los Angeles Times* to extend its coverage beyond a simple report that charges against the Smileys had been dismissed. Judie Choate worked on *Time* and *Newsweek* to no avail.

PREPARING THE SMILEYS

It was risky to bring the Smileys to Washington to testify. They were unsophisticated and might easily become intimidated by the awesome surroundings of the U.S. Senate. We felt, however, that their story was so poignant that, if it received sufficient attention, it might dramatically enhance our cause throughout the country. We took the risk.

The logistics involved in getting John and Patricia to testify were considerable. After their release from jail, they were still regarded as killers in their neighborhood and had moved to San Diego. I asked the president of our San Diego Chapter, Sally Salzstein, to find the Smileys and sound them out about their willingness to testify. Sally reported that they were agreeable but poorly educated, and therefore might make poor witnesses.

Knowing that it would be impossible for the Smileys to prepare their own testimony, I solicited the assistance of a young pediatrician in southern California, Dr. Jay Goldsmith. While a resident at the Children's Hospital in Oakland, Jay had helped organize our Northern California Chapter. At the time he was serving in the Air Force in Victorville, California. (He now is director of pediatrics at the Ochsner Clinic in New Orleans.) Goldsmith, a confirmed activist, readily agreed to help. He drove to San Diego and spent a whole day with John and Patricia and got them each to tell their story into his tape recorder. He had the tape transcribed, sent it to the Smileys for their okay, and thereby produced written statements that could be read. I sent the Smileys airplane tickets, and, on the day they were to depart, Goldsmith returned to San Diego to make sure they got on the plane. Judie Choate met the plane at Dulles Airport, took them to their hotel, and literally babysat for the next 24 hours.

The Smileys were out of their milieu. Two examples: Suspicious of all hotel food, Patricia requested that a full quart carton of milk be brought to her restaurant table. The same day she also purchased a packet of purple dye and attempted to change the color of her dress in the hotel bathtub. It did not work; she had to wear blue jeans.

THE HEARING

The moment I walked into the hearing room I knew that our efforts would be wasted; no television or newspaper reporters were present. The dramatic testimony of the Smileys would be restricted to an audience in the hearing room that did not need convincing that SIDS legislation was necessary. Ellen Hoffman seemed exhausted, probably because she had tried to do everything herself, including soliciting media coverage.

Senator Mondale opened the hearing and heard the administration witness, Henry Simmons, go through his perfunctory spiel. Senator

Ted Kennedy walked in about halfway through my testimony; the room lit up. Though Mondale continued to preside, it was obvious that the sun was shining over the head of the senator from Massachusetts.

After a few more witnesses, including me, John and Patricia Smiley were called to the stand. They were engulfed with shyness as they timidly approached the large table and microphones. "They won't be able to make it," I said to Judie. Senator Kennedy came to the rescue. Speaking directly to John and Patricia in a soft voice he said, "I know you're not used to speaking before a large group, but please understand that we are very interested in what you have to say. Just talk to us in your own words and we will understand. Please remember that we care very much about what happened to you and we want to help." The Kennedy magic worked; the Smileys were put at ease. Some excerpts of John Smiley's testimony follow: (It should be recalled that the testimony John read was prepared with the editing assistance of Jay Goldsmith.)

When we found Genya, Trish, my wife, got quite hysterical. She didn't know what to do. She was telling me to do something, to try to bring Genya back to life. I threw everything out of the makeshift crib to give me room. I reached down to take her pulse. I had had training in the service as a medic and I was employed as an orderly, but I couldn't get a pulse. I noticed that there was rigidity of the arm. I got a queasy feeling in my stomach. Trish ran into the bathroom and was crying hysterically. I went in and told her that I was going to go and call the sheriff's department and get an ambulance. I went next door to try and use their telephone but they didn't have one, so I ran down to the corner phone booth and called the sheriff's department. I told the lady who answered the phone to send an ambulance to our address and she asked why and I told her "because my baby is dead." She said, "How do you know it's dead?" I told her I couldn't get a pulse and she said "o.k."
I ran back home and got my wife out of the bathroom because I didn't want to stay in the house. We sat out on the porch—Trish was sobbing gently for a while and then she kind of went into herself. The Sheriff arrived—there were two men in the Sheriff's car. One talked to Trish, the other asked me where the dead person was, because he didn't know if it was a male or a female, so I took him into the bedroom. He reached down to try to take a pulse and he couldn't get one. He took us outside and asked us a bunch of questions. The younger policeman was very sympathetic and at a later time I found out that he was just a rookie and hadn't been hardened like the rest of them. Sheriff Emerson was rather sarcastic. He asked Tricia if we were married. When she said yes,

he asked if we could prove it. In a short time Detective Orell arrived, asked us questions such as what type of drugs we had been taking to sleep so long, and if we drank. He read me my rights, then asked if he could search the house. I told him yes because we didn't have anything to hide. He found a bottle of wine in our refrigerator with one little glassful taken out. He put that in his police report. He separated my wife and I. I had to sit out in front of the house and my wife had to sit out in the back.

We stayed for at least four hours separated from each other at a time when I felt we could benefit most from the companionship of each other. He forced me to take a frat test, which is a urine test for drugs. He took me over to the police station and made me urinate with a policeman standing there watching me. He took my wife over and she had to give a urine sample also. They took us back to the apartment. All this time Genya was laying in the bedroom in the drawer; she wasn't covered or anything. The doors were open, flies were flying around the house. It was a hot day. Then the coroner arrived, really started bullshitting with us, and gave us really a bad time. At a later time I found out that he had no medical training whatsoever and worked as a bartender. The district attorney arrived and made me go inside and "reconstruct" as he put it, "the scene of the crime."

Finally, after about five hours, I guess, it was really dark, they covered Genya up with a sheet and took her out to the hearse that was setting out in front, right past my wife who was sitting in the police car. All the neighbors were standing around like it was the Fourth of July; it completely destroyed us in the community. We were taken over to the police station and told that we were being arrested for suspicion of involuntary manslaughter. We sat around there for a while until about 8:30 or 9:00 p.m. when a sergeant with all kinds of stripes came and picked us up and took us to Riverside to the county jail. On the way there my wife was handcuffed behind her back. She was put in the back seat and strapped in with the seatbelt. My hands were handcuffed behind me and I was strapped in also. The policeman was really a reckless driver, going into the other lane around corners, and really had me terrified. We arrived at jail and I was taken to one floor and my wife to another. They put me in a little blue room, as they call it. It's a little cage with bars and it's painted blue. It was quite a busy night; they had about 40 people in there, all kinds of drunks and stuff. They booked me and allowed me to call my mother. As a result of that phone call, she was so upset that she was put in the hospital for two days. I was taken to spend the night in a little room with foam rubber on the floor, a drunk tank. We were crowded in like sardines in there with really no place to sleep as there wasn't any room to stretch out on the floor. The next morning I was taken into my cell and the word got around somehow why I was there. Everyone was calling me a "baby killer" and threatening to beat me up. The guards treated me like shit and I was beginning to get a little worried after my second day in jail because I hadn't heard from my mother. I was expecting her to bail me out and I asked the guard if I could talk to a chaplain. He said "No," that I would have to write out a request. So I wrote out a written request to talk to the chaplain and I was refused—I couldn't talk to the chaplain. I wrote my wife two notes which were to be transferred down to her floor but she didn't receive any. I received two notes from her—I guess the matrons down where she was were kinder than the pigs who were on my floor.

After three days, on Friday, April 14, at about midnight I was let out. They opened up my cage and took me to the front and told me I was being bailed out. They sent me in to get my clothes, and I sat around for about an hour while other people were being taken out. I was finally released to my mother's custody on $1,000 bail. My mother informed me that she just got out of the hospital, and she wasn't looking very well. The people there were very abusive toward her and my aunt. My mom asked me some questions and then posted the bail for Trish. We went from there to the house in Elsinore to pick up some things that we needed and went over to the hospital to tell them why I hadn't been at work, which they already knew. I was told by Mrs. Gray, the Director of Nursing, that I wouldn't be able to work at the hospital until this was all settled, but that they had great faith in me, they knew I wouldn't harm my baby in any way, that I had a job when we beat the case. They said they were very sorry that it had happened. So we went back to San Diego to stay at my mother's place, having no reason to stay in Elsinore without any money or anything to support ourselves.

Tuesday, the 17th, we had to go back up to Riverside for our arraignment. We didn't at the time know how we were going to pay for a lawyer or anything. We were arraigned on willfully and without malice killing our daughter, Genomet Rose Smiley. We were given a public defender. While we were at the public defender's office we received a telephone call from Ovidio Penalver but the public defender wouldn't let us talk to him so we called him later. He was from the Foundation for Sudden Infant Death Syndrome. The Foundation got a private attorney for us and helped us immensely. Our attorney was J. David Hennigan of Riverside, who went into great detail with the case with us. When we arrived, on April 27, for our preliminary hearing, the public defender's office didn't know we had an attorney and they said they were ready to represent us in our preliminary hearing. However, they only talked to us about ten minutes in the office right after our arraignment and that was the only time. It's a good thing we had another attorney or we would probably still be in jail.

During the "preliminary," the prosecution's whole case was based on what they thought was neglect. They accused us of beating our child, called us drug addicts, and said that we abandoned our child all night from 6:00 o'clock until 3:00 the next afternoon. They brought up the full trash can in the kitchen which really was irrelevant as the baby didn't sleep in the kitchen. They brought up the cat feces in the litter box which we didn't empty before the Sheriffs got there, which also didn't contribute to the cause of death. They accused us of loving our cat more than our child because we asked after its welfare when we were going to jail as to who would take care of him, which nobody did, and that cost us $54.00.

The preliminary hearing went completely in our favor. The whole case was thrown out of court, thanks to the defense of Mr. Hennigan. After the preliminary hearing we moved back to Elsinore and I went back to work as an orderly at the hospital for a while. But we got accusing looks and general harassment from the Sheriff's Department up there. They were coming to my place of employment and hassling with me and we finally had to move away. We just couldn't take it any longer. We moved back down to the San Diego area.

As a result of this unfortunate death of our child, my wife doesn't want to have any more children. Myself, I would like to have another child, but I think it's better if we don't with the feelings that my wife has. We also have been accused by members of the families on both sides of neglect because they don't understand the situation. Trish's mother couldn't grasp that a child could just overnight suddenly die without screaming or crying. She has feelings that somehow we caused or had something to do with the death from lack of knowledge or neglect or something. I have had to leave the profession that I like the most because who would want to hire someone who has been put in jail and accused of murder. It's really bad. I lost a little bit of my own self respect and all the bad memories. We live four miles from Genya's grave and occasionally I would like to see her, but I don't feel that I can. There are just so many bad memories to the whole situation and I would like to forget, but I know that I will never be able to forget.

I think the Sheriff's Department and the Coroner's Office, and the District Attorney's Office could have handled the whole thing more tactfully with quite a bit more compassion and with a little better understanding. I hope that it never happens to anyone else like it's happened to us. The death of a child is bad enough, but that will heal. It's the harassment and lack of knowledge and lack of understanding and lack of compassion that hurts more than anything else. (U.S. Congress, Senate, 1973a, pp. 54-58)

There were a few more witnesses, but the words of the Smileys had obviously drained the emotions of everyone in the room. I was devastated that there were no reporters present to describe the impact of their testimony. Good old Colman McCarthy, however, came through again with a column about the Smileys in the September 21 issue of the *Washington Post*. I had sent him a copy of their testimony on the previous day. He wrote:

> If we were told this morning that in the next year a dreadful plague would kill 10,000 of America's children, it is likely the nation's medical community would command the front pages of newspapers to announce plans to meet the threat. The sign painters at HEW would be idle because no official would dare leave his post in this emergency. Every local community, including Alabama coroners, would be on the alert. Such a plague is not coming, of course, at least not the Black Death kind of threat. But a year from now, 10,000 infants will have been found dead in their cribs. Afterward their parents will die repeated emotional deaths in private anguish. The research to prevent SIDS may be far off, but a way to prevent the abuse of surviving parents is well known. Perhaps the largest mystery involving SIDS is that we are not acting on facts already available.

I was not privy to the subsequent deliberations of the two subcommittees. I know that Ellen Hoffman drafted the committee report unassisted. Lee Goldman and his colleagues on the staff of the Health Subcommittee not only bought Hoffman's concept of earmarking specific funds for research, but raised the ante. Thus the bill that finally emerged from the Senate Labor and Public Welfare Committee authorized $24 million over a three-year period for SIDS research to be conducted at the National Institute of Child Health and Human Development, as well as authorizing $12 million for education and services to families. The bill was taken up by the full Senate as part of routine business on December 11, 1973, and passed on a voice vote (U.S. Congress, Senate, 1973c). Voice votes are taken for noncontroversial legislation; usually there are only a few senators in the chamber. The end result is the same, however, a Senate-passed bill. We had thought the House passage would follow in a similarly undramatic fashion; however, a humorous but exasperating little minuet was yet to be played out.

13

THE RITES OF
FINAL PASSAGE

In the Senate, once a bill is passed by a committee it can immediately be taken to the floor for action. Not so in the House, the more "deliberative" body. There, after action by both subcommittee and full committee, a bill must be reviewed by yet another body, the Committee on Rules, which ostensibly establishes rules for how a bill is to be debated on the floor. Actually, the Rules Committee serves as a formidable filter at the end of a funnel.

Because the Rules Committee is so deliberative—some would say obstructive—there are alternate ways for relatively noncontroversial bills to reach the House floor. For real "motherhood and apple pie bills," there is the consent calendar. Here the House leadership distributes a menu of bills that require unanimous consent before they can be considered. One nay-sayer can screw up the works. Virtually no legislation that requires the expenditure of money ever makes it onto the consent calendar. Certainly this was so up until 1974, when Congressman H. R. Gross of Iowa retired. This crusty curmudgeon made an entire career out of objecting to *all* federal spending.

Another way around the Rules Committee is called the suspension calendar. Here a two-thirds majority is required to "suspend the rules" and consider a bill on the floor. Once a week the House leadership gathers the bills that are perceived to have little opposition and serves them up. Though not subject to the veto of one person, any perceptible show of opposition will get a bill knocked off the suspension calendar and onto the queue of bills waiting to go through the Rules

Committee. In the fall of 1973, HR 11386, having received sub- and full committee approval, was duly placed on the suspension calendar.

The quaint custom in the House is that the main proponent of a bill (floor manager) is usually the chairman of the *full* committee through which it passed. Thus health legislation was managed, not by the chairman of the Health Subcommittee, Paul Rogers, but rather by Harley Staggers of West Virginia, chairman of the parent House Interstate and Foreign Commerce Committee. The custom is akin to requiring that testimony at congressional hearings be given by the most senior rather than the most knowledgeable Administration witnesses. The custom made for some sticky problems and almost dispatched our SIDS bill to oblivion.

A useful rule of politics is that the majority party should never flaunt their advantage over the minority. Successful legislators assiduously try to avoid partisan divisions by carefully soliciting minority support. Warren Magnuson, an almost fanatic practitioner of this ecumenical philosophy, would not dream of bringing his HEW appropriations bill to the Senate floor without having the ranking Republican at his side to defend it.

In the fall of 1973, Congressman Staggers apparently had not taken such precautions and had inadvertently incurred the displeasure of a senior Republican on the committee, Tim Lee Carter. I say inadvertently, because the source of Carter's displeasure emanated from actions by Stagger's *staff*, of which the Congressman was unaware. Apparently some Democratic staff members of the House Commerce Committee had met with their counterparts on the Senate side to discuss some legislation in conference but had not invited minority staff members. The Republican staff members complained to their patron, Representative Carter, with sufficient eloquence to make the supposed affront an affair of honor.

A POINT OF HONOR

The SIDS bill headed a list of health measures on the suspension calendar that Staggers innocently brought to the floor one afternoon. As he started to explain the measures, the courtly Kentuckian, Carter, rose to complain about the alleged transgressions of Stagger's staff. Witnesses told me that Carter had no intention of blocking the legislation, but simply wanted to give vent to his feelings and receive the usual "sorry, it won't happen again." Staggers, not being aware of what Carter was talking about, did not follow the script. Instead, in high dudgeon, he took great exception to the interruption, and the two veteran law makers began shouting at each other. In frustration, Staggers blurted out, "is the gentleman from Kentucky going to object to consideration of this bill or not?" It was high noon! The cheek had been struck by the glove. The awful words had been spoken. Carter fired back, "yes, I object." A point of honor having been made, a two-thirds majority could never be obtained to suspend the rules. The bill was withdrawn from the calendar, and the warring parties stormed out in a huff.

Weeks passed while the House of Representatives turned its attention to weightier matters. Christmas recess came and went. I was desperate. Not even Paul Rogers, let alone his aide Steve Lawton, could do anything. Staggers' aide, a young physician, Lee Hyde was equally helpless. He told me that his boss would not even allow the matter to be discussed in his presence.

It was too late to send the legislation through the Rules Committee, which would not have worked anyway since Staggers's active support was needed. One day as we sat lamenting, Lee Hyde suggested that an intermediary be enlisted and nominated me for the job.

I made an appointment to see Congressman Carter, and, when the time came, with great trepidation, I was ushered into his office. To my pleasant surprise, he remembered me both from my SIDS testimony, and also from a visit two years previously when I was seeking his support for the National Health Service Corps. At the time we had a pleasant chat about physicians in politics. I again spoke to him as one doctor to another and reiterated the pressing need for the SIDS legislation. Carter was obviously embarrassed by the whole matter. "You know I'm all for that bill," he said, "I want to see it passed just as much as you do. It's just that I don't like getting pushed around by the majority party." He then proceeded to tell me how Paul Rogers would never get into such a bind. "Paul always respects the views of the minority. He and I work together on everything, but Staggers—" his voice trailed off in disapproval. Carter sensed my discomfiture. "Look," he said, "I've made my point; I don't think he'll do it again. You tell Staggers that if he puts the bill on the Suspension Calendar again, I won't object." I didn't tell Congressman Carter that I had never met Harley Staggers, but bubbling over with gratitude, I flew back to relay the happy news to Lee Hyde. Hyde, too, was off the hook since he was among those responsible for the transgression that drew the ire of Carter.

HOUSE DIALOGUE

On January 21, 1974, the first day that Congress returned from its New Year break, HR 11386 was duly placed on the Suspension Calendar and came before the House. Thus it became the occasion for some vintage rhetoric from H. R. Gross. The Iowa Congressman had announced his intention to retire at the end of the term and had therefore redoubled his efforts to protect the federal treasury. Predictably, he objected to the SIDS bill, not on substantive, but on procedural grounds. Here is the dialogue from the *Congressional Record*:

> MR. GROSS: Mr. Speaker, I do not know fully the merits or the demerits of the several bills that have been brought to the floor of the House today from the Committee on Interstate and Foreign Commerce, but I was shocked to find out last week that there were no reports available on these bills, and no other information that would provide guidance with respect to the language changes in the bills—and that there are many in at least two of the bills to follow this one. This is a shocking situation on the first day of the second session of the 93rd Congress where we would be compelled to consider bills regardless, I say again, of the merits or demerits without the reports to accompany them, without the information we ought to have to intelligently legislate. And I point out to my colleagues on the floor of the House that the bills involve an expenditure of many, many millions of dollars.
>
> I should like to have known what the departmental reports were, particularly the Bureau of the Budget, and the justification for spending in these several bills that are called up with no opportunity for amendment, and with a semi-gag rule—in other words, 20 minutes of debate on each side.
>
> Mr. Speaker, I hope that this sort of a performance will not again be repeated.
>
> MR. STAGGERS: Mr. Speaker, I raise briefly to state to the gentleman from Iowa that I can sympathize with the views of the gentleman. I wish to describe to the gentleman from Iowa the extraordinary circumstances under which these bills are brought to the floor. When the Congress adjourned they said—that is, the leadership—that they did not have any legislation to consider at this time, and they wondered if there was any legislation that could come out of our Committee after long hearings, bills on which hearings had already been completed. We had long hearings on these bills, and the hearings had been completed and they were extensive hearings and all of the bills had come out unanimously from the subcommittee, which is one of the finest subcommittees in the House. That is the reason they were brought forth. Also, when they were brought before the full Committee they all came out unanimously with

the exception of one of the bills, which had one vote against it. So I would say to the gentleman that I am sure he understands the extraordinary circumstances under which these bills are being considered. I would also add that we do have reports here on the table and if any member would like to do so they can look at them, peruse them, and we will be glad to answer any questions on any of the bills. We believe these bills are very meritorious, and they ought to be handled now.

MR. GROSS: Mr. Speaker, would the gentleman yield?

MR. STAGGERS: I will be happy to yield to the gentleman from Iowa.

MR. GROSS: Mr. Speaker, on page 2 of H.R. 11386, the bill presently before the House, lines 16 through 19, the language reads:

(B) the provision of information and counseling to families affected by sudden death syndrome.
No grant may be made or contract entered into under this subsection for an amount in excess of $50,000.

What precisely does this mean? Does it mean that $50,000 may be awarded to the family?

MR. STAGGERS: It means that the program which provides counseling cannot be given more than $50,000. This also would cover counseling not only to those who have lost a child, but perhaps those who might lose a child, so that they would have the necessary information. There have been cases of children who have been affected by this syndrome where the parents have been disturbed during the night, and have found the child on the point of death, but through understanding and counseling, knowing something about the situation, they have given the child mouth-to-mouth resuscitation and revived the child, and that child is living today, whereas if they had not known something about it, or in some way been alerted, that child would not be living.
This is all part of the program that the money will go to.

MR. GROSS: But it does not provide indemnification to a family for a loss of this kind?

MR. STAGGERS: No, sir; not a bit.

MR. GROSS: I thank the gentleman.

H. R. Gross, it should be added, was totally sincere. He was probably the only member of Congress to have actually read committee reports before voting. By effectively tying up the machinery of government in procedural wrangles, this unique gentleman probably cost the taxpayers countless millions. I'm also certain that Congressman Staggers had no intention of deluding his colleagues by telling them that HR 11386 was supposed to teach parents mouth-to-mouth resuscitation in order to prevent SIDS. He simply was not familiar with the details of this minor piece of legislation. After all, he was only the floor manager.

The procedural matters taken care of, the love-feast began. Supporting speeches were given by Congressmen Adams of Washington, Hudnutt of Indiana, Carter of Kentucky, Abzug of New York, Rogers of Florida, Harrington of Massachusetts, and Gude of Maryland.

At the conclusion of the brief speeches, the following note appears in the *Congressional Record*:

> THE SPEAKER: The question is on the motion offered by the gentleman from West Virginia [Mr. Staggers] that the House suspend the rules and pass the bill H.R. 11386, as amended.
>
> The question was taken; and (two-thirds having voted in favor thereof) the rules were suspended and the bill, as amended, was passed.

RESOLVING DIFFERENCES

It only remained for differences between the House and Senate versions of the bill to be resolved before it could be sent to the White House. For major pieces of legislation, a group of representatives and senators will sit down and reconcile the different versions in conference. For a minor bill such as ours, staff aides on both sides try to work out an agreement in order to avoid a formal conference.

The major difference in the legislation was that the Senate version called for funds specifically earmarked for SIDS research. Ellen Hoffman told me that she and Lee Goldman would insist on inclusion of the research authorization. When I transmitted this to Steve Lawton, he laughed. By then Saul Goldberg and his associates in the GIS were extremely critical of the House version, claiming "it did nothing." Funds for research were what they wanted. I once again touched bases with Mike Gorman, Harley Dirks, and Gil Woodside. Their opinion was unchanged; the Rogers bill was superior.

Hoffman wanted to sit down and thrash the matter out with Lawton, but, as she plaintively said, "he never returns my calls." The two of them did not know each other. Also Lawton, reflecting the views of his boss Rogers, was not about to accept the opinion of an "outsider" on health legislation. On the other hand, Lawton was in almost constant contact with his Senate counterpart, Goldman, on all kinds of health legislation. There never was even a staff conference, as such, on the SIDS bill. In informal discussions with Lawton, Goldman agreed to accept the House version; Hoffman had no choice but to go along.

On March 6, 1974, Senator Mondale appeared on the Senate floor to obtain a unanimous voice vote for the SIDS legislation.

On April 10 Congressman Staggers asked unanimous consent from the House to concur with the Senate amendments (i.e., authorizing $9 million for three years instead of the original House versions of $6 million for three years). Unanimous consent was obtained, and "the Senate amendment to the House amendment was concurred in." That ended "the dance of legislation."

Had the higher price tag of the Senate bill, with the earmarked authorization for research, prevailed, the SIDS legislation might have caught the attention of the White House. They were making a big show of vetoing "extravagant" congressional legislation. Since only "peanuts" were involved—$9 million over a three-year period—Public Law 93-270 came into being by virtue of President Nixon's signature on April 22, 1974.

Ironically, two congressmen voting for the SIDS bill shortly thereafter lost grandchildren to SIDS, Hugh Carey, who was to become governor of New York, in 1975, and the floor manager, Harley Staggers of West Virginia, in 1976.

14

IMPLEMENTATION:
PUSHING ON A ROPE

In my days of innocence, I would have considered Congress's approval of a sought-after law as a momentous event that called for the raising of flags and the blowing of bugles. In my present skeptical state of mind, I view passage of a law as only one step that can either lead forward or backward, depending on how the law is implemented. Seven years passed before there were any beneficial effects from the Flammable Fabrics Act Amendments of 1967. As far as I know, there has *never* been a decrease in the number of injuries due to power lawn mowers. The Consumer Product Safety Commission has provided much work for lawyers and public relations experts but has had only marginal success in making the marketplace safer.

Those of us who were involved in passage of the Sudden Infant Death Syndrome Act of 1974 strongly felt that our legislative efforts would turn out to be in vain unless we vigorously involved ourselves in implementation. This turned out to be a much tougher job than getting the law passed. When the matter was before Congress, we were dealing with politicians who, whether they are good or bad, are at least accountable to the public. In the implementation phase, we were dealing with a huge bureaucracy, HEW, that did not want the law in the first place, did not request any funds to implement it, and, worst of all, could weave and bob interminably. Let me say once again that the top HEW officials were decent human beings who were not opposed to solution of the SIDS problem. SIDS just ranked too low on their priority lists to receive personal attention. I saw as my first task locating an inside person, not an office, not a bureau, but a living breathing human being in HEW, who would be sufficiently sensitive to the urgency of the problem to make a personal commitment. The department had to take three steps to put the new laws into effect. They tripped up on all three of them.

TRIPPING ON THE STEPS

The first instance was pardonable. PL 93-270 authorized $2 million to be spent in fiscal year 1975. The actual money still had to be appropriated. The Nixon administration, having been opposed to the original legislation, of course, did not request any funds for implementation. This was decided by Nixon's Office of Management and Budget. We would have to get the money ourselves. We tried but failed to get the House HEW Appropriations Subcommittee to provide some money in their version of the bill. Warren Magnuson, however, guided by the hand of Harley Dirks, put $2 million, the full amount authorized, into the Senate version. The difference was split in conference. The program received a baptism present of $1 million. Thanks to the power of Senator Magnuson, the money part was easy.

The next task required HEW to shuffle through their personnel register for a live body who could get the show on the road. That proved too great a challenge. Bureaucracies think of offices, not of persons. The National Institute of Child Health and Human Development (NICHD) was designated as the "lead agency" to implement the SIDS program, despite the fact that the agency's mission clearly was to support research and that no one on their staff had shown the slightest interest in dealing with the human aspects of SIDS. Why this decision? Doubtless, the "assistant secretary for organization charts" found that the only box in all of HEW where the term SIDS was listed was lodged in NICHD. And to make sure that no one person could be held accountable, implementation responsibilities were "turfed out" to an "interagency panel."

A time-motion study of HEW officials would probably show that they spend a high proportion of their workday attending meetings. (Admittedly, this pattern is not unique to government employees.) These meetings ostensibly are for planning programs but in fact serve as ends in themselves for those who wish to project the illusion of activity. Besides NICHD, seats on the interagency panel were given to the Office of Maternal and Child Health, the National Center for Health Statistics, and the National Institute of Mental Health. The panel, charged with designing A PLAN for HEW's implementation of

PL 93-270, met a couple of times a month—in other words: the same old story.

After the funding and designing a plan for implementation, the department's third task was to promulgate regulations for spending the money. In addition to the interagency panel, responsibility for this task was vested in HEW's Office of the General Counsel. This gaggle of lawyers is supposed to review the proceedings of Congress and devise rules consistent with congressional intent. Instead, when any ambiguous matters arise, they very carefully avoid consulting the people on Capitol Hill who drafted the legislation. Power, after all, is the currency of the realm. If you've got it, flaunt it. Lawyers who work for administrative departments get their "day in the sun" when it comes to the drafting of regulations. Perversely, one of the first opinions generated by HEW's General Counsel was that PL 93-270 did not allow funds to be spent for the performance of autopsies.

A JOURNEY THROUGH THE LAND OF OZ

Had I not been involved previously in implementation struggles, I assuredly would have been certifiable for believing I had been transported to the Land of Oz. Two days after PL 93-270 was signed, I wrote to Assistant Secretary Charles Edwards, requesting that the National SIDS Foundation be consulted as the regulations for the new law were being prepared. "The mistreatment of SIDS families can be overcome in less than two years, *if* the new law is appropriately administered," I said.

He responded on May 21 as follows:

Dear Dr. Bergman:

Thank you for your letter of April 24 and your continuing interest in the implementation of the recently-enacted legislation on the sudden infant death syndrome. We are currently considering several options available to us for funding under this legislation, and I can assure you that the decision on the most appropriate method of financing will be made as expeditiously as possible.

We shall be happy to receive any suggestions that you and the National Foundation for Sudden Infant Death wish to offer in connection with the administration of this legislation. It would be extremely helpful to have these suggestions in written form, so that they may be shared with appropriate staff in developing the Department's program.

Sincerely yours,

/S/Theodore Cooper for
Charles C. Edwards, M.D.
Assistant Secretary for Health

I responded on October 14 with a detailed memo giving my suggestions for the implementation plan (Appendix VIII). Prior to writing the memo, I had sought the advice of someone who possessed detailed knowledge of the HEW bureaucratic structure, Gerald LaVeck, who by then had returned to Seattle to teach at the University of Washington. LaVeck's feeling was that the SIDS program should be lodged in an agency that is both oriented toward patient services and linked to local and state health departments. "Your overall objective," he said, "should be to induce local health departments to view services to SIDS families as an integral part of their continuing programs. Therefore you must pick the federal agency that can best bring about this long-term goal. Don't fool around with NICHD," said the former director, "they get into trouble any time they go outside of the research field."

In the meantime, I had found my "live body" in the person of Paul Batalden, a young pediatrician who had suddenly been catapulted into a position of some prominence, director of the Bureau of Community Health Services. This bureau was the "service arm" of HEW, being responsible for such programs as the National Health Service Corps, the Office of Maternal and Child Health, Community Health Centers, and Migrant Health Programs. Batalden seemed like the answer to our prayers. He understood what we were trying to do, and he knew how to play the government power game. "Get me the horses [i.e., mandate and money] and I'll do the job," he said. Getting him the mandate was harder than obtaining the money.

I wrote to Edwards on May 13 and phoned him on May 23, urging that the responsibility for the new law be vested in the Bureau of Community Health Services under Paul Batalden. I also repeated my plea to have a hand in the regulation-writing process. Edwards was cordial and pledged all kinds of *general* cooperation. Like a good politician, however, he was careful to give no specific commitments. The matter was still being "studied." It was the same old problem; SIDS was not a priority problem for Edwards or anyone else in his office. The HEW bureaucracy would be left to work its ways.

The ridiculous confusion about the SIDS program within HEW is illustrated by the following item taken from the June 12, 1974 issue of *Drug Research Reports* (the "Blue Sheet").

SUDDEN INFANT DEATH SYNDROME PROGRAM LANGUISHING
DESPITE NEW LAW: SOME PROJECT PROPOSALS PROMISING,
BUT FUND SHORTAGE IS CRIPPLING

Sudden Infant Death Syndrome (SIDS) research is suffering from neglect and starvation despite a recent law meant to give the problem visibility. Budgets are tight already and the agencies involved have no idea where to cut to start up a new special effort. There is $2 mil. authorized, but nothing appropriated, for fiscal year 1974, and program heads aren't enthusiastic about the prospect of trying to spread so little money among so many worthwhile project proposals.

The month-old law requires HEW to designate a lead agency and to present Congress with an implementation plan within a year. When the Natl. Institute of Child Health and Human Development (NICHD) was queried about the govt.-wide SIDS effort, staffers told "The Blue Sheet" that there was no money for research in the law. Because the money was for education programs, they said they presumed the maternal and child health program was handling implementation. Staffers at maternal and child health div. of the Bureau of Community Health Services told "The Blue Sheet" they thought the Office of Child Development was the lead agency. A child development office spokesman said, "We have nothing to do with that. I don't know why people have that impression.

A PERSONAL TOUCH

Letters are of limited value, particularly when they are read and answered by persons whose only interest is "satisficing" the correspondent. Face-to-face meetings are preferable, especially if the major actors can be gathered in the same room. I was extraordinarily fortunate because I was regarded (and feared) as a friend of Senator Magnuson. HEW brass were obliged to give me a personal appointment whenever it was requested. Political connections ensure *access*, which may or may not translate to influence. Thus on July 15 I went to Washington for a meeting with Drs. Theodore Cooper, deputy to Edwards, Norman Kretchmer, director of NICHD, and Batalden. My version of the meeting was contained in a July 18 letter to Cooper:

> Thanks so much for the opportunity to meet with you on July 15th regarding implementation of PL93-270. I drew the following conclusions from our meeting:
>
> (a) You directed Paul Batalden to proceed with plans for the Office of Maternal and Child Health to be the lead agency in administering the project grants authorized in this bill.
>
> (b) Paul Batalden agreed to begin recruiting appropriate staff.
>
> (c) A draft of proposed regulations would be ready at the Assistant Secretary level by August 30th.
>
> (d) I would have an opportunity to comment on these proposed regulations before they leave the Assistant Secretary's office.
>
> Please correct me if I have drawn any false assumptions.
> Many thanks for the sympathetic hearing that I received.

I assumed far too much; the knights of incompetency still had some turns at bat. Congressman Rogers received the following news from Assistant Secretary Edwards, dated July 29, *after* my meeting with Cooper, Batalden, and Kretchmer:

Dear Mr. Rogers:

Thank you for your letter of July 11 concerning PL 93-270, the "Sudden Infant Death Syndrome Act of 1974", asking where the program will be administered. I am pleased to bring you up to date on the progress the Department has made in implementing the act.

On May 24, I designated the National Institutes of Health (NIH) as the lead agency for development of an implementation plan. A preliminary plan has been developed, which I approved on June 5. I am looking to the National Institute for Child Health and Human Development to take the leadership for implementation and to be responsible for coordination of SIDS operations in the Public Health Service. The coordination will be effected through the DHEW Panel on Sudden Infant Death Syndrome with representation from my office, NICHD, NINDS, NCHS, NIMH and BCHS-MCH. As you know, research programs are already in progress to determine the etiology of the disease and identifying means of prevention. The Health agencies are currently developing individual action plans to develop programs in counseling, information and education data gathering and analysis. We expect a comprehensive implementation plan this Fall. Let me reassure you that we, also, are committed to the success of this program.

Sincerely yours,

/S/ Charles C. Edwards, M.D.
Assistant Secretary for Health

I responded with a loud scream that probably was heard all the way from Washington State to Washington, D.C. "I thought we had made a deal," I wrote in an anguished letter to Ted Cooper. Norman Kretchmer responded on August 21:

Dear Dr. Bergman:

Dr. Cooper has referred your letter to me for reply.

As you indicate, there was consensus that the Office of Maternal and Child Health in the Bureau of Community Health Services would assume a major share of responsibility for implementing Part C of PL 93-270. There is no indication at present that there will be a problem in submitting an implementation plan to the Office of the Assistant Secretary for Health by August 30, 1974.

The Interagency Panel on the Sudden Infant Death Syndrome continues to cooperate in the development of an effective program to alleviate the suffering of bereaved parents and to achieve the means by which crib death can be prevented. Your efforts in this regard are sincerely appreciated.

With best regards,

/S/ Norman Kretchmer, M.D., Ph.D.
Director-Designate
National Institute of Child
Health and Human Development

Sarcasm crept into my letter to Theodore Cooper, dated August 27, 1974.

Dear Dr. Cooper

I received a letter dated August 21 from Norman Kretchmer, responding to my August 7th letter to you. He states, "There is no indication at present that there will be a problem in submitting an implementation plan to the Office of the Assistant Secretary for Health by August 30, 1974." I am delighted! That is one week away. Per your original offer, I look forward to reviewing it.

I also queried him about the letter from Edwards to Congressman Rogers designating NICHD as the "lead agency." Cooper responded on September 17 as follows:

By now you have undoubtedly heard from Norman Kretchmer concerning the implementation plan for the program. I think we all agree that there is really no incompatibility with the overall Congressional intent in what is being devised. The Institute was responsible for developing the implementation plan. The actions of the Appropriations Committees will be compatible with what is recommended in the implementation plan. I am sure that we will keep our word in having your review and advice of the plan when it's in final form. I have indicated the same thing to Mr. Dirks. If there continues to be some need for clarification, we will be pleased to respond promptly. The delay in our schedule was not the fault of either NIH or any of the other agencies. It was associated with a change in our requirements for form of implementation activities, as well as operating plans.
Dr. Edwards sends along his good wishes as do I.

Sincerely yours,

/S/ Theodore Cooper, M.D.
Deputy Assistant Secretary
for Health

WHERE ARE THE REGS?

I knew that the draft regulations were still floating around HEW and was afraid that I would get them after they were "cast in concrete." As far as I was concerned a bunch of middle level amateurs were dabbling with the SIDS program, but since they were called government officials, they had to act as if they knew something about it. The top dogs simply could not get matters straight. I doubt that Edwards or Cooper, both highly intelligent men, ever invested the time necessary to understand the SIDS problem or the purpose of the law. These matters were too small for their personal attention. So agency staff, who were even more ignorant, prepared their letters.

PAYING FOR AUTOPSIES

A new actor briefly stepped onto center stage. Charles Lowe, a well-known pediatrician, had just left NICHD to become special assistant for pediatric affairs to the Office of the Assistant Secretary for Health. "At last," I thought, "a pediatrician with some clout and understanding!" My hopes soared even higher when he presided at a meeting, on October 1, of myself, Kretchmer, and Batalden to "straighten out misunderstandings." We all agreed the program should be in the Office of Maternal and Child Health. Also, Lowe understood the issue about payment for autopsies. He claimed that HEW lawyers had said that the costs of autopsies could not be covered. They would have to be swayed. I promised to generate some congressional letters, which shortly appeared from the offices of our patrons, Magnuson, Mondale, and Rogers.

Senator Mondale wrote to Assistant Secretary Edwards on October 28:

> I am distressed that there might be a delay in implementation of PL 93-270, the "Sudden Infant Death Syndrome Act," because of confusion about whether or not the costs of obtaining autopsies are authorized by law.
>
> As the sponsor of the legislation in the Senate, I can assure you that it was decidedly my intent that assistance should be given to obtain autopsies in infants dying suddenly and unexpectedly. Testimony before my Subcommittee showed that many families are denied this opportunity to find the definite cause of death in their child. One of the major purposes of the legislation was to correct this serious problem.

Would Charles Lowe continue to make policy decisions for the SIDS program from the assistant secretary's office? I was optimistic after receiving the following letter dated October 4:

> Needless to say, I hope that our meeting of October 1 has allayed many of your concerns with regard to implementation of PL 93-270. It is my perception that we isolated at least one of the key issues, that of payment of autopsies and that in further discussion with Paul Batalden you reached a supplementary understanding on the opportunities and limitations of this activity. His office is in the process of developing the programmatic guidelines and award criteria for the awarding of contracts for the demonstration service projects.
>
> I have informed Dr. Cooper as fully as possible on the content of our discussion and on the issues requiring clarification.
>
> Please feel free to communicate with my office should there be other elements that continue to need explanation or clarification. I certainly have the impression that both NICHD and the Bureau of Community Health Services are moving with a well defined plan and crisply identified program goals. We will monitor this program with care and interest.

MORE BITTERNESS

It all came unglued. When Charles Lowe moved in among the high-policy setters in the assistant secretary's office, his interest in small, finite issues like SIDS seemed to quickly wane. While presiding at one meeting concerning SIDS, Lowe appeared appropriately "secretarial" and succeeded in "sucking me in." The weeks ticked by and still nothing happened. I wrote the following letter to Dr. Cooper on November 15:

> I am totally, utterly, and completely frustrated with the delay on the part of HEW in issuing regulations to implement PL 93-270, the Sudden Infant Death Act of 1974. The law was signed by the President last April! The Department was well aware of the contents of the law at least six months prior to that date, let alone aware of the problem that passage of the law was supposed to alleviate. You have expressed resentment of my method of communicating with you through Congressional offices, yet it seems to be the *only* way I can get an answer. I submitted my written comments on the Department's implementation plan to you on October 14th, [Appendix VIII] and pleaded for some direct feedback. It has not been forthcoming. The pity is that this is such a relatively *small* problem for the Department, which is, I am sure, the reason for your inactivity. You are much more comfortable with the biggies, like HMO's, PSRO's, and NHI. Also, there is no significant disagreement

about how the law should be implemented among the agencies that will carry it out; you are hung up on small details. I had thought that when you assigned Charlie Lowe to troubleshoot, the log jam would be broken, but alas, this does not seem to be the case. Dr. Cooper, I am angry as hell, and I do not think I am unreasonable. Must we go through the whole business of congressional letters, oversight hearings, angry confrontations, etc., in order to implement a noncontroversial, desperately needed program? I assure you that is exactly what I will press for, unless you guys get off the dime.

Cooper responded on November 21:

> I have just received your letter of November 15 concerning the responsiveness of the department to your previous letter of October 14.
>
> Prior to receipt of the November 15 letter, I forwarded to you a thorough response to your previous letter. As you are no doubt aware, the response required interfacing with several different agencies and offices within them to provide the information requested.
>
> I have spoken with Dr. Charles U. Lowe about your concerns and the much needed two-way communication. He assures me that every effort is being made to resolve the issues that you have identified. Also, Dr. Lowe indicated that he had recently spoken with you concerning several of the principal issues—in effect, a status report on the activities. I want to reassure you of his continuing interest and dedication to maintaining this program on target and to be a direct point of contact for you.
>
> Your input and criticism have served to alert us of the problems you perceived. Thank you for your continued interest in this important program.

"HARLEY PLEASE HELP!!!"

It was the last sentence that was most insulting. "Thank you for your continued interest in this important program." I was convinced that the missive emanated directly from the Satisficing Stationery Shop. Far too much time had been wasted in composing letters and attending meetings, while more than 20 infants a day in the United States were dying of SIDS. Harley Dirks, who had accomplished so much for us in the past, had to become more directly involved in the mess. It was time for a reckoning in his cluttered office in the Senate Office Building. It was a risky shot. Administration officials hate having to shuffle up for a command performance in a congressional office, particularly when the performance is to be before an outside constituent like me. Ordinarily only senators themselves can summon assistant secretaries and higher into their presence. When it came to HEW,

Harley Dirks had more clout than most senators. Besides Harley, I wanted some other witnesses. Steve Lawton was unable to make it, but Ellen Hoffman did attend, as well as George Degnon from the Academy of Pediatrics. It was important for Cooper, as well as Harley, to know that failure to implement the SIDS law was of concern to more individuals than just Abe Bergman.

I came to like Ted Cooper at that December 5 meeting. He demonstrated two human qualities, which in ordinary people would be considered commonplace but in high government officials is a rarity—a sense of humor and an ability to express anger openly. Cooper had a twinkle in his eye, taking the summons into Dirks' presence in stride. He also was mad as hell at me for my "combative" letters and told me so to my face.

Cooper admitted that the department had lagged too long in issuing regulation, but insisted that this was not due to disinterest at the higher levels, but rather to the press of business. He pointed out that there were several laws where regulations had been delayed. He promised that notice of proposed rules would be published by January 1 and that grant awards would be made in April. Cooper indicated that Joann Gephart, R.N., of the Office of Maternal and Child Health would be in charge of administering the grant program in that office. She would have no authority, however, over any of the other agencies also dealing with SIDS. When pressed to name a single individual responsible for coordinating HEW's activities in SIDS, Cooper demurred. He said he did not want to see a "czar." Hoffman inquired as to why NICHD was designated a "lead agency" when the Office of Maternal and Child Health would receive all the funds for PL 93-270. Cooper stated that that decision was made fairly early at a time when NICHD had "most of the action" in SIDS. He stated that with the program farther "down the pike" another look would be given to the "lead agency" but gave no commitment.

The meeting seemed to be successful; the air was cleared. Cooper, who succeeded Edwards as assistant secretary, appeared to focus on the issue and became truly helpful. Indeed, during the short time that Ted Cooper served as assistant secretary for health and scientific affairs, he was generally considered to be the most capable person ever to have held the office.

THE "REGS" ARE ISSUED

On March 4, 1975, the secretary of HEW proposed in the *Federal Register* draft regulations for project grants for sudden infant death syndrome information and counseling. Funds for autopsies were included. On June 6, 1975, the final regulations were issued and, under a special provision, 22 project grants were awarded for "regional SIDS centers." (See Appendix IX for text of regulations.)

I have documented much frenetic activity on my part. Did any of this activity make a bit of difference in either the content or timing of the regulations? I have no way of knowing. A couple of HEW old-timers expressed amazement that regulations could be issued and grants awarded *only* 14 months after passage of a law by Congress. What an incredible thought!

In politics, one never knows to what extent any campaign efforts affect the eventual outcome. A controlled trial would be interesting. I have never known a politician, however, who had tested the hypothesis. I certainly did not.

15

KEEPING THE
FOUNDATION AFLOAT

You seek a world in which no children starve;
I seek a world in which fewer children starve.

Albert Camus in a statement made at
the Dominican Monastery of Latour-Maumberg in 1948

If the reader discerns a softening of tone when I write about the
National SIDS Foundation, it is no accident. I am an unabashed partisan and ask forgiveness for any lapses in analytic powers when I take
up that organization.

With the enormous investment of time and energy spent on securing passage and implementing the SIDS legislation, it was sometimes
hard to remember that our most important battles had to be fought
at the local community level. Whenever we lost sight of that fact, the
unremitting volume of letters and telephone calls to the Foundation's
New York office set us straight. The main reason we went to Congress
in the first place was to obtain money to cover the cost of autopsies.
No federal law was going to ensure compassionate handling of families.
We could only close up shop when these poignant pleas for help stopped coming in. Keeping the shop open, however, was a perpetual
struggle. Given the responsibilities we had assumed, our expenses were
minimal. We rented two rooms in a shabby office building in the
Broadway theater district that always seemed to stay about two swings
away from the wrecking ball. Our payroll consisted of Judie Choate,
who made less than $2 an hour, a secretary, and some part-time clerks.
Volunteers from the New York area pitched in. For many years, the

books were kept by Ann Siegal. Printing and mailing information were relatively large budget items. Paying the long-distance telephone charges each month was a cause for celebration. Our income was derived from a small but steady stream of memorial donations, and a tithe on our chapters of 50 percent of their fund raising efforts. In 1973 the total income of the Foundation was $110,840 and, in 1974, $141,897.

STATE OF THE CHAPTERS

Though we knew that the development of strong local chapters was imperative to achieve our objectives, they were a mixed blessing. For one thing, the chapters did not have a uniform concept on what they should be doing on a local level, or what the Foundation should be doing on a national level. Some wanted to be exclusively involved in raising money for research, and others as a support group for other parents. The philosophical orientation usually depended on the composition of the group. There were three general categories: (1) "new parents," who had recently lost children and were still in the throes of their grief-guilt reactions, (2) "old parents," who had not lost children within two years and tended to have a more global perspective, and (3) "nonparents," many of whom were health professionals, mostly nurses, drawn to our cause for idealistic reasons.

There was no such thing as a typical chapter. Some, like the ones in Seattle, on Long Island, and on northern California's East Bay were relatively large and contained a mixture of all three groups. A chapter on Chicago's North Shore was made up of mostly suburban housewives, none of whom were SIDS parents. The Alaska chapter centered in Anchorage was organized by public health nurses who perceived a need for a community program after making home visits to SIDS families. Some chapters were in fact energetic couples like the Salzsteins in San Diego, and the Greenes in Maine, who did the work of ten people.

BURNOUT

In our chapters, there could be any number of members listed on the rolls, but only a few could be relied on to do the work. This characteristic, of course, is common to all volunteer organizations, but in the NSIDSF there was an important difference, in that our work engendered such intense emotions. This was not only true in SIDS parents for obvious reasons, but also in the rest of us. It was that we always seemed to be unappreciated underdogs staging guerilla warfare. Very few positive strokes were ever given for Foundation work.

The setup was tailor-made for rapid burnout. With very few exceptions, it was difficult to continue in active chapter work for more than a few years. SIDS parents could hurl themselves into the fray partly as a way to resolve their own grief. As the normal healing process occurred, however, it was only natural, and indeed healthy, to disengage. Leadership necessarily had to be transitory. This meant a waxing and waning of chapter activities based in large measure on the attributes of the current crop of SIDS parents.

Salvation sometimes appeared in unusual ways. Two weeks after they lost their daughter in January 1973, Charles and Anne Barr of Marblehead, Massachusetts, contacted Judie Choate to ask how they could help. Among her other attributes, Judie was a good judge of horseflesh. In no time at all, Anne had become president of our eastern Massachusetts chapter, and Charlie was installed as chairman of the Board of Trustees of the NSIDSF. Working with Charlie was an incredible pleasure. Raised in Alabama and educated at Harvard, he ran an advertising agency in Boston. He coolly steered the Foundation over some rocky shoals.

The phenomenon that never ceased to fascinate and inspire me was the emergence of strong grassroots leaders who, before their children died, never thought of themselves as especially accomplished. Suzie Behr in Omaha, Maria Orr in Honolulu, Sherryl Collins in Kewaskum near Milwaukee, Donna Gimeno in Denver, Lynn Runfola in Buffalo, Judy Roth in Detroit, Ann Barr, Donna Musslewhite in Atlanta, Linda Hash in Oakland, Jane Adams in New Orleans, and many others were all "ordinary" housewives who were drawn into leadership roles only when their lives were touched by tragedy. Though, of course, they would have preferred an alternative means, their work with the Foundation chapters opened new vistas in their lives.

NONPARTICIPANTS

For the most part, our chapters were composed of white middle-class women. Men, minorities, and poor families were notably absent. Men in our culture tend to be less able than women to handle tragedy, especially sudden death. The risk of divorce following "crib death" is high, in large measure due to communication failure. Whereas women tend to express their sadness and want to talk about the death, men are constrained to uphold a "macho image" by holding their feelings within themselves. While a wife may mistakenly interpret her husband's unwillingness to talk about the death as lack of caring, the man may terribly resent being "bugged" by the woman to relive the pain. ("What's the point of talking about it?")

There was much talking about SIDS, of course, at chapter activities. Very few men participated actively. Most supported their wives' involvement, as long as they were not "sucked in." There were still others who were openly hostile, increasing the burden on their spouses.

We were always trying to involve minorities and poor families in our activities, since SIDS occurs more frequently among them and because they lack other forms of support. We had no success whatsoever. We could never organize chapters in the midst of large cities such as New York, Detroit, Chicago, or Los Angeles. One reason may be that poor people appear to deal with a tragedy like "crib death" as one more manifestation of life's cruelty, confirming their powerless state. Joining with others, especially others from a strange milieu, to fight back is just not done.

FINANCIAL REPORTS

We usually discouraged new parents from seeking a formal chapter charter. That's because acceptance of a charter brought with it some bureaucratic requirements, the most onerous of which was the filing of quarterly financial reports. We asked that each chapter designate a medical adviser, an attorney, and, most importantly, a certified public accountant, all of whom, of course, would donate their services. The financial reports were a recurring nightmare for both the chapters and the national office. Why? The NSIDSF had been chartered as a philanthropic corporation in the State of Connecticut (by Lowell Weicker). Rather than each chapter having to file articles of incorporation in their states, as well as negotiate with the Internal Revenue Service for tax-exempt status, the chapters remained under the umbrella of the parent corporation. Of more practical significance was that for the Foundation to have any chance to raise private funds, we needed the philanthropists' equivalent of the Good Housekeeping Seal to certify that we were a legitimate charity. Before we could get that certification from the organization called the National Information Bureau, we needed periodic audits of the books of both the national office and the chapters. To a harassed chapter president already doing the work of five people, filling out bureaucratic forms for "that office in

New York" did not always seem like a top-priority matter. It also meant hounding a local accountant to do free work during tax season when he was invariably busy with paying customers. How hard could we push?

Midwest regional director Suzie Behr from Omaha wrote:

> I'm now receiving complaint after complaint from chapters in my region. Since I've come up the ranks, it's damned hard for me to tell Pat Mounteer [from Salt Lake City] that she can't come to the regional meeting, much less be a chapter, because her audited report isn't in. I see a fellow human being who works from 6:00 p.m. until 3:00 a.m. at Denny's restaurant and then hands out blue [SIDS information] brochures all day at the Utah State Fair for 18 days straight. My job is to reprimand her? I can't do it. I won't do it!

It was not until October of 1975 that the Foundation received a certified audit statement and not until January of 1979 that the Foundation was "cleared" by the National Information Bureau as a legitimate charity.

SEARCHING FOR CELEBRITIES

In our frantic efforts to obtain money to keep our campaign alive, we ceaselessly searched for celebrities willing to take up our cause. The association of Franklin Roosevelt with poliomyelitis, John Kennedy with mental retardation, Jerry Lewis with muscular dystrophy, and Danny Thomas with childhood cancer, among others, are powerful illustrations of how big names draw attention money to disease causes. Sticking pins into dolls named for the children of famous parents was a form of gallows humor we sometimes employed. Rumors periodically surfaced about this or that person who may have lost a child to SIDS. A famous football player for the Dallas Cowboys was said to have lost a child but, when contacted, did not wish to discuss the matter. He had just separated from the baby's mother.

The most tantalizing target was the movie star Robert Redford. A movie magazine had reported that while a poor, struggling acting student in New York City in 1960, Redford had lost a baby to "crib death." Based on this item, Robert and Lola Redford received scores of letters from SIDS parents requesting their help in fund-raising schemes. Saul Goldberg of the Guild for Infant Survival tried hard to attract the Redfords to help his group. I myself, after seeing two Redford movies in one week, *Downhill Racer* and *Jeremiah Johnson*, wrote a sentimental plea with the thought that such a sensitive actor would surely be willing to come to the aid of brutalized families. Eventually the Foundation was contacted by Lola Redford who agreed to help us, but she imposed several conditions: all requests would be channeled through the national office, the family's privacy was to be respected, and, most important, Robert Redford was not to be involved. "My husband," she said, "still cannot talk about the baby's death."

In October 1977 Lola Redford, who agreed to become a member, came to Chicago for a meeting of the Foundation's Board of Trustees. With much trepidation, she consented to an interview by a reporter for the *Chicago Tribune*, which I witnessed. The reason the Redfords were reluctant to hurl themselves into the SIDS fray quickly became apparent; Lola used every ounce of her energy to maintain her composure. She was a "new SIDS mother," not having spoken about the incident for 17 years. Her tale was the by then familiar one of horror and degradation: interrogation and search of the apartment by an investigator, and identification of the corpse at the city morgue. Because the parents were young and poor, the implications of abuse or neglect were pushed with vigor. The Redfords had no family physician, and in 1960 there were no groups to provide information or support. The interview ended with Lola in tears, but at least it appeared that she had been able to exorcise some of her pain. I doubt that Robert ever had a similar opportunity. That the couple survived with their minds and marriage apparently intact is an indication of their inner strength.

Lola Redford's participation in our work was minimal; undoubtedly the interview episode evoked too much pain. She was also heavily involved in a New York-based consumer action network. She did produce her husband for a few movie-premiere benefits, but since advance publicity was prohibited, little money was raised. Nevertheless, the fact that the Redfords were somehow involved with the Foundation was an enormous morale booster to SIDS parents throughout the country. The fact that grief-stricken parents shared a common bond with such a famous couple as the Redfords provided a degree of comfort.

Despite her grief, and other activities, Lola Redford might have been induced to play a larger role in our organization, but for my intemperance. For two years I had been "played along" by a prominent board member of Variety International, an energetic group of mostly "show-biz" types who raise large sums of money for children's charities. When the group held their annual convention in Seattle, Mary

Dore and I made an emotional appeal for money to their charity-dispensing committee. Though the committee members made sympathetic noises, it was clear that Mary and I were not the appropriate supplicants. The committee members were aware both that Robert Redford had lost a child to SIDS and that he usually shunned the Hollywood crowd, e.g., them. The price for Variety Club support was delicately, but definitely, spelled out: Redford would have to make a personal appearance for a hand-out.

I managed to convince my contact that, while Robert Redford's appearance was out of the question, it was conceivable that Lola Redford might be willing to "make the scene." That proved to be acceptable. The next Variety International meeting was to take place in New York City, where the Redfords lived.

I wrote to Lola, "it is hard to escape the concept of exploitation. People in our society—actually in all societies—venerate those with famous names. Are you aware that many families who have lost children to 'crib death' gain some solace from knowing that the Redfords went through a similar ordeal? I suppose you folks have long since reconciled yourselves to being treated as symbols rather than flesh and blood." I asked her to make a half-hour appearance before the Variety International Committee in New York. I did not hear from her for months. As the date grew closer, I tried to call but could not get through. Finally I received a cryptic note from Robert Redford's secretary, saying that neither he nor Lola would be able to attend the meeting.

I remember the moment well. It was the end of a long day that was filled with a host of minor frustrations. I was physically and mentally exhausted. Since that state is not uncommon for physicians, my action was inexcusable. In a cryptic and bitter note, I upbraided Lola for being too selfish to spend a few hours to assist families less fortunate than she. And then in the unkindest cut of all I said, "*I* did not lose a child to SIDS!"

Lola Redford's response written on November 24, 1980, was apt:

> To reassure you, we have not forgotten that we lost a child to SIDS; were that possible, the letters which I receive from bereaved parents, who have found some comfort in identifying with our grief rekindles the pain every time. One of the hardest things I have ever done is talk about our son's death to the press, perhaps (though you were there) it is you who needs a reminder of what pain is—or do you foster the belief that us rich famous folks don't feel pain and don't mind exploitation.

I hope that other parents who live with the guilt of SIDS don't have to live with the additional burden of the guilt thrust on them by your expectations.

Your misplaced anger was not only inappropriate, it was insensitive and unkind.

UNREALIZED EXPECTATIONS

I was not the only one whose expectations were unrealistic and therefore unrealized. The national office and chapters were always in a state of disharmony, as were the chapters with each other. We tried to bridge the communications gap by appointing four regional directors, all of whom were active in their local chapters. The move helped, but did not cure the problem.

In 1975, based on the experience of our vigorous Long Island Chapter, the Foundation embarked on a fund-raising project involving the sale of charms containing our logo, a tree with a broken branch and fallen leaf. The majority of chapter presidents felt that all chapters should be obliged to participate in the charm-selling campaign, or else lose their charters. Tumult ensued when the Board of Trustees accepted this recommendation.

Mary Dore, founder of the Washington State Chapter, wrote:

I feel strongly about keeping demands on individual chapters at a minimum. As long as they operate legally and in good taste and provide service, they deserve PRAISE. In turn, chapters can be proud to belong to a national organization that keeps to this guideline. It would be a shame to break apart over nonsense. Everyone wants the same thing. Growing pains always hurt.

Bruce Beckwith wrote:

It strikes me that a strong centralized authority can only work if it conveys to the chapters the image of a supportive, responsive authority that values input from local sources and gives those localities considerably more autonomy to respond to their varying regional and local needs and capabilities. It has to accept that there will be big, energetic, dominant groups, as well as small, less efficient and visible groups. Whatever the latter type of group can do should be appreciated, rather than criticized.

JUDIE CHOATE RESIGNS

Frustration over our inability to receive timely financial information from the chapters, and hard feelings over the charm-sale project contributed to the "burnout" of my brilliant comrade Judie Choate, who resigned as executive director in April of 1976. No mere mortal could ever have stayed on the battlefield and endured more pressure than Judie. She was truly superhuman. She not only was primarily responsible for forging a *national* organization, but also almost literally, using long-distance telephone wires, for holding it together. Judie was "on call" 24 hours a day for over ten years.

For the first five or six years that I worked in the field, I was a fairly good grief counselor for SIDS parents. The emotional drain of such counseling, however, was so great that in order to maintain my sanity I felt forced to restrict myself to organizational and political matters. My physician status served as an effective shield; laymen are used to seeing doctors stand aloof. Judie Choate, especially because she was a SIDS parent, had no protection whatsoever. It mattered not that she and her marvelously supportive husband Ed were under constant financial strain, or that her two boys had the needs of all normal children. If a shocked SIDS parent anywhere in the country needed to unburden themselves, Judie was obliged to pick up the phone to assume some of those burdens, day or night. There was no "signing out."

The struggle to pay the Foundation's bills never stopped. Every manner of fund-raising "expert" came forward with schemes to make us rich, all of them requiring "up front" money that we didn't possess. Judie had to bear most of the frustration from constantly being rebuffed by wealthy individuals and foundations. Even more frustrating was our inability to obtain chapter financial reports. Judie Choate left the Foundation after the toughest work had been accomplished. By 1976 health professional and public understanding of SIDS was beginning to emerge; there was no turning back. More than any other single person, Judie is responsible for "humanizing" the handling of SIDS in the United States.

MOVING TO CHICAGO

The near-dissolution of the Foundation over the "hard-line" approach to fund raising was cause for much soul searching. A "reduced expectations" campaign was undertaken, with a resolve to employ more warm blankets and less cold water. We despaired at finding anyone with a fraction of the talent and dedication of Judie Choate to serve as executive director, until we fastened upon Carolyn Szybist. She was a magnetic speaker and warm leader who was loved by the chapter volunteers. A draft would be necessary; no one at a chapter or national level ever volunteered for a position of responsibility in the Foundation. Carolyn was persuaded to take the job only because she accurately perceived that if she did not, the organization would dissolve. Her assumption of the director's job entailed moving the national office to Chicago. It was a small price to pay.

16

COLLABORATING
WITH NIMH

With great effort, the Foundation was managing to carry out basic functions, such as printing and distributing literature, arranging for speakers and distributing our educational film, and, above all, answering the mail and telephone. Opening the Regional SIDS Center at Loyola Medical School in Chicago was a big step forward. In communities where we had strong chapters, such as Seattle, Oakland, San Diego, Omaha, New Orleans, and Long Island, we could ensure humane management programs. We were stymied, however, in our resolve to establish humane community management systems in most of the other towns of the United States. Such an effort required sending out trained community organizers, which we could not afford. What about the feds? If it was to take them 14 months just to paint names on their office doors and sharpen their pencils, one could only speculate how many SIDS parents would be thrown in jail waiting for them to swing into action. It was time once again to heed Mary Lasker's advice and go hustling along the banks of the Potomac.

Throughout the 1970s there were two high officials in HEW who by actions rather than words consistently demonstrated that they were more interested in serving the clients of their respective agencies than in making themselves look important in Washington. There must have been more than two, but I am only familiar with Bertram Brown, director of the National Institute of Mental Health, and Emery Johnson, director of the Indian Health Service. Interestingly, even as they constantly took risks by ignoring the HEW "bean counters," as Johnson called the horde of bureaucrats holding down sofa cushions in the administrative offices, both men established record tenures in their respective positions. (It was my privilege to have worked with Johnson in the creation and successful passage of the Indian Health Care Improvement Act of 1975. What a pleasure to have the person responsible for carrying out a law participate in its drafting, despite the official opposition of his superiors.)

It was Bert Brown whom I turned to for help with SIDS. We had met casually a few times in the past. When he was a pediatric intern in the 1950s, Brown had done a nice unpublished study of the pediatric emergency room at Yale-New Haven Hospital. I did a similar study a few years later when I was a resident at Boston Children's Hospital (Bergman, 1962). At that time Brown was a psychiatry resident in Boston, and we met to compare notes.

On June 13, 1973, I wrote to Brown, asking: "Is there any way that the National Institute of Mental Health could help with the 'human' aspects of SIDS? No agency within HEW has taken upon itself a concerted attack on the tragic by-product of this disease, guilt, which is responsible for a great deal of mental illness in the United States." I met the next month in Washington with Brown and his special assistant, a child psychiatrist, Steve Hersh. Hersh impressed me immediately for a single reason: he maintained contact with the lives of real people by working with children one day each week at the National Cancer Institute. Caring for even the occasional sick patient cannot help but broaden the perspective of a physician-administrator. Otherwise the endless meetings and reports take on a life of their own.

The meeting was fruitful. Brown and Hersh could have given me a dozen excuses why they could not find the money. Instead they quickly acknowledged that SIDS caused mental illness that could be prevented by early counseling of families. In February of 1974 a three-year contract was signed between NIMH and the NSIDSF for $163,513 to organize mental health backup services for the families of SIDS victims and to educate mental health professionals about SIDS.

Receiving the money was not quite as simple as Bert Brown writing out a check. Government contracts are administered by a program officer, like Brown or Hersh, who judge whether the work is needed and meritorious, and an independent contract officer, who ensures that all fiscal dealings are on the up-and-up. Strict rules determine how contracts are awarded, and once the award is made, how the money is managed. Though I was always impatient with the inevitable delays, I was aware that, when taxpayers' money was involved, such a system was necessary to deter corruption. Also, my dealings with the HEW contract officers were excellent. They were tough, but fair.

Following "the book," the contract office at NIMH first had to determine whether there were any other qualified groups that could perform the work. There were not. I then had to sit down with a long-faced accountant to justify every cent of our proposal. He was satisfied and the contract was officially awarded. At long last, we had some resources to perform work directly in local communities.

We immediately hired two public health nurses, Barbara French who worked out of the New York office under the direction of Judie Choate, and Kathryn Patterson, who worked out of my office in Seattle. Kathy had worked for me in an injury research project while obtaining her masters degree from the University of Washington School of Nursing. I have already described the extraordinary effectiveness of this sprightly blonde with a will of steel.

FINDING MENTAL HEALTH PROFESSIONALS

It is fortunate that Bert Brown, Steve Hersh, and the eventual project officer, Stephen Goldston, coordinator of Primary Prevention Programs for NIMH, took a broad view of our contract work. Had we limited ourselves to organizing mental health backup services for SIDS families and educating mental health professionals, much time would have been wasted tilting at windmills. That is because the vast majority of mental health workers viewed SIDS in the same fashion as the editors of the *American Journal of Psychiatry*, who rejected our original paper describing the psychiatric toll of SIDS. It was difficult to interest mental health professionals in a subject that seemed so remote to them. Educational seminars on SIDS for mental health workers were sparsely attended. I find that it is the rare mental health worker who feels qualified to deal with organic diseases, even their psychic by-products.

We continued to concentrate, therefore, on implementing a basic coordinated management program in each community for sudden infant death. Sensitive initial handling of the SIDS family was the most effective means of preventing future mental illness, a point that was fortunately understood by our NIMH colleagues. The key targets remained the coroner or medical examiner, and the health department director and/or the director of public health nursing.

As the basic management programs came into existence, the need for mental health consultants became more apparent, more to assist the first-line counselors than to provide direct care to SIDS families. The counselors, usually nurses, needed training in grief counseling, much of which consisted of understanding their own feelings about death. They also needed help in handling unusual or especially severe grief reactions. Just as a small number of saintly pediatricians emerged to help in the early days, it was usually possible to inveigle one or two mental health workers to sign on. They were all breeds: psychiatrists, psychologists, social workers, as well as nurses or clergymen with mental health training. The common qualities were sensitivity to the SIDS problem, and a willingness to serve without recompense.

HELPING TO PREPARE GRANT APPLICATIONS

After the SIDS law was passed in late 1974, it was apparent to us, if not to the HEW bureaucrats floating in circles over its implementation, that funds would soon be available to establish regional SIDS centers. We also correctly surmised that since HEW had opposed passage of the law, and did not understand its purpose, they would not be able to help communities organize projects that could apply for funds. Kathy Patterson and Barbara French therefore spent much of their time organizing regional centers and providing assistance in preparing grant applications. HEW's Office of Maternal and Child Health awarded 22 grants for SIDS educational and counseling projects in June 1975, and eight more the following year. Fifteen of those first 22 projects came into existence as a direct result of the Foundation's technical assistance provided under the NIMH contract. Just as important, community management programs were instituted in an equal number of locales that did not receive federal funds. Not a bad payoff on Bert Brown's investment.

NO MONEY FOR NIMH

Our good working relations with NIMH were in sharp contrast to the constant bickering going on between the Foundation and both the Office of Maternal and Child Health (OMCH), and to a lesser extent, the National Institute of Child Health and Human Development (NICHD). Nevertheless I continued to lobby the assistant secretary's office to place all the money appropriated under PL 93-270 in the OMCH. The irony of this situation was not lost on our NIMH project officer, Steve Goldston. He frequently urged me to try diverting some of the money to his primary prevention program. The idea was not farfetched; I entertained similar thoughts about the wisdom of my actions. There was one big reason why I did not alter my stance. I knew that the *only* reason we got the money, and had good working relations, was because of the personal interest of the NIMH director, Bert Brown. He had vision, and was willing to take risks. If Brown were to leave, the bureaucratic jungle of NIMH would be no easier to traverse than any other part of HEW.

I guessed right. In 1977 Bertram Brown was forced to resign by HEW Secretary Joseph Califano. It was an ironic move. Brown had been positively heroic in keeping the community mental health center movement alive during the administrations of Presidents Nixon and Ford. When President Carter came to office, mental health became the primary interest of Rosylyn Carter. Two strong-minded individuals like Califano and Brown could not share the spotlight as the first lady's "agent" in mental health. The secretary had to prevail.

"RESIGNATION" OF HARLEY DIRKS

Another Washington, D.C., "hatchet job" had more profound effects for me and the SIDS cause. In October 1976 Harley Dirks resigned from the staff of the Senate Appropriations Committee. The tale is sordid but not atypical of life in the political thicket. In a previous chapter I described the hearing ritual of the HEW Appropriations Subcommittee. Because appropriations hearings are pure ritual, and boring at that, Senators are loathe to waste an afternoon in attendance. At the best of times, Dirks had difficulty getting even one senator to chair a hearing. In 1976 the problem was complicated in that six members of the committee were running for reelection. He kept having to cancel scheduled hearings when he could not recruit a chairman. This was inconvenient for witnesses, some of whom had to travel long distances, and it played havoc with the strict schedule laid out in the Senate for final consideration of the bill.

Dirks fastened on a solution to the dilemma. He placed into the hearing record the written testimony submitted by several department witnesses, along with a few simulated questions, making it appear that a hearing had actually taken place. No harm was done, no words were falsified. The department witnesses were no doubt relieved that they did not have to waste their time at a boring hearing. The traditional Capitol Hill game of transposing illusion for reality was played out.

The usually politically savvy Dirks made an elementary miscalculation. In his zeal to save his boss Magnuson from embarrassment, he neglected to guard his own flank. Dirks was not popular with many of his Senate staff colleagues. They were jealous of the enormous power he wielded, and put off by his blunt, and sometimes sarcastic, speech. It was get-even time. A staff colleague on the Appropriations Committee who disliked Dirks contacted Washington columnist Jack Anderson. A couple of big newspaper stories soon followed ("Congressional Aide Fakes Hearing Records"). The integrity of the Senate was called into question; a victim had to be sacrificed to the gods of propriety.

To this day I remain ashamed of Senator Magnuson's conduct in the matter. Harley Dirks had served him with incredible energy, talent, and loyalty. However misguided, it was Magnuson's interests that he was trying to protect. The senator could easily have issued a public admonishment, and the jackals would have had their taste of blood and been satisfied. The senator was in Seattle. I did what I had never done before, calling his residence and asking for an immediate audience. He consented and listened to me politely. It was no use. Without a hint of ambivalence, Magnuson expressed outrage at how Dirks could have brought such embarrassment upon *him* and confirmed that he would have to go.

Dirks was succeeded by one of his subordinates, Terry Lierman, a 28-year-old political science graduate from the University of Wisconsin, who before coming on the staff of the Appropriations Committee had worked at the National Institutes of Health. My influence in the Magnuson operation dropped precipitously. Whereas first Gerry Grinstein, and then Harley Dirks, had trusted me implicitly and thereby imbued me with some of their power, I was now just another, albeit persistent, Magnuson constituent. It was not that Terry Lierman was hostile. Quite the contrary, we maintained friendly personal relations. His style, though, especially contrasted to Dirks, was just cautious. He was going to be judicious. Above all, he wanted to maintain civil relations with the bureaucrats at HEW, and not "push them around." There was joy in the long corridors of HEW's Parklawn Building.

17

A DUAL SYSTEM
FOR HELPING FAMILIES

Securing passage of the Sudden Infant Death Syndrome Act of 1974 (PL 93-270) should have been the crowning achievement of the National SIDS Foundation. Instead we were to discover that we had created a powerful competitor who would come close to destroying us. Mention has already been made of our struggle to get the authority for implementing PL93-270 into the Office of Maternal and Child Health (OMCH). Though I did not exactly expect the officials of that office to lick my hand in gratitude, neither did I anticipate their initial indifference and subsequent hostility toward our efforts to influence how the program would be managed.

I was naive! The first instinct of a government official in a new job is to act to ensure that the job lasts as long as possible. Why should government workers be any different than other human beings? Likewise, it is only logical that advice on how to carry out that job will be sought from colleagues and superiors within one's organization who hold the keys to survival, rather than from zealous outsiders. I did not possess such calm understanding in 1975 when, through a series of memos and personal meetings, I besieged OMCH with queries on the criteria they proposed to use in awarding the federal funds. The pervading theme of the responses was, "don't call us, we'll let you know when we decide."

An immediate complication for us was the departure of Paul Batalden, who had been a covert partner in lobbying to get the SIDS program lodged in OMCH. He had succumbed to burnout and repaired to Minneapolis to practice pediatrics and pursue research in health services. I learned once again the futility of depending on single individuals in government service; their half-lives tend to be short. Batalden, however, was succeeded as director of the Bureau of Community Health Services (of which OMCH was a component) by Edward Martin, who was promoted from his position as director of the National Health Service Corps.

At the time I thought the promotion was fortuitous. I knew and respected Martin for the rescue job he had performed on the corps, which I considered my baby. The corps had floundered for two years after its inception because of indecisive leadership. Ed Martin was anything but indecisive; brilliant and arrogant were the adjectives generally used to describe him. He was president of the Student American Medical Association during 1969-70 at a time when the organization split off from its antediluvian parent to preach social activism. A breeding ground for the medical reformers of the day was Montefiore Hospital in the Bronx, where Martin did a residency in social medicine. The Bureau of Community Health Services, the arm of the U.S. Public Health Service engaged in carrying out client services (as opposed to financing research and education), was an ideal setting for a physician with Martin's background.

The fact that I already possessed a working relationship with Ed Martin was a boon, but the people in charge of the SIDS program in OMCH were one tier down on the management chart. That meant that my outrage at their shenanigans, which unfortunately was almost continuous, forced me to be a "tattle-tale" to the big boss. As mentioned earlier, though it may yield momentary satisfaction, a definite price always is exacted for going over the heads of bureaucrats, and the inhabitants of the Office of Maternal and Child Health "wrote the book" on government bureaucracy at its worst.

When the health mission was taken away from the Children's Bureau in 1963, the bureau's health operatives stayed in place but painted new door signs and printed new stationery under the label of the Office of Maternal and Child Health. The "play your cards close to the vest" style of OMCH's first director, Arthur Lesser, was emulated by his successors as well as the others who worked in the office.

"OLD BOY-OLD GIRL" NETWORK

To survive for more than a few years, any federal program must have an approving constituency outside of the District of Columbia who assure their legislators that the particular operation is vital to the survival of the republic. These constituents are invariably those who depend on the flow of federal dollars that are channeled through the program. The constituency supporting OMCH has been described as the "old boy-old girl" network. Who are those who comprise the network? For the most part they are linked either as past students or present faculty of departments of maternal and child health in schools of public health, most of whom have gone to work in state and local health departments. Whereas physicians have overwhelming influence over the affairs of NIH, other health professionals such as nurses, social workers, and nutritionists have carved out their fiefdoms in the OMCH. At its best, this arrangement fosters cooperative interdisciplinary endeavors. At its worst, it fosters wasteful "featherbedding."

DIFFERENCES BETWEEN NIH AND OMCH

Besides their constituencies, NIH and OMCH also differ in the manner by which they award grants and contracts. NIH has a rigid, formalized system on how applications are acted upon, with defined roles for councils (setting priorities), study sections (merit reviews by peers), and staff. Staff members give advice and can sometimes influence which study section reviews a grant, but, for the most part, they do not determine who gets the money. Nongovernment members are nominated to councils and study sections for defined terms; the composition of these bodies is public information.

The manner by which grants and contracts are awarded at OMCH is murkier. Staff members set the program spending priorities, choose outside consultants to sit on the frequently held ad hoc review panels, sit in on the review panel meetings, and make the final decisions on panel recommendations. Needless to say, the outside reviewers usually have close ties, either past or present, with the OMCH. This incestuous system does not necessarily make for bad decisions. It does mean, however, that if one wants to tap OMCH for money, it is best to stay on the good side of OMCH staff.

The financial stakes at OMCH are much less than at NIH, especially since 1981, when the Maternal and Child Health Block Grant siphoned all but 15 percent of the Title V money and sent it directly to the states. The 15 percent "set aside" for discretionary spending by OMCH is "peanuts" by Washington standards. For example in fiscal year 1984 the total NIH budget was $4.48 billion, while the OMCH "set aside" amounted to just less than $60 million. That is why there has never been any hue and cry to scrutinize the award process.

PLEA FOR OPERATING PHILOSOPHY

What was the basis of my beef with the OMCH? They disbursed between $2 million and $3 million every year in the SIDS program without ever formulating a coherent operating philosophy. I pleaded in vain for a statement of objectives, and for strategies to achieve those objectives. Obviously I was not hesitant to declare my thoughts, which were in fact pretty simple: every family in the United States that lost an infant suddenly and unexpectedly should receive the benefits of the four-point management system. The limited amount of money available should be used to implement the services where they were absent and supplement the services where they were partially available. Last on my priority list for fund giving were areas in which good SIDS management programs were already in operation.

The main implication of my recommendation was that project grants should be made mostly on the basis of unmet needs of families. OMCH did not want to talk about that. Indeed, they did not want to talk about anything. Joann Gephart had been appointed to coordinate the SIDS program in OMCH. She did not return my phone calls and or answer my letters, and even when she came out to Seattle for other purposes, she did not want to meet with me. As it turned out, Ms. Gephart did not last long in the position. An "iron curtain" had already descended between the NSIDSF and the OMCH.

It's important to mention that marked improvement occurred in SIDS management between 1972, when the management study was performed, and 1975 when the first federal project grants were awarded. Several state legislatures, including those of Alaska, North Dakota, Kansas, Texas, and Michigan, passed laws mandating performance of autopsies and providing family support. Legislative fiat, of course, did not in itself provide the money to perform these services, but it did not hurt. More importantly, the states of Florida, Utah, Vermont, and Rhode Island had initiated the four-point management program. It was no coincidence that these states, along with Oregon and Maryland, which had pioneered in SIDS management, all had statewide medical examiner systems where funding of autopsies was not an obstacle.

AWARD OF PROJECT GRANTS

The final regulations for PL 93-270 were published in the *Federal Register* on June 6, 1975. About two weeks later grants worth $1.8 million were awarded to 24 projects. That was not as bad as it sounds.

Table 1

Fiscal Year	Projects Funded	Amount of Awards (millions)
1975	24	$1.8
1976	31	2.0
1977	30	1.8
1978	33	2.5
1979	37	2.8

The draft regulations were in circulation for many months along with application packets. The review and award process followed the pattern described above. During the first go around several nongovernment consultants, including Kathryn Patterson, were asked to review a packet of applications and furnish their comments by mail. In subsequent years ad hoc panels convened to review project grant applications, but the final decisions were always made by OMCH staff. There were no site visits. More awards were made in the next four years, and several projects fell by the wayside. By 1979 there were 37 federally funded SIDS projects located in 32 states. Twenty-four of them came into being as a direct result of consultation provided by the NSIDSF. Table 1 shows the number of projects as well as the total amount of money allocated by fiscal year.

From 1975 to 1979 $10.9 million was spent by HEW for the SIDS projects, which represents 89 percent of the $12.2 million Congress

Table 2

	Number	Amount
State health department	21	$1,226,176
City or county health department	2	163,960
University or hospital	11[a]	1,092,889
Medical association	2[b]	220,060
Regional maternal and child health council	1	84,725
Total	37	$2,787,810

[a]Includes one project operated through medical examiner office.
[b]Projects operated through medical examiner office.

appropriated for the entire program. HEW spent the other $1.3 million for program support and contract activities. One hundred thousand dollars were returned unused to the U.S. Treasury. The project grants were awarded to a variety of organizations as shown in Table 2.

SUCCESSFUL PROJECTS

All too often, especially in government, program success is judged by "effort" rather than "effect" variables. Effort, of course, is much easier to assess than effect. An effort variable commonly used is the number of individuals trained, or the number of conferences held. My sole criterion for judging whether a project was successful was the percentage of SIDS families in the service area who receive the benefits of the four-point management program. Though we did not attempt to replicate the 1972 management study, we charged our chapters with monitoring the projects.

Like most grant programs, some of the SIDS projects were hugely successful, some were marginal, and some were dreadful. The best results occurred in the sites where the coroner or medical examiner, the public health nurses, and the parent volunteers worked as a team. The worst results were in those places where "turf battles" between the three groups took place.

An example of an excellent project is the one in Boston, serving eastern Massachusetts. Previously the autopsy policies were wildly inconsistent due to scores of "districts" each with its own death investigation system, presided over by a political appointee. The project is located at the Boston City Hospital where autopsies are performed, and presided over by two pediatricians, Robert Reece, of the City Hospital, and Fred Mandell, of Children's Hospital. Mandell is medical adviser for the foundation's eastern Massachusetts chapter, as well as vice-president of the NSIDSF. An effective management system began almost overnight.

Other good programs operated in North Carolina, Rhode Island, Vermont, Florida, Utah, New Mexico, and Maryland, and in the counties containing Detroit, Minneapolis, and St. Louis. These all happened to be areas served by capable medical examiners who already routinely performed autopsies on infants who died unexpectedly. Federal funds allowed them to expand their services by adding educational and counseling components. This was also true for areas like Seattle and Long Island, which were able to improve on the services they were already providing. There were other excellent projects; the ones above are listed only as examples.

TRAVESTIES

The most glaring shortcoming in the awarding of project grants was the lack of any direction from the feds for matching resources to community needs. The rich got richer, and the poor got poorer. Existing SIDS management programs with capable grantwriters tended to come away with the bacon, while the communities with a high proportion of poor families, for example in Mississipi, South Carolina, Tennessee, and West Virginia, with scant access to SIDS information and counseling, were ignored. Then there were the travesties in Nebraska and Louisiana.

Spurred by the efforts of Suzie Behr, a good program was organized in Omaha with cooperation from the local childrens' hospital, the medical school, and the Visiting Nurses Association. The Maternal and Child Health (MCH) director for the state of Nebraska, Robert Grant, however, was not pleased. He wanted to direct his own project. Grant therefore submitted an independent grant proposal to be centered in the State Health Department in Lincoln, only 60 miles west of Omaha, and by pulling the wires of the "MCH old boy network," got his money.

Grant also knew how to play hardball. When the administrator of Omaha Children's Hospital, which had housed the Foundation's Nebraska chapter, questioned the wisdom of a competitive SIDS project nearby, Grant suggested that he drop the matter or else the hospital might face the loss of some crucial funds channeled through the health department. The matter was dropped. When Suzie Behr, with the support of the Foundation, screamed to her congressman about the wastefulness of having two competing SIDS projects in Nebraska, the OMCH finally dispatched a team to "investigate." Their response? Both grants were terminated!

New Orleans, with outstanding cooperation between the coroner, health department director, and our local chapter, had an excellent management system before federal money became available. The fate of the project would be good material for those opposed to all federal spending. There was constant bickering within offices of the health department about whether nurses making home visits should have special mental health training. The program deteriorated, and the grant was finally withdrawn in 1977.

California's response to the SIDS funding legislation bothered me more than that of any other state because California was the only state in our 1972 management study whose health department director expressed active disinterest in the SIDS problem. "The health system of the state is committed to preventive care and epidemiology, and will not initiate any efforts in the handling of SIDS," our field investigator, Ovidio Penalver, was told. The attitude scarcely changed when a grant for $118,162 was awarded to the California Health Department in 1975. Our northern California chapter, which was as sophisticated and energetic as any in the country and had an established track record in setting up SIDS management programs in many counties, tried to provide guidance to the project director, Warren Hawes, to no avail. Initially Hawes even refused to convene a project community advisory council that was mandated by the federal regulations. The relationship of the chapter and its medical leader, Dr. Norman Lewak, to the SIDS project mirrored that of the NSIDSF to the OMCH. Draw the wagons into a circle and to hell with zealous activists. The money was frittered away on staff salaries and educational conferences leading nowhere. The Foundation's screaming and yelling to OMCH about the travesty in California resulted in "placing the project on notice" in 1978, whatever that means. In their renewal application in 1980, the California project reported that only 25 percent of the estimated 660 SIDS families in the previous year received services. OMCH patted them on the head and renewed their grant anyway.

THE QUESTION OF LEADERSHIP

As should be apparent my skepticism about HEW bureaucrats is not limited to the SIDS program; those who work with child abuse are worse. I once wrote a piece called "Abuse of the Child Abuse Law," which was published in *Pediatrics* (1978). I offered the following "modest proposal" for administrators of the National Center for Child Abuse and Neglect, were I to be made HEW secretary for a day:

> All administrators should spend at least half of their time in the trenches as Child Protective Services workers. I doubt that many have even seen abused children, let alone worked with them. I am sure that there are enough vacancies within commuting distance of D.C. If the paperwork piles up on their desk while they are away, less mischief will be perpetrated.

Substitute SIDS families and SIDS counseling for abused children and child protective services, and the same would hold true. Geraldine Norris, who succeeded Joann Gephart as coordinator of the OMCH SIDS Program, is a friendly intelligent person. It was a pleasure to talk to her about any subject other than SIDS. When it came to SIDS, however, she had no firsthand experience in counseling families who had just lost their infants, and despite my entreaties, had no intention of obtaining that experience. With rose-colored glasses, I even suggested that since there was no SIDS management project in Washington, D.C., that the staff of the federal SIDS office lend a hand. What a joke! They had far more important duties to attend. Yet is was on the shoulders of a nurse like Geraldine Norris, a fiscal management type like Ralph Pardee, and a public health physician like Vince Hutchins, director of OMCH who had not seen a live patient in 20 years, that the mantle of leadership fell. This triumvirate in the OMCH were the ones providing direction to the 37 federally funded projects on how to carry out their missions.

What form did that direction take? Understandably it was bureaucratic—how to prepare applications, manage grants, file reports, plan conferences, and so forth. They were not about to advise on new methods of reaching SIDS families or set up services where none were present. To HEW a $3 million annual appropriation was a "drop in the bucket." Project personnel were brought together for numerous regional and national conferences on "planning." One regional meeting of project staff held in Seattle in 1975 cost $10,000. A national meeting in New Orleans cost close to $100,000. In 1972 and 1973, the NSIDSF held over ten regional seminars throughout the country for $5,000. The contrast in operating styles was not lost on our Foundation volunteers.

Human nature also decreed that the "wagons in a circle" philosophy of the OMCH would rub off on some of the projects. A definite "us against them" mentality developed between the professionals of OMCH and "their" SIDS organization (e.g., the federally funded projects) and the pesky volunteers who were always critical. The fact that the government programs had the money, and the volunteers were raising nickels and dimes at cookie sales, widened the confidence gulf.

SZYBIST'S LAMENT

On March 17, 1979, in a moment of extreme frustration, Foundation Executive Director Carolyn Szybist wrote the following to all NSIDSF chapters:

When the [SIDS] legislation was written and passed in 1974, I know what we asked for. We asked for regional centers that addressed themselves to the needs of families, and did the professional job that volunteers couldn't do in the way it should be done. We [the Foundation] gave them the tools for the job, the literature, the framework, and the models. We set up the good projects. People working with and for the Foundation assisted in the creation of programs everywhere in this country. It should have worked.

Now with the passing of nearly four years, we have people in our organization who don't know what the law was supposed to do and don't know what it was supposed to accomplish. It wasn't supposed to create what it is creating. We are seeing some of the federally funded projects out raising money, organizing parent groups, and forgetting to take care of families. We have assisted in the creation of a double system, the National SIDS Foundation and the Federal Government SIDS Organization.

I agreed with Carolyn's thoughts at the time and still do today. We had indeed created a double system, with the government portion possessing infinitely more resources than our own, and seemingly dedicated more to its own perpetuation than the goals that had originally brought it into existence. The Foundation's leadership spent much more energy fighting with the Department of HEW over how the law should be administered than in securing its passage. Furthermore, passage of the law resulted in a diminution of our chapters' fundraising and organizational activities. Many of our flock expressed the view that "why should we work so hard or contribute money when the feds are going to take over and get the job done."

Now that a decade has passed, and my personal involvement has lessened, I have a clearer perspective of the SIDS Act. In fact, there were only a handful of individuals from the Foundation and from the feds who lost any sleep over the conflict. No harm was inflicted on those most vulnerable, SIDS families. Some money was wasted, but as Senator Magnuson used to say: "they spill more money on the floor of the Pentagon every day than HEW spends all year for its health programs."

There's a song recited at the Jewish Passover Seder recounting the whole host of miracles wrought by the Lord in delivering the children of Israel from slavery in Egypt. Each verse ends with the Hebrew word *dayenu* which means "sufficient." The point is that any single miracle would have been sufficient to celebrate the exodus. That there were so many is just "frosting on the cake."

My thoughts turn to New York City, and the mistreatment of Edward and Judie Choate, Robert and Lola Redford, and Roy and Evelyn Williams. New York was in the first group of cities to receive a project grant that allowed initiation of a SIDS management program. If only a handful of families in New York were spared the burden of feeling responsible for their infants' deaths, then passage of the law was justified. *Dayenu*!

18

THE MOBILIZATION CONTRACT

In the fall of 1977, I stepped down as president of the NSIDSF. Judie Choate had "burned out" in the job the previous year, and by 1977 Carolyn Szybist was already showing the characteristic premonitory signs. With evidence of a broken marriage on my hands, I was clearly not immune and needed some respite. My resignation was an incredible relief.

I had wanted to quit two years earlier, after the SIDS law had been passed, but two factors deterred me. First, the transition of the central office from New York to Chicago was rocky enough. More turmoil might have swamped us. Second, because there were so few of us active in the trenches, the Foundation had the unwritten rule that no one could quit *any* job without first identifying a successor. Unfortunately there were no candidates clamoring for my job. It took two years to find a credible successor who evinced even the slightest interest. At that point, providentially, Stanford B. Friedman nibbled at the bait; I was not about to let him get away.

I had been an admirer of Friedman since 1959, when we worked together as pediatric residents in Boston. It was apparent that he possessed "the right stuff," which to fellow residents meant that he was cool in emergency situations. His abiding interest has always been the interaction of body and mind, which has led to an outstanding career in both pediatrics and psychiatry. While working at the National Cancer Institute on coping mechanisms in illness, Friedman published a landmark study on the biochemical correlates of grief (Friedman et al. 1963). It was thus not surprising that he was also attracted to studying SIDS.

163

In 1977, as now, Stan Friedman was professor of both psychiatry and pediatrics at the University of Maryland, and director of the federally funded SIDS center in Baltimore. No stranger to the national scene, Friedman is the founder of two important organizations, the Society for Adolescent Medicine and the Society for Behavioral Pediatrics.

In July of 1977, after Carolyn Szybist planted the seed, Charlie Barr and I took Stan to a dinner at a quaint seafood restaurant in Boston. I would like to think that it was our charm that persuaded him to take the presidency of the Foundation. In fact, however, like all of us involved in the fray, the attraction to Friedman was the cause itself and the knowledge that he could make a significant contribution. He's an academic whose horizons have always extended beyond the walls of the ivory tower.

"BEATING THE BUSHES"

A condition of Stan Friedman taking on the presidency was that I become vice-president with responsibility for "government relations," which included remaining as project director for a contract with the OMCH begun, in September 1976, for "The Mobilization of Community Resources for SIDS Programs in Areas Not Served by Federally Funded Projects."

Though the federally funded projects made a huge dent in providing needed services, there were only 24 of them in 21 states in 1975 and 42 in 37 states by 1980. What was to happen to the SIDS families who did not happen to live in project service areas? We steadfastly held that, through mobilization of existing community resources, it was possible to provide appropriate management services without a direct federal grant. OMCH encouraged projects to widen their service areas, but in 1976 that still left over half the communities in the United States in the lurch. Someone had to be out "beating the bushes," in the same fashion as the Foundation's nurses, Kathryn Patterson and Barbara French, did under our contract with NIMH. Bert Brown, the NIMH director, appropriately felt that since OMCH had been given $2 million to assist SIDS families he should no longer have to subsidize this activity. A simple transfer of contract authority from one HEW agency to another seemed the logical step, but the terms "simple" and "logical" did not appear on our roadmap.

The response of Geraldine Norris and her colleagues at OMCH to my proposal for a contract to do community organization was frosty.

They first said that OMCH did not have the authority to contract under the SIDS law until I pointed out that they were already contracting for a new educational film. After a few more desultory letters and phone calls, I recognized that I was in the midst of a "satisficing" game. A meeting with Ed Martin ensued that resulted in a contract for the Foundation "to conduct mobilization activities for health care providers, public safety officials, voluntary organizations concerned with human services following instances of sudden and unexpected infant deaths, and the public generally, in a maximum of 18 states not served presently by federally funded SIDS projects."

FORCING SIDS INTO TITLE V

The contract, with a total value of $264,547, lasted from September 30, 1976, to April 20, 1979. It was canceled and reinstated twice, and modified eight times before finally sinking in a sea of vitriol. The OMCH officials never forgave us for going over their heads to Martin and seemed to do everything in their power to impede the contract work. Though I am sure their love for me doubtless was as negligible as my love for them, I also am certain that OMCH officials were guided in their actions more by ideology than personality. They sincerely felt that the best way for SIDS programs to be initiated and permanently maintained was through funneling the money along familiar channels to state maternal and child health directors. It did not matter that Congress and their superiors in HEW called for a more pluralistic approach. The OMCH officials dug in their heels at every juncture. They were used to hunkering down and outlasting congressional mandates and bright young physicians like Batalden and Martin who flitted through their high offices on brief tours of duty.

One of the more bizarre meetings I attended was at the luxury resort of Snowbird, Utah, in August 1977. OMCH called together the state MCH directors and the directors of the federally funded projects ostensibly to get their views about the position HEW should take when the SIDS authorization law came up for renewal the following year. As is usually the case on such occasions, however, the communications were mostly one-way. The party line was that the SIDS program would be folded into the "program of projects" authorized under Title V of the Social Security Act and channeled through OMCH to state MCH programs.

The OMCH position was no secret. SIDS projects centered in medical schools, hospitals, and medical schools, hospitals, and medical examiner offices had already been given to understand that their grants would shortly be terminated in favor of other administrative arrangements. In their zeal to create a neat administrative package, the OMCH staff never bothered to ask the State MCH directors whether *they* desired to control all of the SIDS projects. At the Snowbird meetings it was clear that most of the state directors did not want the added responsibilities. The glory of managing more federal dollars did not compensate for the additional paperwork requirements.

In the discussion of legislative recommendations, the attendees were asked to vote on a series of options. Most of the choices involved amending Title V of the Social Security Act. From the back of the room, I not so innocently asked Geraldine Norris if she were aware that the House Ways and Means Committee and the Senate Finance Committee, instead of the respective health committees, would have jurisdiction if Title V were involved, since they jealously maintained vigilance over anything involving social security legislation. Norris nervously turned to Ralph Pardee for help. (Pardee, the grey eminence of OMCH since the days of Arthur Lesser, was always looked to for guidance in policy and/or political matters. Though possessing no professional training in the health field, he was probably the most powerful person in OMCH by virtue of having been there a long time and knowing how to skip through the bureaucratic maze. In order to function, every government office must possess a Pardee type. The drawback is that the totally pragmatic Pardee seemed to approach SIDS, or any other health problem, with as much passion as he would employ in obtaining parking permits or ordering pencils for the office.) Pardee made light of the congressional committee jurisdiction issue implying that the matter was too abstruse to occupy the attention of the attendees at the meeting. The whole exercise at Snowbird was vacuous. The secretary of HEW has little enough to say about an administration's legislative position (as opposed to officials at the Office of Management and Budget, or White House), let alone the staff of OMCH.

CONTRACT TRIBULATIONS

Even the Foundation's worst critics (who resided in the Office of Maternal and Child Health) agreed that the government got its money's worth from the mobilization contract. Tangible improvements in SIDS management took place in communities all over the country. Eight "community organizers" were employed at various times over the three years, seven of them being SIDS parents. All had originally been active in local Foundation chapters, with the exception of one, who worked in Virginia and was active in the Guild for Infant Survival. Our workers were not in it for the money; none received enough recompense to cover even their child-care costs when away from home. The cost-effectiveness prize went to North Dakota. We estimated that for a contract allowance of $750 a statewide management program funded by the state legislature came into being. Though at not quite the same bargain rate, similar improvements were wrought in such places as Wyoming, Kansas, Maine, Oklahoma, and Alaska.

The contract also allowed the NSIDSF to breathe. It paid for a secretary in the Chicago office, half of Carolyn Szybist's salary, a lot of telephone bills, and travel for Carolyn and me to speak at seminars. This support of Foundation activities was like a festering wound to Saul Goldberg of the GIS. Goldberg persistently peppered the OMCH with complaints on how they were subsidizing his competitors. Thus it is not surprising that OMCH assiduously kept watch on us to see that their money went for contract instead of Foundation work. Since a purpose of the Foundation was to mobilize community resources for SIDS management, it was hard for us, let alone beady-eyed contract officers, to separate our work into neat compartments. We used our local chapters to spearhead management programs. Yet when our field representatives met with local chapters we ran the danger of being criticized for performing Foundation rather than contract work.

LIAISON WITH HEALTH DEPARTMENTS

HEW, like all federal departments, maintains mini-clones of their various programs in ten regional offices. The power of these regional offices has waxed and waned depending on the prevailing political philosophy in D.C. A requirement of our contract was that our field representatives establish and maintain contact with the regional MCH personnel, as well as with MCH directors in all of the states in which they worked. I was pleased with this clause. If MCH personnel at the regional and state levels were activated by the "mother church" in Rockville, they, theoretically, could enhance our mission. But that was when I early on, thought the OMCH wanted our contract mission to succeed. Two episodes demonstrated that the opposite was true.

When the contract was signed I asked Geraldine Norris to write a letter to the regional and state MCH offices notifying them of the project. She said "yes." After a few months, when the letter had not materialized, I reminded her and she again said "yes." A year and half later, when Norris was away on leave and the "SIDS desk" was being covered by a temporary person, a letter finally went out to MCH personnel describing the mobilization contract.

In September 1976 a three-day meeting of SIDS project directors was held in Oakbrook, Illinois, to which nurse consultants from all the regional MCH offices were invited to learn about SIDS. Our field representatives were also there to meet with Gerry Norris about the contract work. It would have been an ideal time for the two groups to meet each other. Not only did they never get together, but despite Carolyn Szybist's pleading, Norris did not even allow an announcement to be made about the just-signed contract. The lesson was clear. The National SIDS Foundation may have wangled an HEW contract through political contacts, but the Office of Maternal and Child Health would not lift a finger to help make the project a success. Scant attention was paid to the fact that tax dollars from the SIDS appropriation had paid for everyone's trip to Oakbrook supposedly to learn about how to help families who lost infants to "crib death."

CANCELLATIONS

Franz Kafka would have appreciated the machinations of HEW. In his book *The Trial*, the protagonist is suddenly arrested, tried, and convicted without ever knowing the charges or the accusers. Our original contract period was for one year with the understanding that renewal would take place upon evidence of satisfactory performance. Once a contract is signed, even the government has to honor it. In October 1977, at the end of a year's contract work, the games began. The standard ploy was uncertainty about whether money would be available. "Since Congress has not passed the HEW Appropriations Bill, we don't know how much money we'll have next year." Somehow that uncertainty did not stop OMCH from scheduling frequent conferences for the SIDS projects, with travel budgets for each conference exceeding the cost of our entire contract.

I worried at that point that my blunt operating style might be drawing too much hostile fire and asked Stan Friedman, our new president, to enter the negotiations. Stan is a calm person who is a wonderful listener. Changing negotiators did not help. We received a couple of six-week extensions until December, at which point we were informed that the contract was to be terminated.

It was time to call on Ed Martin again. I met with him in January 1978. Our meetings always followed the same pattern. We began by fondly talking about the National Health Service Corps, our mutual "baby:" Next followed the ritual lament about the difficulties of swimming in the bowl of jello, HEW's bureaucracy, and how powerless he was to effect any changes. I acted as therapist; listening, commiserating, and supporting. At the time Martin still seemed idealistic. I told him how important it was for him to continue the fight for the sake of the poor people who were supposed to be helped by the HEW programs he administered. I believed it! The health care of migrants, the inner-city poor, and the rural poor in regions like Appalachia was too important to be left to the likes of pragmatic paper shufflers like Ralph Pardee. The actual subject of my visit was taken up almost as an afterthought. Martin knew, of course, what I wanted and had already decided what to do. The contract would be renewed, and he and I would meet together with the OMCH staff to "knock some sense into their heads." A quaint thought!

The eventful meeting took place on February 10 in Rockville, with Ed Martin presiding. Stan Friedman, Carolyn Szybist, and I represented the Foundation. Ralph Pardee, Geraldine Norris, and Arthur Funke, a psychologist, represented OMCH. Martin did most of the talking. He asked Norris whether our community organization efforts had indeed resulted in improved SIDS management programs. She agreed that we had been successful. "Then why is the contract being terminated?" he asked. She looked to Pardee for help. This time he kept silent. Ralph Pardee had not survived all those years in the HEW bureaucracy by crossing swords with a superior out in the open. Pardee left Norris "to dangle." The best explanation she could offer was that we had not filed timely reports of our activities. Visibly angered by this response, Martin lauded the effectiveness and cost-efficiency of our work in local communities and ordered that we spend the rest of the morning working out the details of how the contract work was to be conducted over the next year. That order, however, could not be carried out. When Martin left the room, Gerri Norris, in tears, became so overwrought that the meeting had to be adjourned. A few days later, Martin removed Norris as project officer for the contract, installing instead his own deputy director of community health services, John Marshall.

JOHN MARSHALL

The quiet Ralph Pardee, "Mr. Inside," who acquired power by knowing the system and maintaining low visibility, was representative of one type of federal bureaucrat. John Marshall was representative of another, albeit rarer, species. He also thrived by knowing how to "work the system," but in contrast to Pardee, enjoyed "representing the agency," either with outside organizations or with members of Congress and their staffs. Because he was bright, facile in writing and speech, and oozed with sincerity, Marshall was the perfect trouble-shooter. Such a role, however, entails great risks, since there are so many powerful egos to please. When one's boss is under attack, the faithful deputy can easily be thrust into the position of sacrificial lamb. The recompense for constant willingness to throw one's body on live grenades is acquisition of considerable power. Marshall, who has a Ph.D. in clinical psychology, has held many jobs at HEW since joining the agency in 1969.

John Marshall demonstrated so much skill at defending the party line of the moment, that I envisioned him functioning equally well as an "apparatchik" in the Kremlin, which is another way of saying that, while Ed Martin always let you know which programs were his favor-ites, Marshall never gave an indication of his favorite causes. He was content to let someone else call the signals; he would see that the job got done.

For the first few months, we were relieved to have John Marshall as our project officer. In contrast to Gerri Norris, who was not al-lowed to make any independent decisions, Marshall understood what we were trying to do, read our reports, and answered our letters and phone calls. Here is what he wrote to Carolyn Szybist on March 31, 1978, after receiving a quarterly report:

> I did read through it and found it to be helpful as a first step in begin-ning to assimilate some grasp of what the contract buys. It left me feel-ing both more comfortable along some dimensions, and less comfortable along others. Perhaps my discomfort comes from not having seen earlier reports so that I am left with only a sense of a series of discrete activities and accomplishments. It is not clear to what extent they represent linear progress toward a goal versus circular or random movement. It was a lit-tle bit like watching sperm seeking the right ovum. That is clearly a ne-cessary but inchoate-appearing process. I feel more comfortable when I can estimate some probabilities of connecting.
>
> On the surface the report appears to support the level of effort for which the Foundation has been reimbursed. Further, it supports it in a manner consistent with our program objectives.

It is not the ordinary HEW official who writes about sperm watch-ing or inchoate-appearing processes. Marshall loved to complain about the onerous bureaucracy, while mastering its intricacies. On April 14 he wrote to Carolyn:

I have not yet received your plan. Was your relief that of having completed it, or of having mailed it? If the latter, I hope it is not lost. As a practical matter in the interest of communication, it is good that you send me copies of pertinent documents. To save the Foundation and the government money, why not put mine and Gerry's [Norris] in the same envelope and let us take care of distribution to the other. Somehow that strikes me as appropriately bureaucratic.

Carolyn was no mean writer herself. She also was wise to the game of "marking the paper trail." She responded to Marshall on April 19:

Your letter of April 14th was received today and caused an appropriate alarm with your indication that you had not received our workscope and project design. Please thank your secretary for her telephone assurances today to me that it is, indeed, in your office. . . . our historical past and contract evolution rather dictated a need to know that you received it.

I appreciate your correspondence and good humor relating to this contract and your interest in cost-effective communication. However, it strikes me as appropriately bureaucratic that any pertinent documents that should be seen by both you and Gerri Norris should continue to be sent independently to both of you. Travel, meetings, etc. can periodically be impediments to even the best-intentioned and accomplished communicators. Since very few documents fall into this "dual" category, my personal evaluation places it on a low priority if one were start on a campaign towards saving money, yours or HEW's. I have found the cost of straightening out lack of communication to far exceed postage costs.

19

CALLING THE COPS

Federal laws authorize the expenditure of funds only for a set period of time, at the end of which the law must either be reauthorized or terminated. The SIDS Act of 1974 was authorized for three years and thus had to be acted on by Congress in 1977 or else face oblivion. I had been involved in the inception of six pieces of federal legislation but for several reasons had never been active when any of them came up for renewal. For one thing, it is difficult for me to summon up the same energy for a repeat performance, especially when my expectations for the legislation have not been fully realized. I always wonder how actors can continue to find the energy for a role after they have been playing it every night for six weeks. Another more important reason for my lowered level of involvement is that to the consternation of conservatives, every time a new government program is created, a constituency automatically arises devoted to the program's perpetuation. Thus many more players are available to pitch in by renewal time.

In the spring of 1976, Ellen Hoffman called to discuss the renewal of the SIDS law. Though this was a full year before action was required, the Senate Subcommittee on Children and Youth was not overburdened, and she thought it would be useful to get this noncontroversial matter out of the way. I attributed Ellen's phone call not just to her desire to keep the wheels of government turning in an orderly and responsible fashion, but also to her expectation that early hearings would be a way to enhance the visibility of her subcommittee and its chairman, Walter Mondale, who was in a relatively quiescent phase of his political career. July 1 was set as the hearing date. I was asked to suggest witnesses, as well as modifications of the law. I duly complied with the request. In the last week of June the hearing was canceled. Mondale had been summoned to Plains, Georgia, to be interviewed by the soon-to-be presidential nominee of the Democratic Party, Jimmy Carter, as a potential running mate. Mondale, of course, was selected by Carter and the Democratic convention in July and in November was elected as vice-president of the United States.

NEW LEGISLATIVE ACTORS

The only person on "the Hill" who held more than a passing interest in SIDS legislation was Ellen Hoffman. With her departure from the scene due to her boss leaving the Senate, and the lack of outside lobbying activity from me or anyone else, the impetus for early action on the renewal legislation dissolved. Since there was no pressure either to go through the renewal process, or to kill the law, Congress passed, in the fall of 1977, a "continuing resolution," which is a commonly employed device that grants a temporary one-year lease on life.

When the next Congress convened in 1978, some new actors appeared on the scene. Mondale's subcommittee received a new chairman, Senator Alan Cranston of California, and a new name, the Subcommittee on Child and Human Development. More importantly, a new staff member, Mary Aronson, replaced Ellen Hoffman.

It was when I sat down to meet with Mary Aronson in the fall of 1978 that I recognized that, just as I was no longer able to effectively counsel new SIDS families, after 12 years I was also "burned out" as a good lobbyist. I committed the cardinal sin of expressing impatience. There was nothing wrong with Ms. Aronson. She was a nurse who was understandably excited about going to bat for the first time in the political big leagues. She knew little about SIDS and less about the political history described in this book. Worse for my ego was that she did not know anything about me. To her I was not a "mover and shaker" on Capitol Hill, but just another doctor with a special interest. Even the magic name Harley Dirks, which used to set Senate staffers quaking, meant nothing. He was gone. I was left to state my case on its merits, and did it badly.

I really did not insult Mary Aronson; I doubt that she remembers the encounter at all. The significance of the episode was that it made me realize that I could not undertake any more lobbying unless I were willing to submerge my own ego on behalf of my cause. Having to influence a constantly changing sea of new faces in powerful positions is a given of political life. Power passes quickly. My success in lobbying should be attributed much more to chance personal relationships with powers like Warren Magnuson, Henry Jackson, Gerry Grinstein, Harley Dirks, Mike Pertschuk, and Steve Lawton, rather than any personal talents of my own, a fact that became abundantly clear when those individuals disappeared from Capitol Hill.

On March 1, 1978, a hearing was finally held on the SIDS law. Senator Cranston presided. I did not attend but heard from unbiased sources that the most impressive testimony was delivered by Carolyn Szybist. In striking contrast to the HEW witnesses, Carolyn was able to provide a picture of SIDS management activities in all 50 states. It was not until December 12, 1979, however, following another continuing resolution, that President Carter signed the new SIDS law, PL 96-142. No House hearings were held. The new law upped the authorization levels to $5 million in fiscal year 1980, and $7 million in fiscal year 1981. A new provision called on HEW to submit a plan "on or before February 1, 1980, to extend counseling and information services to the fifty States and the District of Columbia by July 1, 1980; and extend counseling and information services to all possessions and territories of the United States by July 1, 1981." By that time Paul Rogers had retired from the House of Representatives. He never would have allowed such unrealistic political bombast (fashion a program in two months) to appear in health legislation that he crafted.

BELTWAY BANDITS

Concomitant with the burgeoning number of programs spawned by the federal government in the 1960s, a new growth industry, consulting firms, appeared all over the Washington scene. These firms lived, some would say preyed, on grants and contracts awarded to perform services that could not be carried out by a federal agency, the most common of which was program evaluation. In the classic form, an agency seeking to justify its existence before Congress would come forth with a an embossed multicolored volume prepared by "independent" consultants describing magnificent accomplishments. Criticism of an agency's performance was akin to biting a feeding hand, and thus not conducive to the survival of a consulting firm.

In Washington the consulting firms have come to be known as "Beltway Bandits" because so many are located along I-495, the highway that surrounds the city. In the May 1980 issue of the *Washington Monthly*, Gregg Easterbrook wrote:

> Almost eight million people work for Washington by working for companies under contract to government; meanwhile the official "size" of the government, 2.5 million civil servants, has scarcely changed in 20 years. . . . consulting companies ring the capital drawing at least $2 billion in federal paychecks per year into prosperous, ambiguously named organizations like BDM, ICF, Peat-Marwick, Battelle, and Cresap. . . . the discovery that consultants would tell the government whatever it paid to hear was one of the great visionary moments in modern Washington history. (pp. 13, 14, 18, 21)

Soon after the SIDS projects were established I urged Ed Martin to employ a prestigious and unbiased group like the American Academy of Pediatrics to determine, using methods similar to our management study of 1972, whether the projects were doing their jobs. He demurred. In the summer of 1977 a contract for $86,000 was awarded by OMCH to Lawrence Johnson and Associates, Incorporated (LJA), to develop methodology to evaluate the effectiveness of SIDS projects. To no one's surprise, LJA was shortly thereafter awarded a contract for $183,584 to evaluate the performance of the federally funded SIDS projects.

In their prospectus, LJA describe themselves as "a social-behavioral science research firm with its offices in northwest Washington, D.C. The firm provides research, evaluation and planning, and policy development services in the social, psychological, economic, and health sciences to government and commercial clients." They are also classified as "minority-owned."

When Jimmy Carter came to Washington in 1977, he, laudably in my opinion, tried to steer more government business in the direction of minority firms. Unfortunately this idealistic policy resulted in the creation of a lot of "minority-front" outfits. The higher echelons of the firms were reshuffled to place just enough minority names on the letterhead to legally qualify without changing the composition of the workforce or paycheck distribution. In the case of LJA, I was annoyed not only at their lack of expertise in the health area, but at seeing all the white faces that turned out to work for them. But I never held any malice against the LJA folks themselves. Like everyone else, they were trying to make a living. They did what they were paid to do and certainly stirred no waves for their project officer, Geraldine Norris, which is more than can be said for Carolyn Szybist, Stan Friedman, and me.

CONTRACT TERMINATION

Uncertainty over the future of the mobilization contract made the work of our field representatives difficult. Anne Barr, the Northeast representative, wrote in May 1979:

> During the last nine months it has been difficult to do "contract" work in the Northeast due to month by month extensions which resulted in confusion regarding funding for travel and seminars, and most importantly, a game called "musical states." The target areas constantly change. For instance, I was supposed to work in Western Massachusetts, but was then told to stay away since the area was going to be served by the Boston center. I initiated three programs in upstate New York (Albany, Buffalo, and Binghamton) and then was instructed not to work there anymore because a "grand plan" was being put together for coverage of the whole state. The same is true for Washington, D.C., and Western Pennsylvania. All this would not bother me if I knew that *someone* was available to help these parents. The mail I receive from these areas where I've been directed to stay away from indicates that the parents are getting NO support or counseling. In fact, *they are not even getting any information about SIDS*. A recent letter I received from a mother in Cortland, New York, illustrates the problem. She had read about the NSIDSF in a national magazine, and wanted some information for herself and to share with others. She wondered if the local coroner might have been mistaken in his diagnosis of suffocation of her three month old daughter due to use of too many blankets. She wanted to know if in fact her daughter had died of SIDS, how she could educate the coroner so that he would not inflict guilt on future SIDS parents. Unfortunately this example is neither atypical or unusual for parent mail from upstate New York or Western Pennsylvania.

Try as we might, we could not get a full year's renewal of the mobilization contract and had to settle instead for month-to-month extensions. John Marshall began to talk about the difficulties of defending our "sole-source" contract status. Whenever the subject arose I assured him that we would be happy to bid competitively, since I was confident that no other organization possessed anything close to our capabilities. In November 1978, however, we were reassured by a letter from Marshall saying that our contract was to be extended through December 20, 1979, subject only to approval of a workplan scheduled to take place at a January meeting in Rockville. Inexplicably a signed contract appeared in the mail the very next week extending our work to March 20, 1979. Figuring that a quarter of a loaf is better than none, we were relieved.

The other shoe dropped on January 19, 1979. Carolyn received a call from a private consulting firm in Pennsylvania asking if the Foundation would collaborate with them in responding to a "request-for-proposal" (RFP) from the Office of Maternal and Child Health for "The Mobilization of Community Resources for SIDS Programs in Areas Not Served by Federally Funded SIDS Projects." I wish I could have seen her face! Carolyn immediately called John Marshall, who was unavailable. His assistant came on the line and told Carolyn that she should be able to get a copy of the RFP by calling HEW's contract office, but furtively pleaded with Carolyn "not to tell anyone" that they had talked. On January 23 we received the RFP; proposals were due in Rockville on February 1.

On the same day Carolyn was finally able to reach Marshall. He was apologetic about us not hearing of the decision to put out the contract for competitive bids, saying only that "individuals within my own office were not conforming to my requests. Trust me," he said, "you needn't worry. The review committee is stacked in your favor. And if you aren't awarded the contract, I am prepared to cancel the RFP and extend your old contract." On January 31 our proposal was delivered, by hand, to the Parklawn Building. On February 5, Marshall again reassured Carolyn and promised to call her on March 1, when he would know the results.

March 1 came and went without a word. Despite almost daily phone calls it was not until March 13 that Carolyn was able to get Marshall on the line. He was not authorized to tell her about the contract, he said. She would have to call the HEW contract office. Carolyn knew, of course, that we had lost. Marshall sounded depressed. "The system has broken down around here," he said. "No one in HEW can do their jobs. Political pressure is the only way to accomplish anything." Marshall spoke so convincingly that Carolyn now confesses that she felt sympathy for him at the time. We received the following letter from the contract office dated April 9, 1979:

> Your proposal submitted in response to the above referenced RFP has been carefully evaluated. This is to advise that a contract has been awarded to another offeror. The following information is provided in connection with this negotiated procurement:
> 1. Number of prospective contractors solicited: 88
> 2. Number of proposals received: 2
> 3. Name of Offeror receiving award: Lawrence Johnson & Associates of Washington D.C.
> 4. Total contract amount: $124,242.

Your continued interest in the programs of the Health Services Administration is appreciated.

FIRESTORM

We were enraged by HEW's decision. It had been annoying to see a private profit-making firm with no experience in SIDS win a contract to evaluate the federally funded SIDS projects, but we had not protested. We knew that the worst that could result from the LJA evaluation would be a waste of taxpayers' money. Now, however, a group of uncommitted technocrats was taking charge of our admittedly religiouslike crusade started in 1972, and that was more than we could bear. It seemed blatantly unfair.

What could we do? We wrote many anguished letters and made many pleading telephone calls. In retrospect I can see that all of our protests were ineffective. We should have realized that we had been resoundingly beaten on the turf of government bureaucracy by pros like Ralph Pardee and John Marshall, and we should have moved on to more constructive activities. Instead, in venting our wrath, we acted like amateurs and succeeded only in expending more energy and money in an orgy of self-pity.

The press were uninterested; we could not stimulate one story about the contract termination. Like the police reporters in the Bronx covering the Williams trial, government contract abuses are not news unless they involve billions, not thousands, of dollars. Our stable of congressional friends fired off the standard searing letters to the secretary of HEW, all asking for an immediate explanation of the dastardly deed. The responses, which of course were forwarded immediately on to us in order to provide an illusion of action, were identical, bearing what to me were unmistakable signs of John Marshall's craftsmanship. Here is an example of a letter to Senator Cranston dated July 26, 1979:

> In accordance with the Department's emphasis on competitive procurements, it was determined that it was in the Government's best interest to compete the SIDS mobilization effort this fiscal year rather than to obtain this service as a sole source procurement. The NSIDSF was given an opportunity to compete and they did submit a proposal. As with all competitive situations, Federal procurement regulations and guidelines were adhered to strictly. There were no irregularities in the manner in which this competitive procurement was solicited, evaluated and awarded.

This particular letter was signed by Julius B. Richmond, M.D., assistant secretary for health, and surgeon general of the Public Health

Service. How can a senator fight that? Of course everything was on the up-and-up; the surgeon general assured him so. The presence of Dr. Richmond's signature on the letter was ironic. I was his pediatric fellow at the Upstate Medical Center in Syracuse from 1961 to 1963. He was a solicitous father-figure to all his past and present trainees. He had an even closer relationship with Stan Friedman, who had followed him as a disciple in the scholarly field of behavioral pediatrics. Since he was at the "top of the heap" in HEW, why not just go to our friend, Julie Richmond, and ask him to "fix" the situation? Alas, we knew him too well.

Julius Richmond always has been more a philosopher, inspiring others to look at the big picture, than a nuts and bolts administrator. He had more commitments at any one time than anyone I have known. For instance, in the mid-1960s Richmond simultaneously held down the posts of chairman of the pediatric department at Syracuse, dean of the medical school, medical director of the Office of Economic Opportunity and director of Project Head Start. I once began to tell him of our tribulations with OMCH, but when he interrupted to ask me about my children, I took the hint and never bothered him about the program again.

Terry Lierman, Senator Magnuson's chief health aide, took pity on me and did summon "the department" to his office for a personal accounting. I was expecting nothing less than an assistant secretary. Who should waltz in, however, but John Marshall, accompanied by a smoothie from HEW's legislative liaison office, whose job it was to mollify congressional egos. I had not seen Marshall for months. He was as charming as ever. He even apologized for making promises that he could not keep. What could he do now, however? A legal contract had been awarded to LJA. If HEW tried to withdraw the contract, court action would almost certainly ensue. Check and checkmate!

Since HEW made a big point in their letters of saying that the NSIDSF proposal was "not technically acceptable," and that LJA submitted a proposal that was judged by an "unbiased review panel" to be "meritorious," we tried mightily to find out the composition of that panel. It was not easy. The Foundation's attorney finally filed a "Freedom of Information" request. The "unbiased review panel" turned out to consist of Joann Gephart, Geraldine Norris, and one other OMCH staff member.

SEEKING CALIFANO'S ASSISTANCE

One of our more desperate, and again, in retrospect, laughable attempts to secure redress, was attempting to get Secretary of HEW

Joseph Califano to intervene on our behalf. We knew that Califano, a consummate political animal, would not hesitate to use a blunderbuss if provoked. It was a blunderbuss that we wanted. It turned out that a SIDS parent, Phillip Schaefer, of Belvedere, California, was an early supporter and fund raiser for Jimmy Carter. He succeeded in arranging an appointment on June 1 for Stan Friedman, Carolyn Szybist, and Jim Mills, a business executive who was then Board Chairman of the NSIDSF, to meet with Secretary Califano. Our hopes soared. At the last moment the secretary was summoned to the White House, the Hill, or to some other equally important engagement, and asked his "deputy executive secretary" Cliff Stromberg to sit in for him. Every important personage in Washington has a pinch hitter like Stromberg ready to step into the batter's box at a moment's notice. Washington types like Stromberg must possess the ability to mollify the disappointed meeting seekers and convince them that, if not for the summons to the Mount, a cage full of snarling tigers could not have kept their boss from this vital meeting. The script was followed. The director of population affairs came to represent Assistant Secretary Richmond "personally," and a policy coordinator from Secretary Califano's office appeared, to add heft. The villain of the piece was John Marshall. He dutifully accepted the flaying administered by Stromberg and confessed to uncounted sins. As Stromberg escorted our impressed delegation out the door he solemnly promised to *personally* conduct an investigation on behalf of the Secretary and get back to us *soon*. We never heard from him again.

THE GAO INVESTIGATION

At last we came to the realization that we had been robbed so we decided to call the cops. But that's a little difficult when the perpetrators are representatives of the United States government. There happens to be an official police department, however, that exists just for the purpose of investigating claims of wrongdoing in the federal government. This independent "watchdog" agency, serving at the behest of Congress, is called the General Accounting Office (GAO). Because the GAO prides itself on its independence, and because I had seen some excellent evaluations of health programs performed by the agency, I had been after Terry Lierman for over a year to "sick the GAO gumshoes" onto the SIDS program. He put me off with the excuse that a GAO investigation was too cumbersome and too expensive. At the time I chalked up Terry's reluctance to his natural cautiousness.

That HEW appeared to be getting away with both their chicanery and stonewalling caused me to lose all perspective. I was obsessed with getting a GAO investigation. Against his better judgment Lierman finally relented just to get me off his back. Since Senator Magnuson was beginning his reelection campaign, I suspect Terry also wanted to make sure that I would be pulling my oar and not running around half-cocked, which is just what I was doing.

THE GUMSHOES ARE LOOSED

On February 22, 1980, Senator Magnuson, joined by Senator Cranston, and Representative Henry Waxman, the new chairman of the House Subcommittee on Health and the Environment, wrote to the comptroller general of the United States "to request a GAO audit of the Sudden Infant Death Syndrome Counseling and Information Project program authorized by Part B of Title XI of the Public Health Service Act." The gumshoes were loosed and I was elated. I was even more elated when the GAO official heading the investigation, Bernie Ungar, appeared in my Seattle office and spent a whole day pouring through my files, which I felt contained abundant evidence documenting HEW's perfidy.

My emotional roller coaster began to descend when Carolyn Szybist reported on her encounter with a GAO investigator in Chicago. "The guy spent the whole day going through our files, and never asked me any questions about the Foundation or SIDS. He didn't seem interested in what we did." It turned out that all the members of the GAO team were accountants, none with any health background.

The GAO investigation took six months to conduct and cost over one-quarter of a million dollars. When I told this to Terry Lierman, all he could do was smile at me reproachfully. He was kind. Their 127-page report (U.S. General Accounting Office 1981) was not entirely a whitewash. Improvements were called for in the award and administration of project grants, as well as in HEW's administration of contracts. John Marshall's knuckles were lightly tapped: "the official who acknowledged telling the Foundation that its contract would be extended was not authorized to make such a statement" (GAO p. 48). Regarding the panel that reviewed the two contract proposals, GAO said: "although two of the three panel members who reviewed the technical proposals had previous disagreements with the Foundation, we found no evidence that the proposals were not evaluated objectively and equitably" (GAO p. 48). On comparative performance on the mobilization contract, GAO said:

The Bureau of Community Health Services (BCHS) project officer told us that Johnson & Associates performed satisfactorily under the contract *and was extremely responsive to the expectations of the project office.* BCHS believed that the contractor was effective in mobilizing SIDS resources, but had not generated as many mobilization results as the Foundation. (GAO p. 53) (emphasis added)

GAO's main recommendation to Congress was that the SIDS information and counseling program be consolidated within the Maternal and Child Health program authorized under Title V of the Social Security Act.

GAO was good enough to circulate draft copies of their report to all interested parties, and print the responses along with their final comments. My response, on behalf of the Foundation, was eight pages long. Probably no more than a dozen persons in the whole land read the document, but my soul rested easier with the knowledge that our case had at least been laid out in some official archive.

FINALE

All of our furor over administration of the SIDS program faded into insignificance as President Ronald Reagan successfully carried out his pledge to abolish most of the federal categorical health programs. The Omnibus Budget Reconciliation Act of 1981 removed almost all the grant and contract authority from the Office of Maternal and Child Health, and instead parceled the money out to the states to be spent at their discretion as part of a maternal and child health block grant. Thus the SIDS projects, as well as all the other child health programs, were left to seek their money from state capitals instead of from Washington, D.C.

Excerpts of correspondence between Carolyn Szybist and John Marshall written in June 1979 should serve as an appropriate coda to this narrative:

Dear John,
Someday after a cause and cure of SIDS has been found, I'd like to stop by your office and say hello. One of the Foundation's programs before PL93-270 was the mobilization of communities for SIDS. It is still a Foundation program in June of 1979. That means that we don't do this kind of thing just for the feds; we do it for the sake of SIDS. We have made only one mistake that I can see clearly. We sat back and waited for direction from the federal program, not wishing to interfere or overlap those programs. There are those who think we were not noisy enough

at the very beginning, and there are those who thought we should give the government a chance. We were patient in the tedious "in-house" paper work. I held that feeling, I know. And when Abe began to make noises, they should have been made sooner. I know there are people who don't agree with Abe's style. I'm not worried about their opinions. Abe is right. We did give the feds the know-how, the manpower, and the money. If the programs had gone reasonably right, you wouldn't have heard from us. It hasn't gone right. The (mobilization) contract is one of the examples, although not anywhere near the top.

For the record, the Foundation is not subsidized by the federal government. We have lent our skills for the return of funds and some peculiar rules. We have been guilty of not screaming loud enough. I feel guilty for knowing that our screaming sooner might have made the difference for parents.

Marshall's response:

I have to disagree with you, Carolyn, screaming earlier would not have helped. In fact, screaming doesn't help. Steady and inexorable pressure does. Beware of folks who credit screaming as an effective stimulus for things that would have happened anyway. Keep up the pressure, Carolyn, for an effective national SIDS program. Bang us when we need banging. Bang other folks when they need banging. If it gets too personally frustrating, go do something else. You are a competent, effective person, and there are lots of things that need to be done, and you can make a contribution in many other areas. That's my personal standard and when I get to the point where I can't perform effectively with a sense of integrity, I plan to do something different. Maybe it will be as a bureaucrat in some other program; maybe it will be fixing small engines on the Eastern Shore. Whatever, I hope I will have learned and grown from my relationship with the Foundation and with you, Stan, and even Abe.

EPILOGUE

You are not required to complete the work,
but neither are you at liberty to abstain from it.
Rabbi Tarfon in *Ethics of the Fathers*

The NSIDSF, never destined to thrive, still manages to stay afloat with offices in Landover, Maryland. Marie Valdes-Dapena succeeded Stan Friedman as president in 1984. Penelope Williamson, a psychologist, is now executive director, ably assisted by Edith McShane, a lively and warm octogenarian nun, who among other things in her rich past, used to be a college president. A SIDS grandfather, John Ward, a retired executive of Sterling Drug Company, who is the father of Anne Barr, serves as chairman of the Board of Trustees.

The Council of Guilds for Infant Survival, founded by Saul and Sylvia Goldberg, is no longer active on the national scene, but local guilds currently operate in Alabama, Virginia, Texas, Iowa, Louisiana, and California. Several other groups, however, have emerged in recent years. Alfred Steinschneider, who has continued to be active in SIDS research, founded the American SIDS Institute in 1983, which is based in Atlanta. The organization raises money and conducts research, mainly in the area of infant respiratory and cardiac function. The National Center for the Prevention of SIDS was organized in 1982, with offices in Baltimore, to raise and distribute money for SIDS research. Aided by a sizable subsidy from Citibank/Citicorp of New York, the center has retained entertainer Ben Vereen for a series of highly publicized fund-raising ventures throughout the country. When asked why they

184

felt the need to create a new organization, representatives of the center said that they didn't think the NSIDSF was sufficiently interested in SIDS research.

WHERE ARE THEY NOW?

After leaving the staff of the Senate Appropriations Committee, Harley Dirks spent some time lobbying for the American Medical Association before starting his own health lobbying firm in partnership with his son. Harley also has been fighting a courageous battle with cancer for over five years.

Jehu Hunter and Ralph Pardee have both retired from government service. Geraldine Norris remains in the Office of Maternal and Child Health coordinating what SIDS activities are left for that agency. She serves on the Medical Research Board of the NSIDSF. Almost alone among his compatriots from HEW during the Carter days, the former radical of the late 1960s, Edward Martin, remains in a position of power in the Reagan administration. He is director of the Bureau of Health Care Delivery and Assistance. John Marshall has not yet realized his fantasy of making a living fixing small engines on Maryland's eastern shore. In fact he has finally moved up to fill a box at the top of his own organization chart, serving as director of the National Center for Health Services Research.

In 1982 I left Childrens' Orthopedic Hospital and Medical Center (COHMC) and moved crosstown to the county hospital, Harborview Medical Center. Not coincidently, this move took place a year after my boss, Jack Docter, retired as chief of staff at COHMC. In that tumultuous year, I gained new appreciation for the importance of a protective shield over a person who engages in outspoken advocacy. One episode illustrates the dilemma. I wrote a guest editorial for a local newspaper criticizing the Washington State Department of Social and Health Services for failing to provide adequate protective services for abused children. Privately, officials of the agency were delighted, viewing the piece as assisting their efforts to obtain additional funds from the legislature. COHMC's new chief executive officer (the current "buzz-word" for administrators) did not see it the same way. He upbraided me for publicly criticizing an agency that channeled so much money to our institution. I was instructed to henceforth "clear" all verbal and written statements on issues that could conceivably affect the hospital through the public relations office. I was faced with the prospect of always having a "satisficer" perched on my shoulder. Mercifully for both my superiors and me, a "lateral transfer" to another institution within the University of Washington system was arranged.

PROGRESS IN SIDS

It was when I attended a meeting of the NSIDSF in Cincinnati in September 1983 that I finally began to appreciate the tremendous progress that had been achieved in the field of SIDS. Due to the chronic shortage of funds, it was the first national meeting of chapter representatives in eight years. I was struck with the mood of the meeting, which was in sharp contrast to that of the first meeting I attended in Chicago in 1971. Even though most of the attendees had lost babies to SIDS in the previous five years, there was not the air of desperate tension that permeated the Chicago meeting. A few parents did want to talk with me about their baby's death, but the questions mostly concerned research developments. Clearly, they had all spoken previously with knowledgeable physicians. I was no longer called on to be a source of absolution for their guilt.

Of course, the parents of the SIDS victims grieved, but seemingly, as a group, no more or less than the parents of children who died of other entities. The huge difference between 1971 and 1983 is that SIDS is now generally recognized among both health professionals and the lay public as a distinct disease entity that cannot as yet be prevented. SIDS is now described in all pediatric textbooks and discussed in medical schools and residency training programs. Health professionals, emergency medical personnel, firemen, policemen, clergymen, and morticians are now being taught about the proper management of SIDS families.

Services to SIDS families have not appeared to deteriorate as a result of the Maternal and Child Health Block Grants directly to states that started in 1981. In 1983 Rhode Island Health Services Research, Inc., conducted a survey on the fate of the federally funded SIDS projects and concluded, "In general, the projects appear to be thriving and optimistic about the future" (Rhode Island Health Services Research, p. 15).

By no means are the families of all SIDS victims receiving adequate management services. Deficiencies still exist, most notably in poverty areas where other health services are also lacking. Nevertheless, the trend toward "humanization" of "crib death" continues. Few of the attendees at the Cincinnati meeting had ever heard of the one person most responsible for this achievement, Judie Choate. Judie now owns

Table 3 Grants and Contracts Awarded by NICHD for SIDS and SIDS-Related Research, FY 1964-FY 1983

| Fiscal Year | Total Grants and Contracts Funds (thousands of dollars) | | | | | | Number of Projects | | |
| | Total | | Primary | | Related | | | | |
	Annual	Cumulative	Annual	Cumulative	Annual	Cumulative	Total	Primary	Related
1964	$1,173	$1,173	$23	$23	$1,150	$1,150	55	2	53
1965	1,634	2,807	18	41	1,616	2,766	64	1	63
1966	2,127	4,934	242	282	1,886	4,651	63	3	60
1967	2,314	7,248	208	490	2,106	6,758	73	3	70
1968	2,060	9,308	81	571	1,979	8,737	64	1	63
1969	2,196	11,504	87	658	2,109	10,845	59	2	57
1970	1,787	13,291	34	692	1,753	12,599	50	2	48
1971	2,593	15,884	46	738	2,547	15,146	47	1	46
1972	3,550	19,434	420	1,158	3,130	18,276	66	6	60
1973	4,181	23,615	604	1,762	3,578	21,854	74	11	63
1974	5,300	28,915	1,758	3,520	3,542	25,395	88	22	66
1975	6,321	35,236	2,266	5,785	4,056	29,451	102	26	76
1976	7,445	42,681	2,421	8,206	5,024	34,475	102	28	74
TQ	1,462	44,143	397	8,604	1,064	35,539	20	5	15
1977	9,704	53,847	4,672	13,276	5,032	40,571	112	41	71
1978	8,709	62,556	3,989	17,265	4,720	45,291	97	34	63
1979	11,116	73,673	4,912	22,178	6,204	51,495	105	38	67

Table 3 (continued)

Fiscal Year	Total Grants and Contracts Funds (thousands of dollars)						Number of Projects		
	Total		Primary		Related				
	Annual	Cumulative	Annual	Cumulative	Annual	Cumulative	Total	Primary	Related
1980	8,302	82,475	2,704	24,882	6,098	57,593	111	30	81
1981	9,682	92,157	3,367	28,249	6,315	63,908	97	28	69
1982	8,212	100,369	2,763	31,012	5,449	69,357	80	22	58
1983	7,499	107,868	1,780	32,791	5,719	75,076	71	15	56

Source: Report from the Pregnancy and Perinatology Section of the National Institute of Child Health and Human Development, December 15, 1983.

Note: Grants and contracts are classified as to whether they directly involve some aspect of SIDS (called primary), or whether in the course of investigating a broader subject area, for example, infant respiratory or cardiac functions, knowledge might be gained that would be helpful to understanding SIDS (called SIDS-related).

a small catering business in New York. Her tireless successor, Carolyn Szybist, tried graduate school for awhile but found the academic life too sedate. She now manages a hospital-based home-health agency in Chicago.

RESEARCH

Harley Dirks, Gilbert Woodside, and Mike Gorman had been right. It was not necessary to include a separate authorization for research funds in the SIDS Act of 1974. The momentum, started when Senator Magnuson earmarked $4 million for SIDS research in the NICHD appropriation for 1973, continues, as seen in Table 3.

A National Library of Medicine Medlars II citation list shows 36 articles on SIDS published in the world scientific literature just in the three-month period of January through March 1985. Naturally, not all of the works are of the highest quality, but several of them are important contributions. I doubt that any of the authors of these papers have ever heard of Mary Dore, Harley Dirks, or even Warren Magnuson. But then there is no particular reason why they should know of these individuals. The task of the scientists is to find the cause or causes of SIDS, along with a means of prevention. The scientific world is now aware of SIDS; it will not be necessary to advertise for research proposals again. The clock will never be turned back.

BIBLIOGRAPHY

Adelson, L, and Kinney, ER. 1956. Sudden and unexpected death in infancy and childhood. *Pediatrics* 17:663-669.

American Academy of Pediatrics. 1972. Committee on infant and pre-school child: The sudden infant death syndrome. *Pediatrics* 50:964-965.

Beckwith, JB. 1970. Observations on the patholgocial anatomy of the sudden infant death syndrome. *In* Bergman, AB, Beckwith, JB, and Ray, CG. *Sudden Infant Death Syndrome*: Proceedings of the Second International Conference on the Causes of Sudden Death in Infants. Seattle. University of Washington Press.

Beckwith, JB. 1973. The sudden infant death syndrome. *Curr Probl Pediatr* 3:1-36. (Reprinted by U.S. Department of Health, Education, and Welfare, Public Health Service, 1975 [HSA] 75-5137)

Beckwith, JB, Ray, CG, and Bergman, AB. 1975. The apnea monitor business. *Pediatrics* 56:1-2.

Bergman, AB. 1962. The emergency clinic: A study of its role in a teaching hospital. *Amer J Dis Child* 104:36-44.

Bergman, AB. 1965. Power lawn mowers are dangerous weapons. *Northwest Medicine* 64:261-263.

Bergman, AB, Pomeroy, MA, and Beckwith, JB. 1969. The psychiatric toll of sudden infant death syndrome. *General Practice* 40:99-105.

Bergman, AB, Beckwith, JB, and Ray, CG (Eds.). 1970. Sudden infant death syndrome. Proceedings of the second international conference on causes of sudden death in infants. Seattle and London. University of Washington Press.

Bergman, AB, Ray, CG, Pomeroy, MA, Wahl, PW, and Beckwith, JB. 1972. Studies of the sudden infant death syndrome in King County, Washington. III. Epidemiology. *Pediatrics* 49:860-870.

Bergman, AB. 1973. "The management of sudden infant death syndrome (SIDS) in the United States." Report in pp. 324-762 of U.S. Congress: Senate, Sudden Infant Death Syndrome Hearings. Committee on Labor and Public Welfare, Subcommittees on Health and on Children and Youth, 93rd Congress, 1st session, September 20, 1973. Washington, D.C.: U.S. Government Printing Office.

Bergman, AB, and Choate JA. 1975. *Why did my baby die?* New York: Third Press.

Bergman, AB, Beckwith, JB, and Ray CG. 1975. The apnea monitor business. *Pediatrics* 56:1-2.

Bergman, AB. 1978. Abuse of the child abuse law. *Pediatrics* 62:79-80.

Brecher, EM. 1968. "What doctors now know about crib deaths." *Redbook*, July.

Cleveland, AP. 1975. Sudden infant death syndrome: A burgeoning medicolegal problem. *Am J Law Med* 1:55-69.

Drew, EB. 1967. "The health syndicate—Washington's noble conspirators." *Atlantic Monthly*, December.

Easterbrook, G. 1980. "The art of further study: Life in the consulting cult." *Washington Monthly*, May, pp. 12-27.

Friedman, SB, Mason, JW, and Hamburg, DA. 1963. Urinary 17-hydroxycorticosteroid levels in parents of children with neoplastic disease: A study of chronic psychological stress. *Psychosom Med* 25: 364-376.

Garrison, FH. 1923. *History of Pediatrics* in Abt, IA (Ed.): *Pediatrics*, Vol. III. Philadelphia: W.B. Saunders.

Levin, A. 1970. *The Satisficers*. New York: McCall.

Lewis, A. 1964. *Gideon's Trumpet*. New York: Alfred Knopf.

Lindemann, E. 1944. Symptomatology and management of acute grief. *Am J Psych* 101:141-148.

Magnuson, WG. 1965. "Grant to the Children's Orthopedic Hospital and Medical Center in Seattle for research on the sudden death syndrome in infancy," U.S. Congress: Senate, *Congressional Record*, 89th Congress, 2nd session, September 10, 111:23451-23452.

McCarthy, C. 1973. *Disturbers of the Peace*. Boston: Houghton-Mifflin.

Naeye, RL. 1973. Pulmonary arterial abnormalities in the sudden infant death syndrome. *N Engl J Med* 289:1167-1170.

National Center of Health Statistics. 1984. Births, Marriages, divorces, and deaths for 1983. *Monthly Vital Statistics Report*. Vol. 32, No. 12, March 26.

Neustadt, RE, and Fineberg, HV. 1978. *The swine flu affair: Decision-making on a slippery disease*. Washington, D.C., U.S. Department of Health, Education, and Welfare. U.S. Government Printing Office (Number 017-000-00210-4).

Raring, RH. 1975. *Crib Death: Scourge of Infants—Shame of Society*. Hicksville, N.Y.: Exposition Press.

Raven, C. 1967. Study of sudden deaths of infants. *J Amer Med Women's Assoc* 22:319-320.

Ray, CG, Beckwith, JB, Hebestreit, NM, and Bergman AB. 1970. Studies of the sudden infant death syndrome in King County, Washington. I. The role of viruses. *J Amer Med Assoc* 211:619-623.

Redman, E. 1974. *The Dance of Legislation*. New York: Simon & Schuster.

Rhode Island Health Services Research. January 1984. *Sudden Infant Death Syndrome Survey Final Report*. Providence. Mimeographed. 15 pp.

Savitt, TL. 1975. Smothering and overlaying of Virginia slave children: A suggested explanation. *Bull Hist Med* 49:400-404.

Shannon, DC, Kelly, DH, and O'Connell, K. 1977. Abnormal regulation of ventilation in infants at risk for SIDS. *N Engl J Med.* 297: 747-747.

Southall, DP. 1983. Home monitoring and its role in the sudden infant death syndrome. *Pediatrics* 72:133-138.

Steinschneider, A. 1972. Prolonged apnea and the sudden infant death syndrome: Clinical and laboratory observations. *Pediatrics* 50:646-654.

Strickland, SP. 1972. *Politics, Science and Dread Disease*. Cambridge, Mass.: Harvard Univ Press.

Szybist, CM. 1976. *The Subsequent Child*. Rockville, Md.: U.S. Department of Health, Education and Welfare. Public Health Service (HSA) 76-5145. 20 pp.

Templeman, C. 1983. Two hundred and fifty-eight cases of suffocation in infants. *Edinburgh Med J* 38:322-329.

Tildon, JT, Roeder, LM, and Steinschneider, A. 1983. *Sudden Infant Death Syndrome*. New York: Academic Press.

U.S. Congress, House of Representatives
    1973. Sudden Infant Death Syndrome Hearings. Committee on Interstate and Foreign Commerce, Subcommittee on Public Health and Environment, 93rd Congress, 1st session, August 2. Washington D.C.: U.S. Government Printing Office.
    1974a Sudden Infant Death Syndrome Act of 1974. Report to Accompany H.R. 11386. Committee on Interstate and Foreign Commerce. 93rd Congress, 2nd session. H. Rept. 758. Washington, D.C.: U.S. Government Printing Office.

1974b "Amending Public Health Service Act respecting sudden infant death." Congressional Record, 93rd Congress, 2nd session, January 21, 120:105-109.

U.S. Congress, Senate.
1972a Rights of Children: Examination of the Sudden Infant Death Syndrome Hearings. Committee on Labor and Public Welfare, Subcommittee on Children and Youth, 92nd Congress, 2nd session, January 25. Washington, D.C.: U.S. Government Printing Office.

1972b "Sudden infant death syndrome." Congressional Record, 92nd Congress, 2nd session, June 7, 118:19985-19992.

1973a Sudden Infant Death Syndrome Hearings. Committee on Labor and Public Welfare, Subcommittees on Health and on Children and Youth, 93rd Congress, 1st session, September 20. Washington, D.C.: U.S. Government Printing Office.

1973b Sudden Infant Death Syndrome Act of 1973: Report to Accompany S. 1745. Committee on Labor and Public Welfare, 93rd Congress, 1st session, Sen. Rept. 606. Washington, D.C.: U.S. Government Printing Office.

1973c "Sudden Infant Death Syndrome Act of 1973." Congressional Record, 93rd Congress, 1st session, December 11, 119:40627-40634.

1978   Sudden Infant Death Syndrome Act Extension Hearings. Committee on Human Resources, Subcommittee on Child Health and Human Development, 95th Congress, 2nd session, March 1. Washington, D.C.: U.S. Government Printing Office.

U.S. General Accounting Office. 1981. Report by the Comptroller General. The Sudden Infant Death Syndrome Program Helps Families but Needs Improvement. HRD-81-25. Gaithersburg, MD.

Valdes-Dapena, M. 1963. Sudden and unexpected death in infants: The scope of our ignorance. Pediatr Clin N Amer 10:693-704.

Wedgwood, RJ, and Benditt, EP (Eds.). 1963. Sudden death in infants: Proceedings of the conference on the causes of sudden death in infants. Public Health Service Publication No. 1412. Washington, D.C.: U.S. Government Printing Office.

Werne, J, and Garrow, I. 1953. Sudden apparently unexplained death during infancy: Pathologic findings. Amer J Path 29:633-653.

Wilson, AJ, Stevens, V, Franks, CI, Alexander, J, and Southall, DP. 1985. Respiratory and heart rate patterns in infants destined to be victims of sudden infant death syndrome: Average rates and their variability measured over 24 hours. *Br Med J* 290:497-501.

Wooley, PV. 1945. Mechanical suffocation during infancy: A comment on its relation to the total problem of sudden death. *J Pediatr* 26:572-575.

.

GLOSSARY OF NAMES

(The positions described are those held by these individuals during the events described in the book.)

Adelson, Dr. Lester: coroner's pathologist in Cleveland—a pioneer in "modern" SIDS research.

Aldrich, Dr. Robert: University of Washington pediatric professor who became the first director of the National Institute of Child Health and Human Development (NICHD).

Aronson, Mary: staff assistant to Senator Cranston responsible for SIDS renewal legislation.

Barr, Anne: SIDS parent who was one of the organizers of the Massachusetts chapter of the National SIDS Foundation (NSIDSF), who also served as Eastern Regional Director.

Barr, Charles: husband of Anne who served as chairman of the Board of Trustees of the NSIDSF.

Bataldan, Dr. Paul: pediatrician who was director of HEW's Bureau of Community Health Services while the SIDS-law regulations were being drafted.

Beckwith, Dr. J. Bruce: pediatric pathologist who directed the SIDS research team at Children's Orthopedic Hospital in Seattle.

Brown, Dr. Bertram: director of the National Institute of Mental Health (NIMH).

Califano, Joseph: Secretary of HEW in Carter Administration.

Carter, Rep. Tim Lee (R. Kent.): ranking Republican on the House Health Subcommittee.

Choate, Judie: SIDS parent, executive director of the NSIDSF who organized the campaign to "humanize" the management of SIDS.

Colin Jr., Ralph: friend of Jed Roe who was Abe Bergman's predecessor as president of the NSIDSF.

Connelly, Dr. John: chairman of the pediatric department at Loyola University Medical School who helped organize the Chicago SIDS management program.

Cooper, Dr. Theodore: HEW Assistant Secretary for Health and Scientific Affairs in the Ford Administration when regulations for the SIDS law were drafted.

Cranston, Senator Alan (D. Calif.): succeeded Senator Mondale as chairman of the Senate Subcommittee on Child and Human Development.

Degnon, George: director of the Washington office of government liaison of the American Academy of Pediatrics.

Dirks, Harley M: professional staff member of the Senate HEW Appropriations Subcommittee (Senator Magnuson's chief health aide).

Docter, Dr. Jack: medical director of Children Orthopedic Hospital and Medical Center in Seattle (Abe Bergman's boss).

Dore, State Senator Fred: SIDS parent who also chaired the Washington State Senate Appropriations Committee.

Dore, Mary: SIDS parent who founded the Washington State chapter of the NSIDSF ("Disturber of the Peace").

DuVal, Dr. Merlyn (Monte): succeeded Charles Edwards as Assistant Secretary of HEW for Health and Scientific Affairs in Nixon Administration.

Edwards, Dr. Charles: Assistant Secretary of HEW for Health and Scientific Affairs in Nixon Administration.

French, Barbara: nurse employed by NSIDSF under NIMH contract to organize community management programs.

Friedman, Dr. Stanford: University of Maryland pediatrician-psychiatrist who succeeded Abe Bergman as president of the NSIDSF.

Gephart, Joann: nurse who was the first director of the Office of Maternal and Child Health's (OMCH) SIDS program.

Goldberg, Saul and Sylvia: SIDS parents from Baltimore who founded the Guild for Infant Survival (GIS).

Goldman, Leroy: aide to Senator Kennedy who was staff director of the Senate Health Subcommittee.

Goldsmith, Dr. Jay: California pediatrician who helped prepare testimony of John and Patricia Smiley.

Goldston, Dr. Stephen: coordinator of primary prevention programs for NIMH. Project director for contract with NSIDSF.

Gorman, Mike: preeminent Washington, D.C., health lobbyist, associated with Mary Lasker.

Grinstein, Gerald: former administrative assistant to Senator Magnuson who acted as Abe Bergman's "political guru."

Gross, Rep. H. R. (R. Iowa): notorious "nit-picker" of the House of Representatives.

Hasselmeyer, Dr. Eileen: Coordinated SIDS research program for NICHD.

Helpern, Dr. Milton: famous "crime doctor" who was medical examiner of New York City.

Hennigan, Frank: SIDS parent from Chicago who testified at Mondale Committee hearing.

Hersh, Dr. Steven: child psychiatrist who was special assistant to the director of NIMH.

Hoffman, Ellen: aide to Senator Mondale assigned to the staff of the Senate Subcommittee on Children and Youth.

Hunter, Jehu: administrator at NICHD who was project officer for the SIDS Management Study.

Hutchins, Dr. Vincent: director of HEW's OMCH.

Hyde, Dr. Lee: aide to Rep. Staggers assigned to staff of House Interstate and Foreign Commerce Committee.

Johnson, Dr. Emery: director of HEW's Indian Health Service.

Kennedy, Senator Edward (D. Mass.): chairman of the Senate Health Subcommittee.

Kretchmer, Dr. Norman: succeeded Gerald LaVeck as Director of NICHD.

Lasker, Mary: New York philanthropist and health lobbyist.

LaVeck, Dr. Gerald: Succeeded Robert Aldrich as director of NICHD.

Lawton, Steve: aide to Rep. Rogers assigned to House Health Subcommittee.

Lesser, Dr. Arthur: veteran of Children's Bureau who became first director of OMCH.

Lewak, Dr. Norman: pediatrician who was advisor to Northern California chapter of NSIDSF.

Lierman, Terry: aide to Senator Magnuson who succeeded Harley Dirks as chief clerk of Senate HEW Appropriations Subcommittee.

Lowe, Dr. Charles: HEW pediatrician assigned to Secretary's office who "helped" draft regulations for SIDS law.

McCarthy, Colman: Editorial page writer for *Washington Post*.

Magnuson, Senator Warren (D. Wash.): powerful senator who chaired HEW Appropriations Subcommittee.

Mandell, Dr. Fred: Boston pediatrician who was advisor to Western Massachusetts chapter of NSIDSF.

Marshall, Dr. John: deputy director of HEW's Bureau of Community Health Services.

Martin, Dr. Edward: director of HEW's Bureau of Community Health Services.

Mondale, Senator Walter (D. Minn.): chairman of the Subcommittee on Children and Youth.

Naeye, Dr. Richard: pediatric pathologist from Hershey, Pa., who theorized that SIDS victims suffer from chronic oxygen-lack prior to death.

Norris, Geraldine: nurse who directed OMCH's SIDS program.

Pardee, Ralph: "grey eminence" of OMCH.

Patterson, Kathyrn: nurse employed by NSIDSF under NIMH contract to organize community management programs.

Penalver, Ovidio: University of Southern California medical student who assisted Smileys after they were jailed.

Perthuck, Michael: aide to Senator Magnuson who served as chief counsel of the Senate Commerce Committee.

Price, John and Billie Ann: South Carolina couple jailed after their baby died of SIDS.

Ray, Dr. C. George: pediatrician-virologist who was a member of the SIDS research team at Children's Orthopedic Hospital and Medical Center in Seattle.

Redford, Lola: SIDS parent who became a Board Member of the NSIDSF.

Richmond, Dr. Julius: assistant secretary of HEW for Health and Scientific Affairs in the Carter Administration.

Roe, Jed and Louise: SIDS parents who founded the NSIDSF.

Rogers, Rep. Paul. (D. Fla.): as chairman of the Health Subcommittee, became the most powerful member of the House of Representatives on health matters.

Siegal, Ann and Arthur: SIDS parents who "kept the NSIDSF afloat" by housing it in their New York advertising agency.

Simmons, Dr. Henry: deputy assistant secretary of HEW for health and scientific affairs who testified before Congress on SIDS.

Smiley, John and Patricia: Southern California couple who were jailed when their baby died of SIDS.

Southall, Dr. David: London physician investigating breathing and sleep patterns of normal infants.

Staggers, Rep. Harley (D. W. Va.): chairman of the House Interstate and Foreign Commerce Committee that had jurisdiction over health matters.

Steinschneider, Dr. Alfred: pediatrician from Syracuse (and later Baltimore) who first proposed possible relationship between apnea and SIDS

Stromberg, Cliff: deputy executive secretary to HEW Secretary Califano.

Szybist, Carolyn: SIDS parent from Chicago who became Executive Director of the NSIDSF.

Ungar, Bernard: headed the Government Accounting Office's investigation into the SIDS program.

Valdes-Dapena, Dr. Marie: eminent authority on SIDS research who headed the Medical Research Board of the NSIDSF.

Walcher, Dr. Dwain: NICHD's first "patron" for SIDS research.

Weicker, Senator Lowell (R. Conn.): attorney-friend of Roes who drew up papers incorporating the Foundation.

Williams, Evelyn and Roy: Bronx couple who were imprisoned when their baby died of SIDS.

Woodside, Dr. Gilbert: associate director of NICHD.

APPENDIX I

IN THE LEGISLATURE
of the
STATE OF WASHINGTON

CERTIFICATION OF ENROLLED ENACTMENT
SENATE BILL NO. 180
Chapter 178, Laws of 1963

HUMAN REMAINS–JURISDICTION–AUTOPSY–DISSECTION

Passed the Senate March 3, 1963
Yeas 48   Nays 0
Passed the House March 11, 1963
Yeas 97   Nays 0

CERTIFICATE

I, Ward Bowden, Secretary of the Senate of the State of Washington do hereby certify that the attached is enrolled Senate Bill No. 180 as passed by the Senate and the House of Representatives on the dates hereon set forth.

(Signed by) _____
Secretary of the Senate

CHAPTER NO. 178
SENATE BILL NO. 180

State of Washington   By Senators Dore, England and
38th Regular Session   Petrich

Read first time January 28, 1963, and referred to Committee on Cities, Towns and Counties.

AN ACT Relating to coroners; and amending section 3, chapter 90, Laws of 1917 as amended by section 1, chapter 188, Laws of 1953 and RCW 68.08.010; amending section 237, chapter 249, Laws of 1909 as amended by section 2, chapter 188, Laws of 1953 and RCW 68.08.100; amending section 7, chapter 188, Laws of 1953 and RCW 68.08.104.

BE IT ENACTED BY THE LEGISLATURE OF THE STATE OF WASHINGTON:
Section 1. Section 3, chapter 90, Laws of 1917, as amended by section 1, chapter 188, Laws of 1953 and RCW 68.08.010 are each amended to read as follows:

The jurisdiction of bodies of all deceased persons who come to their death suddenly when in apparent good health without medical attendance within the thirty-six hours preceding death; ((;)) or where the circumstances of death indicate death was caused by unnatural or unlawful means ((;)); or where death occurs under suspicious circumstances; ((, or bodies upon which)) or where a coroner's autopsy or post mortem or coroner's inquest is to be held ((, or dead bodies)) ; or where death results from unknown or obscure causes, or where death occurs within one year following an accident; or where the death is caused by any violence whatsoever, or where death results from a known or suspected abortion; whether self-induced or otherwise; where death apparently results from drowning, hanging, burns, electrocution, gunshot wounds, stabs or cuts, lightning, starvation, radiation, exposure, alcoholism, narcotics or other addictions, tetanus, strangulations, suffocation or smothering; or where death is due to premature birth or still birth; or where death is due to a violent contagious disease or suspected contagious disease which may be a public health hazard; or where death results from alleged rape, carnal knowledge or sodomy, where death occurs in a jail or prison; where a body is found dead or is not claimed by relatives or friends, is hereby vested in the county coroner, which bodies may be removed and placed in the morgue under such rules as are adopted by ((him)) the coroner with the approval of the county commissioners, having jurisdiction providing therein how the bodies shall be brought to and cared for at the morgue and held for the proper identification where necessary.

Sec. 2. Section 237, chapter 249, Laws of 1909 as amended by section 2, chapter 188, Laws of 1953 and RCW 68.08.100 are each amended to read as follows:

The right to dissect a dead body shall be limited to cases specially provided by statute or by the direction or will of the deceased; cases where a coroner is authorized to hold an inquest upon the body, and then only as he may authorize dissection; and cases where the spouse or next of kin charged by law with the duty of burial shall authorize dissection for the purpose of ascertaining the cause of death, and then only to the extent so authorized: PROVIDED, That the coroner, in his discretion, may make or cause to be made by a competent pathologist, toxicologist, or physician, an autopsy or post mortem in ((all)) any case ((s)) in which ((death occurred by violence, or suspicious circumstances, or where an inquest is to be held, or where death occurred in prison, jail or while serving a sentence, or where death occurred suddenly and without medical attendance, or from unnatural causes, or under circumstances indicating the possibility of death by the hand of the deceased or through the instrumentality of some other person)) the coroner has jurisdiction of a body: PROVIDED, FURTHER, That the coroner may with the approval of the University of Washington and with the consent of a parent or guardian deliver any body of a deceased person under the age of three years over which he has jurisdiction to the University of Washington medical school for the purpose of having an autopsy made to determine the cause of death. Every person who shall make, cause, or procure to be made any dissection of a body, except as above provided, shall be guilty of a gross misdemeanor.

Sec. 3. Section 7, chapter 188, Laws of 1953 and RCW 68.08.104 are each amended to read as follows:

The cost of autopsy shall be borne by the county in which the autopsy is performed, except when requested by the department of labor and industries, in which case, the said department shall bear the cost of such autopsy; and except when performed on a body of an infant under the age of three years by the University of Washington medical school, in which case the medical school shall bear the cost of such autopsy.

Passed the Senate March 3, 1963.

President of the Senate.

Passed the House March 11, 1963.

Speaker of the House.

Approved March 26, 1963

Governor of Washington

**FILED
MAR 26 1963
VIC MEYERS
SECRETARY OF STATE
TIME**

APPENDIX II

(Manifesto drafted by Judie Choate in 1971 outlining the "battle plan" of the National SIDS Foundation.)

The goals of the Foundation remain as they stood in 1962—the ultimate prevention of SIDS and the eradication of the needless guilt reactions in families stemming from ignorance about the disease. However, we can no longer solely depend on the determination and financial support of the Foundation family and volunteers. The problem is so enormous and urgent that we have resolved to both expand our activities and solicit the support of other organizations in achieving our goals. Therefore:

"NO LONGER CAN WE ACCEPT:"

1. . . . a death certificate diagnosis, in SIDS cases, of "interstitial pneumonitis," "tracheal bronchitis," "suffocation" or any other meaningless diagnosis. Physicians must know that SIDS is a disease, readily diagnosed during the course of a simple autopsy. More important, parents must know that their babies have died from a specific entity.

2. . . . callous coroners' or medical examiners' administrative procedures whereby families are kept waiting months for autopsy results or subjected to cruel inquests in SIDS cases.

3. . . . physicians confusing all sudden, unexpected infant deaths with true SIDS. The condition can be diagnosed and must be for the sake of statistical identification and the emotional health of the family.

4. . . . suspicion of neglect on the part of firemen, policemen, morticians, newspapermen, and even clergymen with the unexpected death of an infant. These people are most often the first in contact with the stricken family; their lack of information can only further add to the feelings of guilt, grief, and frustration in the family.

5. . . . the fact that some families are denied autopsies because of lack of funds or that low-income families, not receiving private medical care, rarely receive any information about the syndrome.

6. . . . the lack of instruction about SIDS in medical and other health professional schools. Without knowledge, there will be no impetus for new research nor will young physicians and nurses be prepared to deal with the syndrome should it occur in the course of their professional careers.

7. . . . the existence of only a handful of research projects into the cause (or causes) of SIDS.

8. . . . the lack of knowledge of the syndrome on the part of pediatricians and family physicians. Every doctor should be prepared to offer the family more than the small consolation of "these things happen."

9. ... newspaper articles of syndicated doctors' columns discussing suffocation, allergy, or countless other unsubstantiated theories as the cause of SIDS. This kind of misinformation has done in the past, and continues to do, incalculable harm.

10. ... the fact that volunteer families alone have been asked to form local parent groups.

WE, THEREFORE, PROPOSE...

1. ... a standardized procedure in every community for handling cases of infants who die suddenly and unexpectedly that is both compassionate and medically sound. Autopsies must be performed and parents promptly informed of the results.

2. ... that the criteria for the diagnosis of SIDS be disseminated to coroners and medical examiners throughout the United States, and that the term, "sudden infant death syndrome" be utilized on the death certificates.

3. ... that every SIDS family receive authoritative information about SIDS from a physician, nurse, or other health professional who is both knowledgeable about the disease and skilled in dealing with characteristic grief reactions.

4. ... that a major effort be undertaken to increase the amount of research being conducted on SIDS through solicitation of the scientific community by the National Institute of Child Health and Human Development.

5. ... that parent volunteer groups be available in every state or large community to promote the aims of the Foundation on a local level. Close ties should be maintained with local physicians, particularly pediatricians and pathologists.

STRATEGY

1. *Strengthening of national office of NSIDSF to provide*:
a. Authoritative public information,
b. A speaker's bureau
c. Consultants to assist in formation of local chapters, and
d. Liaison with other organizations.

2. *Alliance with professional medical and health organizations* (e.g., pediatricians, pathologists, nurses, social workers, etc.) *so that they can educate their own members* about SIDS.

3. *Involvement of national, state and local government* to:
a. Promote SIDS research,
b. Upgrade autopsy procedures, and
c. Disseminate authoritative information through health department, coroner's and medical examiner's office and law enforcement agencies by means of literature, seminars, consultants, etc.

4. *A dignified public relations campaign to educate the public* about SIDS without producing undue anxiety. Educational efforts will be specifically directed towards those most apt to come into contact with SIDS, such as morticians, clergy, police and firemen, and media representatives.

A PLEA

While 1 in every 350 live births will be a victim of the sudden infant death syndrome, the National SIDS Foundation asks the assistance of all agencies and individuals concerned with the welfare of not only the child, but the entire family unit. With the lack of knowledge in the community, the inhumanity of most of our autopsy systems and continuing medical misinformation, the family of the SIDS victim is shattered.

The National SIDS Foundation asks that each and every family experiencing SIDS be given the chance to face the death with knowledge and dignity. We have pledged our entire resources to this end. We request your help in making dignity a part of the lives of 10,000 families a year.

APPENDIX III

Reprinted from *Pediatric Research*, Vol. 6 No. 4, April, 1972

THE SUDDEN INFANT DEATH SYNDROME

Data from carefully conducted epidemiologic studies suggest that the sudden infant death syndrome, also known as "crib death," is the major cause of infant death after the first month of life. Crib death is the unexpected demise of an infant not known to have had a serious disease, whose death remains unexplained after complete autopsy. In the majority of cases, the baby does not have a cold or other infection and takes his feedings without difficulty. The infant is then placed in his crib for a nap or for the night; several hours later, or in the morning, the baby is found dead. The sudden infant death syndrome occurs more frequently in families of lower socio-economic status, a factor which may explain its higher incidence in non-white infants. It occurs in infants with a history of prematurity, particularly those born between the 34th and 35th weeks of gestation. Male infants appear to be more at risk than females. Victims are mostly between the ages of one and six months; the frequency is highest around the third month of life. The largest number of deaths occur between the months of November and March. These numerous epidemiologic associations with the sudden infant death syndrome may be independent or merely part of a whole set of circumstances commonly associated with low socio-economic class. The etiology of the sudden infant death syndrome is probably rooted in a factor or set of factors found in all socio-economic classes but most prevalent among the poor.

Numerous pathologic mechanisms involving several body systems have been implicated in the etiology of the sudden infant death syndrome. In the past a steady succession of single-factor explanations were offered. More recently several multifactorial etiologic theories have been advanced. For example, one current theory implicates a combination of factors involving infection, instability of the nervous system, and sleep. Realistically, however, it must be admitted that although etiologic theories abound, very few specific hypotheses have been thoroughly eliminated.

On August 16, 1971, the National Institute of Child Health and Human Development held a planning workshop to define new directions in research into the causes of the syndrome utilizing the data presented at the Second International Conference on Sudden Infant Death Syndrome in February 1969 as well as more recent research findings. As a result of this workshop, three broad areas have been identified in which the development of new knowledge would most likely contribute to the understanding and eventual control of the sudden infant death syndrome. The Institute wishes to support research through grants for studies in these areas:

Abnormal neurophysiological development in the fetus and young infant, with particular emphasis on abnormal development of sleep patterns as these relate to the sudden infant death syndrome.

The relationship of central chemoreceptor response and irregular vagal control to respiratory problems in young infants which may precipitate the sudden infant death syndrome.

Abnormal perinatal development of immune response mechanisms with emphasis on the relationship of deficits in immunologic competence to susceptibility to the sudden infant death syndrome.

Please write for research grant application kits and other sudden infant death informational documents to:

Dr. Eileen G. Hasselmeyer
Program Director
Perinatal Biology and Infant Mortality Branch
National Institute of Child Health and Human Development
Room 3A-21, Building 31
Bethesda, Maryland 20014

APPENDIX VI

Reprinted from *The Washington Post*, Friday, December 31, 1971, Page A10

THE SUDDEN INFANT DEATH MYSTERY:
Neither Predictable Nor Preventable

By Colman McCarthy

Perhaps no other death is more difficult for the survivors to bear or the community to understand than the death of an infant. The special kind of funeral— the white coffin the size of a toy box—the mother's grief on carrying a baby inside her for nine months only to lose the child after it is soon outside, the straining of religious faith that says the infant's death is somehow in "God's plan": little of this helps. Yet, about 10,000 to 15,000 babies die of what is called sudden infant death syndrome (SIDS) every year in the U.S. One infant in 350 is a victim. According to HEW figures, 77 infants died of SIDS in the District of Columbia in 1969; 220 died of it in Virginia and 169 in Maryland. Popularly called crib death, SIDS is a major American health problem. Excluding the first week of life when infants die from complications of prematurity, SIDS is the nation's largest cause of death in infants under one year and second only to accidents as the largest cause of death to children under age 15. A news story occasionally appears on the subject and magazine "health columns" refer to it periodically; but the ones who know it best are the parents of the victims. The subject is topical this week because the National Foundation for Sudden Infant Death in New York has announced that Dr. Abraham Bergman is its new president. Bergman is a Seattle pediatrician who for years was a leader in the fight to get flammable clothing off the market.

The mystery of crib death is that it always occurs in sleep. It is neither predictable nor preventable. Parents who give their infant its last feeding of the day —either by bottle or breast—never dream that death is about to strike. The child runs no fever, is not coughing and sounds no louder than usual in the final cry before falling off to sleep. Not many parents even know about SIDS, but even if they did, obsessive worrying about it would be neurotic. Research groups at the University of Washington and Children's Orthopedic Hospital in Seattle, where Bergman teaches, believe that SIDS babies die from a sudden spasm of the vocal cords that close off the airway during sleep. This is often associated with a viral infection. Yet the viral infection does not cause the death, only causes the vocal cords to be more susceptible to a sudden spasm. Even more mysterious is why a viral infection in a 2- or 3-month baby is different than in a 3- or 4-year-old, or an adult. One researcher has reported that sudden unexplained infant deaths "tend to occur most frequently during cold weather in a sleeping 2- to 4-month-

211

old infant born prematurely or of low birth weight, who at the time had an upper respiratory infection. However, one of the major problems that continues to require solution concerns the means by which these characteristics result in or lead to SIDS."

Two international conferences, in 1963 and 1969, were held on crib death, but research is only beginning. Although Bergman reports that some critics say the federal government is purposely doing nothing in the field, he believes the opposite is true. To date he says the National Institutes of Child Health and Human Development has never turned down a qualified research application on SIDS. "The problem," notes Dr. Gerald LaVeck, the institute's director, "is mostly a lack of trained scientific investigators interested in conducting research into the problem."

While the physical mysteries of crib death are explored, there is no confusion about the emotional and social pains suffered by the surviving family. "There is a large amount of ignorance in the U.S. medical profession and the lay public about SIDS," says Bergman. "In the majority of communities, parents who lose children to SIDS are treated as criminals. In many places, they can't get autopsies or else must pay themselves. Usually, families must wait many months to hear the results of these autopsies from a medical examiner's or coroner's office. Many examiners and coroners still call the disease 'suffocation' or a variety of other wrong names. This only reinforces the natural guilt that parents feel anyway. Many are subjected to coroner's inquests and questioned by police. This is a national scandal and must cease."

The destructive emotional effects of crib death can last long after the regular mourning period. Tremendous after-guilt may be felt by fathers or mothers who did not "go in to check" when the baby cried during its last night; physically, though, it would have made no difference, because crying does not occur during the baby's agonal period. Other parents suffer excessive guilt at not having taken the infant to the pediatrician, especially if coughing or a fever was present. If they did just visit the doctor and the baby dies, parents wonder "what the doctor missed." Curiously, Bergman reports, "physicians themselves harbor the same doubts, often for many years. A discussion of SIDS at a medical meeting invariably turns into a confessional for physicians who feel the need to stand up and re-live their traumatic experience and be convinced of the known facts."

It is not that easy for parents. Occasionally, divorce follows a crib death, the father refusing to live with the mother who "let a baby die." If a babysitter or relative was home at the time, they may be blamed, with the parents always feeling guilty about going out for the evening. "In the weeks following the death," Bergman says, "there is often marked change of moods. The parents have difficulty concentrating and frequently express hostile feelings toward their closest friends and relatives. Denial of death is common; the mother may continue to draw the baby's bath or prepare his food. Dreams about the dead child are common, as is a fear of being left alone in the house . . . Other common reactions are anger, helplessness and loss of meaning of life. Parents are fearful, particularly about the safety of their surviving children. A fear of 'going insane' often occurs in the first few days and may last for several weeks. Guilt is universal and pervasive. Whether they say so or not, most if not all the parents feel responsible for the death of their babies."

The last point is the most crucial if the surviving parents are to lead normal lives. In medical fact, they are not responsible. Doctors, medical examiners, counselors and friends have the obligation to inform the parents that they did nothing wrong and could *not* have prevented the death. Guilt or anxiety may never be totally removed, but at least it can be lessened so that life can go on. If families can be consoled after a member dies of cancer, a car crash or other common causes of death, why not with SIDS? Perhaps if the disease is recognized as a disease, and not as a form of suffocation or pneumonia, more can be learned about it. Preventive medicine has conquered other diseases of mystery; it can conquer this one too.

APPENDIX V

92d Congress
2d session

S.J. RES. 206

IN THE SENATE OF THE UNITED STATES

February 17, 1972

Mr. Mondale (for himself, Mr. Beall, Mr. Cranston, Mr. Eagleton, Mr. Hughes, Mr. Javits, Mr. Kennedy, Mr. Magnuson, Mr. Nelson, Mr. Packwood, Mr. Pell, Mr. Randolph, Mr. Schweiker, Mr. Stevenson, Mr. Weicker, and Mr. Williams) introduced the following joint resolution; which was read twice and referred to the Committee on Labor and Public Welfare

JOINT RESOLUTION

Relating to sudden infant death syndrome.

Whereas sudden infant death syndrome kills more infants between the age of one month and one year than any other disease; and

Whereas the cause and prevention of sudden infant death syndrome are unknown; and

Whereas there is a lack of adequate knowledge about the disease and its effects among the public and professionals who come into contact with it: Therefore be it

Resolved by the Senate and House of Representatives of the United States of America in Congress assembled, That it is the purpose of this joint resolution to assure that the maximum resources and effort be concentrated on medical research into sudden infant death syndrome and on the extension of services to families who lose children to the disease.

SEC. 2. The National Institute of Child Health and Human Development, of the Department of Health, Education, and Welfare, is hereby directed to designate the search for a cause and prevention of sudden infant death syndrome as one of the top priorities in intramural research efforts and in the awarding of research and research training grants and fellowships; and to encourage researchers to submit proposals for investigations of sudden infant death syndrome.

SEC. 3. The Secretary of Health, Education, and Welfare is directed to develop, publish, and distribute literature to be used in educating and counseling coroners, medical examiners, nurses, social workers, and similar personnel and parents, future parents, and families whose children die, to the nature of sudden infant death syndrome and to the needs of families affected by it.

SEC. 4. The Secretary of Health, Education, and Welfare is further directed to work toward the institution of statistical reporting procedures that will provide a reliable index to the incidence and distribution of sudden infant death syndrome cases throughout the Nation; to work toward the availability of autopsies of children who apparently die of sudden infant death syndrome and for prompt release of the results to their parents; and to add sudden infant death syndrome to the International Classification of Disease.

APPENDIX VI

Current Classifications of Primary Counties in each Standard Metropolitan
Statistical Area (SMSA) with Reference to Management of SIDS Cases

Excellent Management (9)
Sacramento, California
San Diego, California
Orleans, Louisiana (New Orleans)
Baltimore, Maryland
Hennepin, Minnesota (Minneapolis)
St. Louis, Missouri (County)
Multnomah, Oregon (Portland)
Allegheny, Pennsylvania (Pittsburgh)
King, Washington (Seattle-Everett)

Good Management (8)
Broome, New York (Binghamton)
Erie, New York (Buffalo)
Nassau, New York
Cuyahoga, Ohio (Cleveland)
Philadelphia, Pennsylvania
Dallas, Texas
La Crosse, Wisconsin
Milwaukee, Wisconsin

Fair Management (22)
Alameda, California (Oakland)
San Francisco, California
Santa Clara, California (San Jose)
San Joaquin, California (Stockton)
Denver, Colorado
Hartford, Connecticut
Washington, D.C.
Dade, Florida (Miami)
Marion, Indiana (Indianapolis)
Jefferson, Kentucky (Louisville)
Yellowstone, Montana (Billings)
Wayne, Michigan (Detroit)
Hillsborough, New Hampshire (Manchester-Nashua)
Bergen, New Jersey (Patterson-Clifton-Passaic)
Essex, New Jersey (Newark)
Brooklyn, New York
Ector, Texas (Odessa)
Harris, Texas (Houston)

Midland, Texas
Weber, Utah (Ogden)
Prince William, Virginia
Kenosha, Wisconsin

Generally Poor Management (*35*)
Jefferson, Alabama (Birmingham)
Montgomery, Alabama
Mobile, Alabama
Pulaski, Arkansas (Little Rock)
Los Angeles, California
Orange, California (Anaheim-Garden Grove)
San Bernadino, California
San Mateo, California
Alachua, Florida (Gainesville)
Hillsborough, Florida (Tampa-St. Petersburg)
Palm Beach, Florida
Fulton, Georgia (Atlanta)
Ada, Idaho (Boise)
Cook, Illinois (Chicago)
Winnebago, Illinois (Rockford)
Vigo, Indiana (Terre Haute)
Wyandotte, Kansas (Kansas City)
Bristol, Massachusetts (New Bedford)
Suffolk, Massachusetts (Boston)
Worcester, Massachusetts (Fitchburg-Leominster)
Genessee, Michigan (Flint)
Ingham, Michigan (Lansing)
Kalamazoo, Michigan
Boone, Missouri (Columbia)
St. Louis, Missouri (city only)
New York, New York
Franklin, Ohio (Columbus)
Hamilton, Ohio (Cincinnati)
Jefferson, Ohio (Steubenville-Wierton)
Comanche, Oklahoma (Lawton)
Richland, South Carolina (Columbia)
Davidson, Tennessee (Nashville)
Cameron, Texas (Brownsville-Harlingen-San Benito)
Potter, Texas (Amarillo)
Utah, Utah (Provo)

APPENDIX VII

July 10, 1974

TO: Eileen G. Hasselmeyer, Ph.D.
             Program Director, Perinatal Biology
               and Infant Mortality Branch
             NICHD

FROM: Abraham B. Bergman, M.D.
             President, National Foundation
               for Sudden Infant Death

SUBJECT: Thoughts on implementation of PL93-270, the
               Sudden Infant Death Syndrome Act of 1974

Background of legislation

There are two aspects to the problem of sudden infant death syndrome (SIDS). The first is discovering the cause and possible prevention through biomedical research. Other than language encouraging an increased effort and reports to Congress on progress in research, PL93-270 does *not* deal with research. The sponsors of the legislation felt that adequate authority already exists through NIMH mechanisms and that specific authorizations for SIDS research would not be particularly helpful.

The law does address itself to the "human" aspect of the problem, the tragic grief and guilt reactions experienced by surviving family members. Because of mystery and mishandling of SIDS, the surviving family members tend to suffer greatly. The legislation was prepared in response to an NICHD sponsored study, "The Management of SIDS in the United States—1972." This was performed by me in 1972 and presented to the Congressional committees during testimony on the legislation. The underlying assumption is that all communities in the United States should have a standardized procedure for the handling of cases of sudden unexpected infant death. This can most practically be done by establishing "regional centers" where autopsies could be performed, and parents provided with information and counseling about SIDS. The law thus provides for *education* of personnel on proper management of SIDS and *services* to families who lose children to SIDS.

Current Status of HEW Activities in SIDS

NICHD has been the lead agency in that they support biomedical research. Their research program will not be effected by the new law other than the necessity of filing regular reports with Congress. Other agencies with interest are NIMH, Maternal and Child Health Services, and the National Center for Health Statistics.

218

All of these programs have representatives on an interagency council. No one program has taken the lead in dealing with the education and service activities prescribed by the new law.

It is anticipated that at least 1.5 million dollars will be appropriated in the FY 75 budget for implementation of the new law.

Recommendations for implementation

I propose that responsibility for administering PL93-270 be given to the MCH division of the Bureau of Community Health Services. A "public health" approach is needed with liaison to health departments, coroner and medical examiner offices and health professional organizations in states and local communities. It logically falls within the mission of the MCH program.

A small staff (three persons) should administer the program at the central office; the majority of activities should take place in the HEW regional offices. Approximately 15% of the funds should be used for a *directed* educational campaign to coroners, medical examiners, physicians, public health nurses, emergency room personnel, policemen, firemen, morticians, and clergymen. The NFSID has found that regional educational seminars provide the "biggest bang for the buck" in terms of altering community management systems. This program should be continued and augmented. The expertise of the NFSID in conducting such an educational campaign for the past two years, should be utilized. The Guild for Infant Survival (GIS) should also be utilized in areas where they have active chapters.

The bulk of the money should be utilized for "seed grants" to establish regional centers for the study of sudden unexpected infant deaths. So that the available funds can be spread over as wide an area as possible and achieve maximum results nationally, the yearly federal contribution to any one project should not exceed 50 thousand dollars.

The funds should support the performance of autopsies, transportation of bodies, and the salaries of a counselor (public health nurse) and secretary. Funds from this program should not support SIDS research. Scientists wishing to conduct SIDS research should apply through the usual NICHD channels.

Successful prototypes of SIDS regional centers exist in such communities as Seattle, Portland, Chicago, Omaha, New Orleans as well as some other communities.

The law is meant to be a "carrot and stick"; the grant program should reflect that philosophy. Thus, the grant should be given to a coroner/medical examiner office or hospital that promises to provide the following services:

A. Autopsy all cases of sudden unexpected infant death, regardless of the family's ability to pay;
B. Promptly notify the family of the results of the autopsy;
C. Use the term "SIDS" on appropriate cases on the death certificates;

D. Provide follow-up information and counseling by a knowledgeable health professional; and

E. Make information available about local parent groups where applicable.

The centers should serve a population area of at least 1 million persons. Preferences in awarding grants should be given to communities which have the most limited resources and have the "lowest standards" as revealed in the 1972 Management Study. (In other words, don't make the rich richer.)

Though not called for specifically in the law, applicants should make some contribution to the project and show evidence of plans to continue it beyond termination of federal support.

The overall aim should be that families who lose babies to SIDS should feel no more guilty than families who lose children to other diseases, such as meningitis or cancer. I feel that a concerted effort by HEW to implement PL93-270 will result in this goal being achieved for the vast majority of American families within two years.

ABB/km

APPENDIX VIII

Federal Register
FRIDAY, JUNE 6, 1975
WASHINGTON, D.C.
Volume 40 • Number 110

PART II

DEPARTMENT OF HEALTH, EDUCATION, AND WELFARE

Public Health Service

SUDDEN INFANT DEATH SYNDROME
INFORMATION AND COUNSELING

Project Grants

24436, Rules and Regulations

Title 42—Public Health

CHAPTER I—PUBLIC HEALTH SERVICE, DEPARTMENT OF HEALTH, EDUCATION, AND WELFARE

PART 51a—GRANTS FOR MATERNAL AND CHILD HEALTH AND CRIPPLED CHILDREN'S SERVICES

Project Grants for Sudden Infant Death Syndrome Information and Counseling

On March 5, 1975, there was published in the *Federal Register* (40 FR 10318) a notice of proposed rulemaking regarding the implementation of the grant program established by section 1121(b) of the Public Health Service Act (42 U.S.C. 300c-11, as added by section 3(a) of the Sudden Infant Death Syndrome Act of 1974, Pub. L. 93-270). Interested persons were given until April 4, 1975, to submit written comments or suggestions thereon. Comments and suggestions received with regard to the notice of proposed rulemaking, responses thereto, and changes in the proposed regulation are summarized below.

1. It was suggested that the definition of "sudden infant death syndrome" in proposed § 51a.502(d) be changed to incorporate certain specific clinical findings, such as bronchiolitis. However, since it was felt that the definition set forth in § 51a.502(d) accorded with the weight of medical authority in the field, no change was made in the regulation.

2. The definition of "family" in proposed § 51a.502(f) has been revised to incorporate a specific reference to "parents" in view of the many references to parents in the legislative history.

3. A suggestion that the requirement that projects include "both" types of activities specified in proposed § 51a.503(b) be dropped was rejected as inconsistent with the statutory language.

4. A suggestion that the words "the causes of" in proposed § 51a.503(b) (1) be deleted was also rejected as inconsistent with the statute.

5. It was suggested that the requirement of "appropriate community representation" in proposed § 51a.504(c)(2) be dropped. This suggestion was rejected, since such representation is required by the statute.

6. A proposal that a subsection specifying organized parents' groups and similar voluntary organizations be added to § 51a.505(a)(10) was rejected as redundant.

7. Several suggestions were received that the role of the social services professions and child protective agencies in the information and counseling program should be more explicitly recognized. Sections 51a.505 and 51a.506 were revised accordingly.

8. General and specific objections to the project community council as required by proposed § 51a.506 were raised. However, aside from the change discussed in paragraph 7, the section was retained unchanged as an appropriate means of obtaining the community representation required by the statute.

9. A suggestion that the waiver provided for in proposed § 51a.506(c) be made available to private non-profit organizations as well as to State and local governmental agencies was rejected as inconsistent with the purpose of the section as a whole.

10. Several comments were received objecting to the priority to be given projects in areas with populations of one million or more (§ 51a.507(b)(1)). However, the criterion is considered to be reasonable as a means of allocating resources and maximizing program impact and hence was retained.

11. A proposal that a criterion giving priority to already existing organizations be added to the criteria set forth in proposed § 51a.507(b) was rejected as unwarranted.

12. Section 51a.509 was revised to include a provision requiring the obtaining of legal consent to medical investigations which are paid for with project funds.

13. In accordance with a comment received, proposed § 51a.509(c) and 51a.511 were revised to make it clear that information may be released where required by applicable law.

14. A technical amendment was made to proposed § 51a.510 to add language consistent with the requirements of section 504 of the Rehabilitation Act of 1973, Pub. L. 93-112.

15. It was proposed that applications for grants under this subpart be subject to State health department approval. However, establishment of such a requirement was considered to be unwarranted by the statute or legislative history.

16. One comment implied that appropriate research into the cause(s) of SIDS should include more than "medical investigations * * * such as autopsies." However, it is believed that the functions of a project as set forth in § 51a.505 adequately reflect the intent of the statute as a whole and no change was made.

17. Minor editorial changes were made and typographical errors corrected.

Effective date. These regulations are effective June 6, 1975.

Dated: May 9, 1975.

THEODORE COOPER,
*Acting Assistant
Secretary for Health.*

Approved: May 29, 1975.
CASPAR W. WEINBERGER,
Secretary.

Part 51a of Title 42 is hereby amended by adding thereto a new Subpart E as set forth below:

Subpart E—Project Grants for Sudden Infant Death Syndrome
Information and Counseling

Sec.

AUTHORITY: Sec. 215, 58 Stat. 690, as amended (42 U.S.C. 216); Sec. 1121, 88 Stat. 91 (42 U.S.C. 300c-11).

Subpart E—Project Grants for Sudden Infant Death Syndrome Information and Counseling

§ 51a.501   Applicability.

The regulations of this subpart are applicable to grants to public and nonprofit private entities pursuant to section 1121(b) of the Public Health Service Act (42 U.S.C. 300c-11) for projects for the collection, analysis and furnishing of information relating to the causes of the sudden infant death syndrome and the provision of information and counseling to families affected by the sudden infant death syndrome.

§ 51a.502 Definitions.

As used in this subpart:

(a) "Act" means the Public Health Service Act, as amended.

(b) "Secretary" means the Secretary of Health, Education, and Welfare and any other officer or employee of the Department of Health, Education, and Welfare to whom the authority involved has been delegated.

(c) "Nonprofit" as applied to a private entity means that no part of the net earnings of such entity inures, or may lawfully inure, to the benefit of any private shareholder or individual.

(d) "The Sudden Infant Death Syndrome," for the purpose of this regulation, means the sudden death of any infant which is unexpected by history, and in which a thorough post mortem examination fails to demonstrate an adequate cause for death.

(e) "SIDS" means the sudden infant death syndrome.

(f) "Family" means the parents or other relatives of a SIDS victim or any persons functioning in loco parentis to such victim at the time of a SIDS death.

(g) "Applicant" means a public or nonprofit private entity which applies for a grant.

§ 51a.503 Eligibility.

(a) *Eligible applicants.* Any public or nonprofit private entity is eligible to apply for a grant under this subpart.

(b) *Eligible projects.* Grants to eligible applicants may be made by the Secretary for projects which include both:

(1) The collection, analysis, and furnishing of information (derived from postmortem examinations and other means) pertaining to the causes of SIDS; and

(2) The provision of information and counseling to families affected by SIDS.

§ 51a.504 Application for a grant.

(a) An application for a grant under this subpart shall be submitted to the Secretary at such time and in such form and manner as the Secretary may prescribe. The application shall contain:

(1) A full and adequate description of the project and of the manner in which the applicant intends to conduct the project and carry out the requirements of this subpart;

(2) A budget and justification of the amount of grant funds requested;

(3) Such other pertinent information as the Secretary may require.

(b) The application must be executed by an individual authorized to act for the applicant and to assume for the applicant the obligations imposed by the regulations of this subpart and any additional conditions of the grant.

(c) The application shall:

(1) Provide that the project will be administered by or under the supervision of the applicant;

(2) Provide, in accordance with the provisions of § 51a.506, that the project will have appropriate community representation in its development and operation;

(3) Set forth such fiscal controls and fund accounting procedures, in accordance with the provisions of § 51a.516, as may be necessary to assure proper disbursement of and accounting for grant funds paid to the applicant; and

(4) Provide for making such reports, in addition to the performance report required by § 51a.514, in such form and containing such information as the Secretary may from time to time reasonably require.

§ 51a.505 Project requirements.

An approvable application must contain each of the following:

(a) A description, together with supporting materials, of how the project will:

(1) Establish a mechanism, or utilize a mechanism already existing in the community by which to identify possible SIDS deaths.

(2) Encourage and, where necessary, arrange for or provide appropriate medical investigations of the cause of death performed in accordance with appropriate medical standards when possible SIDS deaths are identified.

(3) Obtain and provide pertinent information from medical investigations of probable SIDS deaths by board qualified or board eligible medical pathologists or other persons authorized by law to perform such investigations.

(4) Identify and, where possible, utilize third-party sources of payment for appropriate medical investigations of probable SIDS deaths.

(5) Encourage the use of SIDS as a diagnosis on death certificates, or as the cause of death on death certificates, when medically determined.

(6) Provide information concerning SIDS to families affected by SIDS, including providing or arranging for prompt diagnosis of the cause of death and notification of the family of the diagnosis within 24 hours of the diagnosis where possible.

(7) Provide for voluntary counseling of families affected by SIDS, including home visits and other followup in accordance with the families' needs, by personnel qualified by training and experience to provide such services. Such personnel must be fully knowledgeable about the management of SIDS and of problems associated with death, grief, and mourning. Such counseling services shall be provided by:

(i) project personnel; and

(ii) as necessary or appropriate to meet the families' needs, other counseling resources within the community.

(8) Maintain consultation and arrangements with other official and voluntary community resources, such as clergy, police, emergency personnel, health

and mental health services, and organized parents' groups, and other voluntary organizations, for

(i) Referral of families affected by SIDS, as appropriate, to such resources; and

(ii) Furnishing directly or indirectly information and suggestions for dealing with SIDS cases to such community resources.

(9) Collect information on SIDS cases in the project area including demographic data, epidemiological data, and therapeutic management data.

(10) Provide information gathered under subparagraph (9) above, in accordance with § 51a.511, to:

(i) Appropriate public officials; and

(ii) Interested members of the general public in the project area.

(b) Assurances that:

(1) Services will be made available without the imposition of any durational residence or referral requirement;

(2) Services will be made available without regard to religion, creed, age, sex, parity, marital status, or income; and

(3) Services will be made available in such a manner as to protect the dignity of the individual.

§ 51a.506 Project community council.

(a) A project community council shall be established by the grantee and shall consist of a minimum of nine and a maximum of fifteen members. At least one-third of such members shall be representatives of the community being served by the project, including representatives of parents' groups or other voluntary civic or community organizations. The membership shall also include representatives of health care, social services, or public safety professions, such as medical examiners, public health nurses, social workers, private physicians, police and fire department representatives, and funeral directors.

(b) The process of selection of its members shall be stipulated in the council's bylaws, which shall be subject to approval by the Secretary and must provide that:

(1) Members shall serve for definite terms which shall not exceed four years, so staggered as to assure that the terms of not more than one-third of the members shall expire in any calendar year.

(2) The council shall meet as often as necessary, but not less than six times per year, for the purpose of considering and, as appropriate, consulting with and advising the grantee with respect to:

(i) The project's progress toward achieving its goals of service to the area; and

(ii) Review and modification of the project's existing functions, as necessary.

(iii) All recommendations of the council with respect to the project's activities shall be available to the public.

(iv) Written minutes shall be kept of all council meetings.

(c) The Secretary may, for good cause shown, allow a grantee a period of time, not to exceed three months from the date of the receipt of a grant awarded under section 1121(b) of the Act, for compliance with the requirements of this section. In addition, in the case of a grantee which is a State or local governmental agency and which has demonstrated to the satisfaction of the Secretary that it is unable, under State or local law, to establish a project community council pursuant to paragraph (a) of this section, the Secretary may allow such grantee a reasonable period of time to take the appropriate steps to have such legal disability removed. *Provided that,* such grantee, in the interim, must establish alternate procedures, approved by the Secretary, to assure maximum community participation in the development and operation of the project.

§ 51a.507 Evaluation and grant award.

(a) Within the limit of funds available for such purposes, the Secretary may award grants to assist in the establishment and operation of those projects which will, in his judgment, best promote the purposes of section 1121(b) of the Act, taking into account:

(1) The need for the project's services and informational materials to be provided, including the relative extent to which the project will contribute to the development of a nationwide distribution of such services and materials;

(2) The applicant's demonstration of an understanding of the problem, including the incidence of SIDS and the handling of the problem in the project area;

(3) The capability of the applicant to provide services and informational materials of high quality and effectiveness; and

(4) The degree to which the project plan adequately provides for the elements set forth in § 51a.505.

(b) In determining priority in awarding grants under section 1121(b) of the Act, the Secretary will take into consideration the relative extent to which the project:

(1) Would serve an area with a population of one million or more persons;

(2) Would be located in an area with an infant mortality rate higher than the national average;

(3) Has community resources available which will enable it to meet the requirements of § 51a.505 and;

(4) Is assured of community support and provides an indication of how continuation of its services will be maintained after Federal funding is concluded.

(c) The amount of any award will be determined by the Secretary on the basis of his estimate of the sum necessary for the proper performance of the project. In determining the grantee's share of project costs, if any, costs borne by Federal funds, or costs used to match other Federal grants may not be included except as may be otherwise provided by law.

(d) All grant awards shall be in writing, shall set forth the amount of funds granted, and the period for which support is recommended.

(e) Neither the approval of any project nor any grant award shall commit or obligate the United States in any way to make additional, supplemental, continuation, or other award with respect to any approved project or portion thereof. For continuation support, grantees must make separate application periodically at such times and in such form as the Secretary may direct.

§ 51a.508 Payments.

The Secretary shall from time to time make payments to a grantee of all or portion of any grant award either in advance or by way of reimbursement for expenses incurred in the performance of the project, to the extent he determines such payments necessary to promote prompt initiation and advancement of the approved project.

§ 51a.509 Use of project funds.

Any funds granted pursuant to this subpart as well as other funds to be used in performance of the approved project may be expended solely for carrying out the approved project in accordance with the applicable statute, the regulations of this subpart, the terms and conditions of the award, and the applicable cost principles prescribed by Subpart Q of 45 CFR, Part 74. Project grant funds may be used for an appropriate medical investigation of a probable SIDS death, such as an autopsy performed in accordance with appropriate medical standards, by a board certified or board eligible medical pathologist or other person qualified by law to perform such a medical investigation, but only where legal consent to the medical investigation is obtained and the following conditions are met:

(a) No other source of funds for such an investigation is available;

(b) The cost of such investigation is reasonable;

(c) Consistent with § 51a.511, the result of such investigation is used only for the collection, analysis and furnishing of information relating to the causes of SIDS; and

(d) The result of such investigation is made available to the family of a suspected SIDS victim unless medically contraindicated.

§ 51a.510 Civil rights.

(a) Attention is called to the requirements of title VI of the Civil Rights Act of 1964 (78 Stat. 252 (42 U.S.C. 2000d et seq.)) and in particular section 601 of such Act which provides that no person in the United States shall on the grounds of race, color, or national origin be excluded from participation in, be denied the benefits of, or be subjected to discrimination under any program or activity receiving Federal financial assistance. A regulation implementing such title VI, which applies to grants made under this part, has been issued by the Secretary with the approval of the President (45 CFR Part 80). In addition, no person shall be denied employment in or by such program or activity on the grounds of age, sex, creed, or marital status.

(b) Attention is also called to the requirements of section 504 of the Rehabilitation Act of 1973, as amended, which provides that no otherwise qualified handicapped individual in the United States shall, solely by reason of his handicap, be excluded from participation in, be denied the benefits of, or be subject to discrimination under any program or activity receiving Federal financial assistance.

§ 51a.511 Confidentiality of information.

All information as to personal facts and circumstances obtained by the project staff in connection with the provision of services under the project shall be treated as privileged communications, shall be held confidential, and shall not be divulged without the individual's consent except as may be otherwise required by applicable law (including this subpart) or necessary to provide services to the individual. Such information may be disclosed in summary, statistical, or other form which does not identify particular individuals.

§ 51a.512 Publications and copyright.

Except as may otherwise be provided under the terms and conditions of the award, the grantee may copyright without prior approval any publication, films or similar materials developed or resulting from a project supported by a grant under this part, subject, however, to a royalty-free, nonexclusive, and irrevocable license or right in the Government to reproduce, translate, publish, use, disseminate, and dispose of such materials and to authorize others to do so. Royalties received by grantees from copyrights on publications or other works developed under the grant shall first be used to reduce the Federal share of the grant to cover the costs of publishing or producing the materials and any royalties in excess of the costs of publishing or producing such materials shall be distributed in accordance with Chapter 1-420 of the Department of Health, Education, and Welfare Grants Administration Manual.[1]

§ 51a.513 Grantee accountability.

(a) *Accounting for grant award payments.* All payments made by the Secretary shall be recorded by the grantee in accounting records separate from the records of all other grant funds, including funds derived from other grant awards. With respect to each approved project the grantee shall account for the sum total of all amounts paid by presenting or otherwise making available evidence satisfactory to the Secretary of expenditures for direct and indirect costs meeting the requirements of this subpart. *Provided, however,* That when the amount awarded

---

[1] The Department of Health, Education, and Welfare Grants Administration Manual is available for public inspection and copying at the Department and Regional Offices' information centers listed in 45 CFR Part 531 and may be purchased from the Superintendent of Documents, U.S. Government Printing Office, Washington, D.C. 20402.

for indirect costs was based on a predetermined fixed percentage of estimated direct costs, the amount allowed for indirect costs shall be computed on the basis of such predetermined fixed-percentage rates applied to the total, or a selected element thereof, of the reimbursement direct costs incurred.

(b) *Grant closeout.* (1) Date of final accounting. A grantee shall render, with respect to each approved project, a full account, as provided herin, as of the date of the termination of grant support. The Secretary may require other special and periodic accounting.

(2) Final settlement. There shall be payable to the Federal government as final settlement with respect to each approved project the total sum of:

(i) Any amount not accounted for pursuant to paragraph (a) of this section.

(ii) Any credits for earned interest pursuant to paragraph (b) of this section.

(iii) Any other amounts due pursuant to Subparts F, M, and O of 45 CFR Part 74. Such total sum shall constitute a debt owed by the grantee to the Federal government and shall be recovered from the grantee or its successors or assignees by setoff or other action as provided by law.

§ 51a.514 Performance report.

With each continuation or renewal application or with each financial status report at the end of a project period, whichever is appropriate, grantees shall submit a performance report for each grant which briefly presents the following for each program, functions, or activity involved:

(a) A comparison of actual accomplishments to the goals established for the period. Where the output of grant programs can be quantified, such quantitative data should be related to cost data for computation of unit costs.

(b) An explanation when established goals have not been met.

(c) Other pertinent information including, when appropriate, analysis and explanation of cost overruns or higher than anticipated unit costs.

§ 51a.515 Additional conditions.

The Secretary may with respect to any grant award impose additional conditions prior to or at the time of any award when in his judgment such conditions are necessary to assure or protect advancement of the approved project, the interests of public health, or the conservation of grant funds.

§ 51a.516 Applicability of 45 CFR Part 74.

The relevant provisions of the following subparts of 45 CFR Part 74, establishing uniform administrative requirements and cost principles, shall apply to all grants under this subpart:

45 CFR Part 74

Subpart
A—General
B—Cash Depositories

C–Bonding and Insurance
D–Retention and Custodial Requirements for Records
F–Grant–Related Income
K–Grant Payment Requirements
L–Budget Revision Procedures
M–Grant Closeout, Suspension, and Termination
O–Property
Q–Cost Principles

[FR Doc. 75–14752 Filed 6-5-75; 8:45 am]

INDEX

ABOUT THE AUTHOR

Abraham Bergman, born in Seattle in 1932, was graduated from Reed College in 1954, and Western Reserve University School of Medicine in 1958. He received his postgraduate training in pediatrics at Boston Children's Hospital, St. Mary's Hospital Medical School (London), and Upstate Medical Center in Syracuse. He is currently Director of Pediatrics at Harborview Medical Center, and Professor of Pediatrics and Health Services at the University of Washington in Seattle. He served as president of the National SIDS Foundation from 1972-1977, and is the author of 26 publications concerning Sudden Infant Death Syndrome.

In 1966 Dr. Bergman began the practice of what he calls "political medicine," which he defines as "employment of the political system to achieve improvements in health." To this end, he has been the major instigator of such national legislation as the Flammable Fabrics Act Amendments (1967), the Poison Prevention Packaging Act (1970), the National Health Service Corps (1972), the Sudden Infant Death Syndrome Act (1974), and the Indian Health Care Improvement Act (1976). He received the Rockefeller Public Service Award in 1979 for his work in public health. He is married to Ann Bergman, publisher of *Seattle's Child*, and is the father of five children.